YOU&YOUR
DOG

D0109590

YOU&YOUR
DOG

DAVID TAYLOR B.V.M.S. F.R.C.V.S.

with PETER SCOTT M.R.C.V.S.

DORLING KINDERSLEY · LONDON

Project Editor	Caroline Ollard
Art Editor	Derek Coombes
Assistant Editor	Janice Lacock
Senior Art Editor	Peter Luff
Managing Editor	Alan Buckingham

First published in 1986 by
Dorling Kindersley Publishers Limited,
9 Henrietta Street, London WC2E 8PS
First published in paperback in 1987 by
Dorling Kindersley Limited

British Library Cataloguing in Publication Data
Taylor, David, 1934 –
   You and your dog.
   1. Dogs
   I. Title
   636.7 083 SF427
   ISBN 0-86318-111-2 (hardback)
   ISBN 0-86318-287-9 (paperback)

Printed in Italy by A. Mondadori, Verona.

Contents

INTRODUCTION

We will never know for sure how it happened – the first coming together of man and dog. The original domesticated dogs were probably wolf-like scavengers, haunting the midden heaps round the dwellings of early Man somewhere in the Middle East. Perhaps Homo sapiens preyed on the animal for food, perhaps he took puppies and brought them up as pets, quickly realizing their potential as helpers in a wide range of human endeavours. Whatever the origins of the unlikely partnership, the canid and the Great Ape quickly struck up a relationship which, although perhaps not having the history-forging significance of the domestication of the horse, led to a symbiosis that was to have enduring and significant effects on human society and culture.

Dogs aren't the most numerous of our pets, but they're arguably the most important. Apart from its practical uses, from seeing-eye to sheep herder to property guard, the dog has a positive, therapeutic psychological effect on the human beings around it. Stroking a dog lowers heart rate and blood pressure. The company of a faithful canine friend is known to aid convalescence in the sick. And, because of the dog's need for regular exercise, it helps keep its master fit into the bargain.

Of course, there's the other side of the coin – dogs can be dangerous and convey disease, and they do demand more care and attention than some owners are willing to give. A cat or a budgerigar is simpler to maintain. But I doubt whether anyone can truly be complete, who has not at least at some time in his or her life kept – and been kept by – a dog. The dog comes in an amazing range of types and sizes. There is a breed for everyone, and the variety is far more exciting than in any other domestic animal.

This book, which isn't designed for the expert, but rather for the ordinary dog-owner, is an introduction to the world of the dog – what it is, how it functions and how to make the most of it. It is for the amateur, the enthusiast and the aficionado, and it contains the latest information and theories, flavoured with my own opinions after almost thirty years as a veterinarian working with canines, not just of the domestic variety but also of the more exotic species represented by the wild cousins of the dog – among them the wolf, the jackal, the dhole and the fox.

Dogs in art (above left)
Dogs have been portrayed in decorative and fine arts for centuries. This 19th century example shows a faithful group gathered around their mistress.

A love of water (above right)
Three Labradors playing on the beach.

The appeal of a puppy (right)
Puppies are amongst the most delightful of baby animals. Here a newborn Great Dane explores.

Stained glass showing huntsman and hounds. Chartres, 13th century.

The canine hunter

Both temperamentally and physically, dogs are built as carnivorous hunters and their predatory instinct is very strong. Dogs are courageous and persevere in the field, so early man relied on the hunting prowess of his dogs to provide him with food. Dogs have acted as hunting companions for their masters down the ages and still carry out this function today, working singly or in packs.

Depending on its breed, the well-trained hunting dog can spot its quarry in the distance or track it by scent, then indicate its position to its master, retrieve the game and bring it back in its mouth. This gift for retrieving means a dog will tirelessly play games of "fetch" for hours – if you're prepared to throw a stick or ball for it.

The best nose in the business

Dogs are endowed with a highly developed sense of smell, many times more efficient than our own. They make expert sniffers and trackers and, as well as locating hunting quarry, are used to sniff out criminals, drugs, explosives and even truffles. The most famous

The gamekeeper's dog (above)
A Labrador accompanies its master in the Scottish Highlands, alert to each new scent and movement around it.
The tireless sheepdog (right)
The Border Collie, bred to be the most outstanding of working sheepdogs.

breed of tracker dog is the Bloodhound, but others are just as gifted and widely used by the police and the army.

A fast runner
Several breeds are extremely fleet of foot, their fast running speed enabling them to capture their prey while hunting. The best-known of these is the sleek Greyhound which reaches incredible speeds of over 40 mph. The sport of Greyhound racing is popular on both sides of the Atlantic. Other "streamlined" breeds include the Saluki, Whippet, Afghan and Borzoi. Running at full stretch, these dogs display some of the marvels of canine "engineering".

The aquatic dog
Many breeds love water and are good swimmers – chief among them the Golden Retriever, Labrador, spaniels, poodles and the Newfoundland. Dogs seem to know how to swim inherently without going through the agonies of learning. A walk beside a pond or river or by the sea is irresistible to many dogs and if allowed, they'll be splashing in the water at the first opportunity.

The canine worker

Over the centuries, man has learned to employ dogs in a rich variety of ways as guards, hunters, war-machines, seeing-eyes, rodent controllers, draught animals, footwarmers, providers of hair and meat and, most important of all, as good companions.

In many parts of the world, local necessity has created some interesting occupations. Carts pulled by dogs were used in Belgium, Holland, Germany and Switzerland until quite recently. Australian aborigines used dingoes for warmth on cold nights, sleeping with one clasped in their arms. Aborigine women, when not carrying young children, often "wore" a dog draped across their lower back as a kidney warmer. The Aztecs, apart from using dog hair to make cloth, fattened a non-barking, hairless dog for eating.

Dogs were once used to harvest the most magical of plants. The mandrake was the source of a coveted narcotic and aphrodisiac extract. Primitive peoples believed that the plant, whose split root often presents the two-legged appearance of a manikin, couldn't be pulled from the earth without producing fatal effects on the puller. So one end of a cord was attached to the root and the other was tied to a dog. The theory was that when the dog was chased away, out would come the mandrake root (often, it was said, with an awful shriek) and down would drop the poor dog.

Dogs of war

Mastiffs in light armour carrying lethal spikes and cauldrons of flaming sulphur and resin on their backs, were used in warfare by the Romans and in the Middle Ages, particularly against mounted knights. As a sad update of this, dogs were trained by the Russians in the last War to carry out suicide missions against German tanks. They would run between the tracks of the vehicles with mines strapped to their backs. The mine would explode as soon as a vertical antenna attached to it touched the metal tank.

Working dogs

As well as assisting man in his sport, dogs have always helped him in his work. A dog's alertness, interest, exuberance and stamina fits it for a busy "career". Some dogs are born to work and should be given the opportunity. A working sheepdog is a heartwarming sight, and one which you can see in action at Sheepdog Trials. Herding and droving dogs love their work and are used all over the world, working with cattle and sheep, often in remote areas. Their terrific strength and powers of endurance make dogs from snowy regions, such as Huskies, able to pull heavy loads on sledges.

Guide-dogs

There can be no friend more faithful than a guide-dog. These wonderful dogs — usually Labradors, Golden Retrievers or German Shepherds – are specially trained to act as "eyes" for blind people, and are complete professionals. A blind person relies so completely on his or her dog that the training must be rigorous and thorough. The reassurance and security a guide-dog gives makes this possibly the most important and worthwhile canine "job".

Turkish sheepdogs (above)
These sheepdogs are wearing spiked collars to protect them against wolves on the lonely grazing grounds.
Sledge race (above right)
Aside from their normal duties, teams of haulage dogs such as Huskies are organized to take part in special sledge races.
Household helper (right)
Apart from the "career" jobs, intelligent dogs can be trained to perform particular tasks at home.

Children and puppies (left)
Young people and dogs will amuse each other for hours.
Two's company (above)
Many elderly people enjoy the company of a dog.
An obedient pet (right)
Show younger family members how to reinforce training.

The canine companion

In every age across the globe, it seems that folk have in one way or another echoed the words of St Bernard (c. A.D. 1150) – "Who loves me will love my dog also." Today, well over a hundred different breeds are kept as pets in Britain and America. Although their appearance varies enormously, all dogs are essentially built to the same animal design, not far removed from their primitive ancestors. They are highly adaptable creatures and the process of evolution hasn't found it necessary to alter them much. Dogs can give great enjoyment if treated with care and common sense.

The perfect protector

Protective instincts are naturally strong in a dog. The desire to guard and keep safe extends to the dog's owner and family, the house and garden. A good watch-dog is one of the most reliable burglar alarms you can have. It doesn't have to be a huge Great Dane or a Mastiff; smaller dogs will put up the alarm vocally just as well. A dog can be trained as an excellent security guard. Other assets such as its senses of smell and hearing help it to do the job well. And dogs are inquisitive – nothing if not curious when it comes to a stranger or an unfamiliar scent.

Man's best friend

Dogs are sociable animals and love human company. In fact, dogs require company to be happy, and to deprive them of it is unfair. Children and the elderly – probably the people with the most free time – are likely to be the most constant companions to their dogs and able to build up a special relationship with them.

The power of the pack is one of a dog's strongest instincts. In the absence of a real pack of its own kind, a dog views the family as its own "pack", with the head of the family as the "pack leader". A friendly dog is interested in all the family activities and loves to be at the centre of things. Even a dog that appears to be in the deepest of slumbers in front of the fire will soon open an eye or twitch an ear if it senses anything going on.

Your dog is your greatest fan – its loyalty is unquestioning. If you respect your dog, it will respect you. By taking the trouble to train your pet, you're doing both of you a good turn, and helping it to fit in more easily with your own lifestyle.

The saying "it's a dog's life" has a strongly pejorative ring to it. After dipping into this book and I hope enjoying what it has to offer, I trust the words will take on for you a more positive and delightful meaning.

THE ANATOMY OF THE DOG

Like many animals, a dog is a miraculous amalgam of organs and systems which carry out specific jobs as well as interrelating to keep the dog "running efficiently". Although anatomy is a huge subject, a concise consideration of how the dog moves, sees, hears, smells, breathes, eats and digests its food helps us to understand why it is built the way it is. Despite the changes undergone since the time when it needed to fend for itself in the wild, the domestic dog is still basically a carnivore and adapted as such. The dog was designed to run fast, to capture and kill its prey as part of a pack. It retains astonishing senses of hearing and smell – both superior to man's. The reasons and treatment for disorders of the dog's body are described in *Health Care* (see pp.226–75).

The basic design of the dog

Dogs come in all shapes and sizes, but the basic design of the "standard" dog equips it for being a carnivorous animal. A dog is designed to chase, capture, kill and eat its prey. It has the mark of the carnivore – the huge carnassial teeth. And yet, the dog is not such a refined carnivore as some, the cat for instance. Dogs have retained a few molar teeth for chewing and grinding. Domestic cats, on the other hand, have reduced their molars to the point that they have very little chewing ability.

Although the teeth are specially modified, the general skeleton of a carnivore is fairly primitive. Carnivores have not emulated herbivores in reducing their number of toes and converting them to a hoof. A dog needs to be agile, capable of rapid changes of direction and able to use its claws as weapons. The wild herbivores may be speedy, but their movement is essentially forward and they're not as adept at recovering from falls sustained while running at speed.

Over the years, selection of dogs to develop the various breeds has modified the anatomy considerably, giving the many variations on the basic shape.

A member of a pack
Its basic design allows for sufficient bursts of speed for the dog as a pack hunter, whereas a solitary hunter like a cheetah needs the refinement of extra speed. In fact within a pack, the dogs will pace each other when hunting. In addition, the wild dog is well muscled for endurance and long-distance foraging.

EXTERNAL ANATOMY

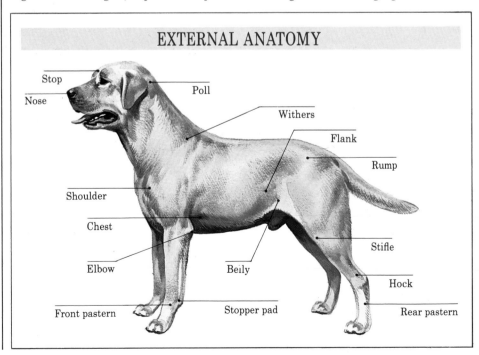

Stop
Poll
Nose
Withers
Flank
Rump
Shoulder
Chest
Stifle
Elbow
Belly
Hock
Front pastern
Stopper pad
Rear pastern

Natural and artificial selection

In the wild, if a certain physical element becomes beneficial to a species over a period of time, then those animals with that particular modification become more successful at surviving and therefore more numerous. Charles Darwin, the originator of this idea, called it "Natural Selection". Darwin developed his theories after watching finches and other animals on the Galapagos Islands.

Over the years of domestication, man has selected various characteristics in the dog which fulfil a particular requirement. He has interceded (some would say interfered) and encouraged certain characteristics that wouldn't succeed in the wild. Since man is a part of nature and has himself changed the environment, it is perhaps permissible that he has modified the dog to fit into his world rather than excluding it and forcing its extinction. One thing is certain – most of us find the world enriched by our furry canine friends. Whatever your lifestyle, there's a dog to suit you.

The box (right) shows several examples of man's selective breeding of dogs. Of course, this doesn't represent the whole range of dogs and there are several exceptions to these basic patterns, but many original breeds evolved from this type of selection. Some breeds have been designed purely for the show-ring and most present-day dogs have been considerably modified from their original purpose. Today's Bulldog, for instance, couldn't carry out the tasks that early Bulldogs (which had straighter legs and more of a nose) were bred for.

It is interesting to speculate what might happen to the dog in years to come. Future developments are in the hands of breeders and Kennel Clubs.

The old, familiar breeds will probably change gradually as working dogs become refined into show animals, although the former hopefully won't be lost. New "old" breeds will probably be introduced from far-flung corners of the world and congenital problems eradicated to produce healthier dogs.

SELECTIVE BREEDING

Large fighting dogs
Mastiffs, Bulldogs
Big, strong dogs with powerful jaws to grab and hold men or other animals.

Running dogs
Saluki, Afghan Hound, Greyhound, Lurcher, Deerhound
Slim, sleek dogs with long legs, capable of great speed.

Small hunting dogs
Terriers
Compact dogs with great tenacity for hunting as a pack or putting down underground burrows.

Mountain dogs
Pyrenean Mountain Dog, Bernese Mountain Dog
Powerful dogs for guarding herds and flocks in mountains, with thick coats and plenty of fat.

Scenting, tracking dogs
Bloodhound, Basset Hound
Powerful dogs with a good nose, capable of following a scent (the ears are said to stir the air and "lift" scents).

Herding dogs
Border Collie
Basic shape, selected for obedience.

Water dogs
Poodles, Water Spaniel
Tight, curly coat which sheds water well.

The dog's skeleton

There are two major types of bone in the dog's skeleton: long bones (tubular bones like the limb bones and spine), and flat bones (the skull, pelvis and shoulder blade bones). Although the basic design is unaltered since the early days the limbs have been considerably modified between the breeds. Just think of the difference between the shapes of a Dachshund and a St Bernard. The reason is that man has bred dogs selectively with bones of different lengths and thicknesses.

How the skeleton works
The skeleton is a system of bony levers moved by muscles which are anchored at crucial points on the bones. The bones are linked together at joints which act like shock absorbers. Bones have a complicated structure which gives great stability and yet allows movement. They are anchored by ligaments which permit a given degree of movement in specific directions.

Each joint is surrounded by a joint capsule which contains the joint lubricant, *synovial fluid*. The ends of the bone involved in the joint are covered in *cartilage* – a smooth surface which helps the joint move easily and helps to absorb any concussion as the dog's weight comes down on the leg.

How bones grow and develop
Long bones begin in the foetus as cartilage stuctures, which are replaced by true bone in the latter weeks of pregnancy. A limb bone can be considered as a tubular structure with a joint or articulation at each end. The

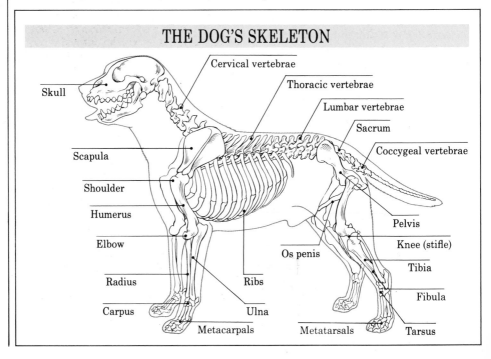

THE DOG'S SKELETON

Skull

Cervical vertebrae

Thoracic vertebrae

Lumbar vertebrae

Sacrum

Coccygeal vertebrae

Scapula

Shoulder

Humerus

Elbow

Pelvis

Knee (stifle)

Os penis

Tibia

Radius

Ribs

Fibula

Carpus

Ulna

Metacarpals

Metatarsals

Tarsus

parts of the bone shaft not involved in the joint are covered with a tough, fibrous *periosteum*. In young, growing dogs the inner layer of the periosteum is actively growing and producing bone, increasing the diameter of the bone. On the inside of a tubular bone, to prevent it becoming too thick and heavy, the older bone is reabsorbed and remodelled, keeping the actual bony wall or *cortex* the same thickness.

Once the dog has stopped growing the periosteum becomes relatively inactive, although if a fracture occurs and needs repairing, it can become active again in that area. To avoid this process weakening the bone, the inside is filled with fine bony struts or *trabecullae*. The spaces between these are filled in the young animal with bone marrow, replaced by fat as the dog gets older.

Growth in length occurs in regions of the bone near the joints called growth plates or *epiphyseal plates*. These growth plates are areas where cartilage is still being produced as an advancing layer behind the growth plate, in the *metaphysis*. (For parts of a bone see X-ray below.) The cartilage is being converted to bone, and so the bone grows in length. In most dogs all growth in length of long bones is complete by ten months of age.

Fuel for growth

Bone growth requires fuel, and this is provided by blood vessels. The main shaft of each bone is supplied by one or two large nutrient arteries which enter the bone through a hole in the shaft, the *nutrient foramen*. The epiphysis receives blood from a ring of arteries inside the joint capsule. These arteries penetrate the whole of the epiphysis to feed the growing bone. They also supply nutrition to the inside layer of the articular cartilage; the rest of its nutrition comes from the synovial fluid inside the joint.

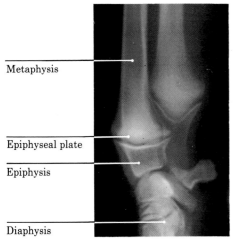

Metaphysis

Epiphyseal plate

Epiphysis

Diaphysis

X-ray showing carpal joint of young dog.

THE DOG'S SPINE

The spine is a tube made up of individual bones called *vertebrae*, linked together by strong ligaments. Through the centre of this tube runs the *neural canal* which houses the precious spinal cord. The vertebrae continue into the tail, although these are much smaller than the main vertebrae; most of the nerves leave the neural canal further up the body to go to their target.

Between each vertebra and the next is a fibrous pad called an *intervertebral disc*, which absorbs excessive shock and movement. Its structure is like an onion – numerous thin "skins" and a fluid, shock-absorbing centre like a golfball.

As a dog gets older, its vertebral discs become less fluid and its spine less supple. In some breeds, particularly the Dachshund, Pekingese and Basset Hound, this happens earlier. These breeds are prone to disc protrusion, often inaccurately referred to as a "slipped disc" (see p.265).

Muscles and movement

Collectively, the dog's muscles are the largest organ in its body. Although selective breeding has brought about great changes in body shape and skeleton, dogs' muscles vary very little between breeds.

How muscles work

Most of the muscles are attached to bones. The flat bones are the main anchorage points for the muscles responsible for moving the legs. When muscles contract, the bones to which they are joined are brought closer together, and when they relax, the bones can move apart again. Extra bending of limbs and extension of joints is carried out by muscles running down the legs and attached to the long bones at critical points to obtain maximum leverage. At the point of contact with the bone, the muscles become fibrous tendons.

The wild dog is well-muscled – it needs to be in order to hunt for its food. Man's best friend – the domestic dog – often has rather soft muscles through insufficient exercise. Of

THE DOG'S MUSCLES

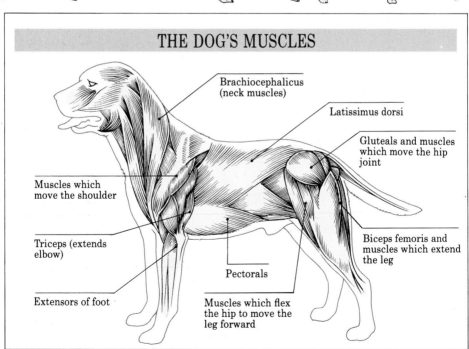

Brachiocephalicus (neck muscles)

Latissimus dorsi

Gluteals and muscles which move the hip joint

Muscles which move the shoulder

Triceps (extends elbow)

Biceps femoris and muscles which extend the leg

Pectorals

Extensors of foot

Muscles which flex the hip to move the leg forward

today's breeds, the Husky is close to the wolf and shares its strength and endurance. Working Husky teams can pull a load of twice their own weight all day at up to three miles per hour.

How the dog moves

The apparatus of the dog's locomotion consists of bones, joints, muscles and nerves. The nervous system initiates and co-ordinates muscular activity. It sends messages to the muscles, which work to move the limb bones.

The action of the dog's limbs can be likened to the spokes of a wheel, each in turn exerting pressure against the ground, then being rotated until able

noted for their speed and agility such as Greyhounds and Borzois. With gundogs, breeders usually try to achieve a happy medium in the centre of gravity because of the need for them to carry heavy game in their mouths.

Most of the forward drive comes from the powerful backward thrust of the hind paws against the ground. Considerable force has to act through the hind legs, so the articular surfaces of the bones fit closely together and are held in position by a complex system of muscles and ligaments.

Jumping

Dogs aren't so good as cats at jumping and climbing. This is partly because

to repeat the process. The larger a wheel, the more ground it covers in one revolution and the longer a dog's limbs, the greater its stride. The further forward its centre of gravity, the faster a dog can move, because its hind legs aren't supporting too much weight and are more readily available for propulsion. This is true of breeds

they can't control their claws or twist their legs in the way a cat does. Dogs can be trained to jump obstacles by using their own weight to gain momentum when running. But a dog's power is really developed for endurance running rather than the sudden muscle contraction needed for the action of jumping.

SIGHT HOUNDS

Certain of the hound breeds, such as the Afghan Hound, Saluki, Greyhound, Deerhound and cross-breeds of these, are sometimes called "long dogs", "gaze hounds" or "sight hounds". These are breeds which hunt by sight, and their long legs make them capable of

great speed. The flexibility of their bodies makes them seem closer to the cheetah than to some of their fellow dogs. These dogs can reach speeds of up to 35–40 mph; a cheetah can run at 55–60 mph.

Speed relates partly to how a dog places its feet. Although these sight

hounds have long backs, they also have long legs, and at full speed the hind legs land ahead of the point that the forelegs are leaving. This contrasts with the long-backed breeds with short legs like the Basset, which place their hind legs well behind the foreleg take-off point.

The skull

There are three basic skull shapes in dogs:

● *Dolichocephalic* – long-nosed breeds like the Rough Collie, Afghan Hound, Dobermann and Fox Terrier.
● *Brachycephalic* – short, snub-nosed breeds like the Pug, Bulldog and Pekinese.
● *Mesocephalic* – A group including dogs which fall between the other two extremes.

Parts of the skull

The features of the skull tend to vary with the overall shape and type of the skull.

The eye sits in the space called the *orbit*, within the *zygomatic arch*. The two zygomatic arches govern the total width of the skull. They vary in shape between the breeds – long-nosed breeds have a fairly straight arch while in short-nosed breeds it is very curved.

The jaw

The shape of the jaw varies quite considerably between breeds (see box below). The official breeds standards

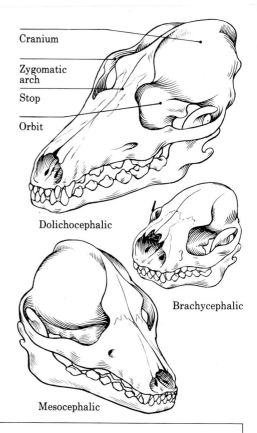

Cranium

Zygomatic arch

Stop

Orbit

Dolichocephalic

Brachycephalic

Mesocephalic

TYPES OF BITE

The diagrams (right) show the four different types of bite a dog may have. Brachycephalic types tend to be "undershot" – the lower jaw extending beyond the upper. Other dogs may have a level bite (teeth meeting), a scissor bite (top teeth fit neatly over lower teeth) or be "overshot" – the upper jaw extending beyond the lower.

Undershot

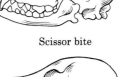

Scissor bite

Level bite

Overshot

include requirements for the "bite" of each dog.

The jaw muscles are very powerful. It is said that a 20 kg mongrel can exert a bite of 165 kg; the pressure of an average human bite is 20–30 kg.

The cranium

The upper part of the dog's skull, it houses the brain and also varies between breeds. In the Chihuahua, a high-domed shape has been specially selected over years of breeding. Unfortunately this has led in certain cases to people breeding from dogs with hereditary brain deformities such as hydrocephalus (water on the brain).

The stop

This is the point where the sagittal crest ends and the skull outline drops down to the nasal bones. Some breeds, such as the Boxer, are required by the breeds standards to have a pronounced stop, while others like the Greyhound or Bull Terrier, are not.

At the back of the skull, the sagittal crest ends in the occipital bone, which gives the Basset Hound its peak. This feature doesn't usually appear in puppies until the age of nine to ten weeks.

The brain

The dog's brain differs from man's mainly in the cerebrum; man has much more grey matter than a dog. Although both need to co-ordinate and control bodily functions and movements, man does this with more sophistication. Most of a dog's brain is involved with senses and recognition. Very little of the brain is available for association of ideas. A dog can be taught to recognize a £1 coin, but would never understand the concept of money and how many cans of dog food the coin would buy. For more about the intelligence and awareness of a dog see *Understanding Your Dog*, pp.210–25.

A large breed like the St Bernard which is similar in weight to a man has a brain about 15 percent the weight of a man's brain. Interestingly, the area of the dog's brain responsible for the sense of smell has 40 times the number of cells of the equivalent area of a man's brain (see p. 27).

The teeth

A dog's teeth adapt it for being a carnivore. It has large, strong shearing teeth (called "carnassials") which it uses to chew through tough materials. In addition, this last premolar in the upper jaw has become elongated and developed a cutting ridge which overlaps with the first molar on the lower jaw when the dog bites. The long, pointed and slightly curved incisors, often called "dog teeth", are useful stabbing weapons for catching and holding prey.

In a dog, the different teeth erupt at different times (see pp.136–7).

Dental formula

This is the number of each type of tooth normally present *in one side* of the upper and lower jaws of a dog
Upper jaw: 3 incisors, 1 canine, 4 premolars, 2 molars.
Lower jaw: 3 incisors, 1 canine, 4 premolars, 3 molars.

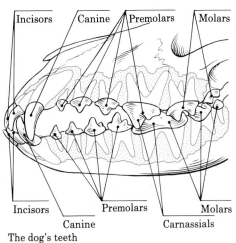

The dog's teeth

The eye

In its basic structure, the dog's eye is much like a human's but there are a few differences which mean that the dog has a different type and range of vision.

The eye is split into two main sections by the *lens*. As a dog grows, the lens grows too, being produced from a living layer around the outside of it, called the *lens capsule*.

The three "coats" of the eye

The dog's eye is made up of three layers. From front to back, these are the *sclera*, the *uvea* and the *retina*. The sclera incorporates the transparent *cornea* at the front of the eye. The uvea consists of three parts –*choroid*, *iris* and *ciliary body*. The choroid contains a reflective layer called the *tapetum*.

The iris (a muscular ring) is controlled by the nervous system and moderates the amount of light entering the eye, like the aperture of a camera. The ciliary body (a ring of tissue behind the iris) is the point of attachment for the suspensory ligament which holds and moves the lens. It also plays a part in focusing the image on the retina and secretes fluid for nourishing the cornea.

The retina

This is the light-sensitive inner layer of the eye. It contains light-sensivitive cells of two types – rods and cones. Rods are very sensitive and work well in low light levels. They only appreciate black and white. Cones operate under good lighting conditions and can appreciate colour. In a dog's retina, only about five percent of the cells are cones and the remainder are rods, so a dog is probably largely colour blind, seeing in black, white and shades of grey.

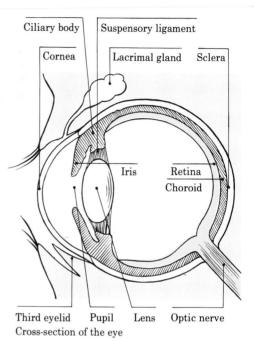

Cross-section of the eye

The eyelids

A dog's eyelids have a number of special features. Under the upper lid is the *lacrimal gland* which produces tears to keep the cornea moist and prevent it from drying out and becoming inflamed. To avoid tears flowing down the face continually, there's a special drainage system. Both top and bottom lids have a short duct at the inner corner; the two ducts fuse to form a single *lacrimal duct* for each eye, leading tears to the nasal cavity. Various problems can cause blockage of these ducts and it is important to treat such problems seriously (see p.256).

The eyelashes

A dog has eyelashes on both upper and lower lids. If these point the wrong way, they may hurt the eye. The eyelid deformities known as entropion and ectropion are fairly common and affect certain breeds more than others.

The third eyelid

Dogs have a third lid on each eye, known as the *haw* or *nictating membrane*. This is mainly hidden under the lower lid and just a small part of the pigmented edge is visible in the corner of the eye close to the nose, although in some breeds it is very prominent. The membrane acts like a windscreen wiper for the eye – a defence mechanism to sweep away foreign bodies. When the eye is suddenly drawn back into its socket or becomes sunken through age or disease, the third eyelid becomes more prominent. If it appears suddenly and remains visible, this may be an indication of disease or slight pain. Watch the dog for other symptoms (see *Health Care*, pp.256–7).

THE DOG'S VISION

Dogs see better in the dark than man, partly because a dog's retina is dominated by rods which are sensitive to low light, and partly because of the *tapetum lucidum* which lies underneath the rod cells and reflects "concentrated" light back through them. This is a help to wild dogs who are likely to be hunting in poor light conditions. As a further aid to hunting, dogs are particularly sensitive to seeing movement in the distance. They perceive stationary objects relatively poorly, though, which makes some individuals seem clumsy.

Field of vision The way a dog's eyes are positioned on its head, combined with good muscles for moving them around, gives the dog a comparatively wide field of view. The variation in the shape of dogs' heads alters the placement of the eyes and modifies the field of vision between the breeds. In general, the brachycephalic, (short-nosed) breeds like the Pug and Bulldog, have eyes situated on the front of the head, giving better overlap in the field of vision than longer nosed breeds.

The dolichocephalic (long-nosed) breeds tend to have obliquely placed eyes with only a small overlap, and the poorest stereoscopic vision of all but a narrow field of view directly ahead of them. This may partly account for the ease with which the elegant "sight hounds" (dogs like the Borzoi and Saluki, see p.21) run into ditches or trip over small obstacles when running at full tilt.

In man, the fields of vision of our two eyes overlap, so we have stereoscopic vision and a good appreciation of depth and distance. Although dogs have a wider field of vision, they're not so good at judging distances.

Dolichocephalic type

Brachycephalic type

Man

The ears and nose

The two most highly developed senses of a dog are its hearing and its sense of smell. Both are superior to man's and adapt the dog as a hunter.

Ears and hearing
Dogs' ears vary tremendously in appearance, but they all have excellent hearing and can detect very high-frequency sounds inaudible to man.

Ears range in shape from large, floppy, sleepy-looking Basset Hound ears, to the pert, pricked ears of some terriers. Cocker Spaniels' ears are floppy and very hairy – they merge into the head. In contrast. French Bulldogs' ears are covered with short hair and stand proud, like radar dishes.

Examples of ear types: bat ears and drop ears.

Parts of the ear
Although the outer ear varies so much between breeds, the structure and function of the middle and inner ears is the same for every dog.
The pinna
The external ear is a cartilage framework, covered with muscles and skin. In most dogs the pinna is fairly mobile, its muscles moving it to follow sounds. The pinna leads into the external auditory canal – a short tube which runs vertically, then turns horizontally towards the eardrum (*tympanic membrane*).
The middle ear
The dog's middle ear incorporates the tympanic membrane (eardrum), and the tympanic cavity, within which are the smallest bones in the body, the *auditory ossicles*. Because of their shape and function, these are known as the hammer, anvil and stirrup (the *malleus, incus* and *stapes*). The three bones are linked, and operate as a system of levers. Sounds received by the inner ear make the eardrum vibrate. This moves the ossicles which transmit the sound to the inner ear.

This system helps to make the ear sensitive to sound by amplification, yet the ossicles protect the inner ear against violent vibrations from very loud noises by restricting the range of their movements.
The inner ear
Further inside the ear are the sound-sensitive spiral *cochlea* and the organs of balance associated with the semicircular canals. The semicircular canals can detect movement, the *saccule* and *utricle* give information on the alignment of the head. This arrangement is the same as that in the cat and in man.

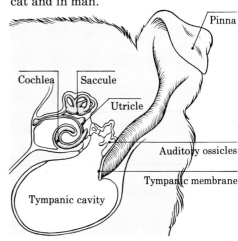

Cross-section of the ear

SILENT DOG WHISTLES

These so-called "silent" whistles aren't silent to a dog! They give out a high-pitched whistle outside the audible range of humans, but within that of a dog. These high-pitched sounds travel further than lower pitched noises and so are ideal for giving long-distance commands to a dog. Dogs can detect sounds from up to four times the distance that most humans can.

The nose and sense of smell

One of the most remarkable features of the dog is its sense of smell. All dogs have an innate desire to sniff everything – places, people, other dogs. The dog's sense of smell gives it all kinds of information and is about *one million times* more sensitive than our own. A dog also has 40 times the number of brain cells involved in scent recognition than the number in a human. Man makes use of this ability in dogs by training them as sniffer dogs (for finding drugs and bombs), detectors of gas leaks, or truffle hounds.

Part of the increased sensitivity of a dog's nose is due to its having a much larger sensory area (*olfactory area*). In man, this is about three square cm, but in the average dog it is 130 square cm. The sensory area is folded many times

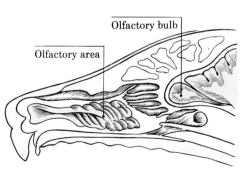

Cross-section of the nose

over, creating ridges which form a trapping mechanism for capturing smells. The sensory cells are more closely packed, giving more cells per square centimetre.

Why is a dog's nose wet?

The nose is kept moist by the secretions of special cells. These are stimulated when new odours are detected. Scents, present as small particles, are dissolved by the secretions, and brought into contact with the sensory cells.

Respiration

The *pharynx* is the area at the back of the mouth where the *trachea* and the *oesophagus* (breathing and alimentary passages) begin. The soft palate – a floppy extension to the roof of the mouth – hangs down and divides the pharynx in two.

The dog is basically a nose breather, with the soft palate closing off the mouth. By circulating most of the normal air supply to the lung through the nasal passages, the dog filters, warms and moistens the air before it reaches the lungs. Mouth breathing becomes far more important to a dog when the air temperature is high, if it has been exercising or if it has a nasal disease.

Problems of short-nosed breeds

In the more brachycephalic (short-nosed) breeds, the soft palate can cause respiratory problems because it is effectively pushed further back into the head which constricts the pharynx, making mouth breathing very difficult for some dogs.

It can be dangerous to hold the mouth of some of these short-nosed dogs closed because when excited they cannot breathe effectively through the nose alone. A combination of nose and mouth breathing is needed to prevent the soft palate sticking in the larynx.

The chest

The boundaries of the chest are the rib-cage and the diaphragm. Most of the dog's chest is occupied by its lungs. The heart sits in the centre of the chest with its lower point just touching the rib-cage. Both of these organs – the heart and lungs – move within the chest; to avoid them interfering with each other or sticking together, each is housed in its own slippery sac.

Also traversing the chest is the tubular *oesophagus*, carrying food from the mouth to the digestive system in the abdomen.

The heart
The dog has a "standard" four-chambered mammalian heart. Two *atria* empty blood into the powerful *ventricles* which drive the blood around. The right ventricle pumps blood to the lungs to eliminate carbon dioxide and to pick up oxygen. This blood from the lungs returns to the left atrium, which empties it into the left ventricle to be pumped around the

body (see diagram p.263).

The resistance to the heart's pumping is greater in the bulk of the body than it is in the lungs, so the left ventricle is larger and stronger than the right. Built into the wall of the heart are two "pacemakers" which send co-ordinated impulses to the muscles telling them when to contract and when to relax.

The trachea and lungs
The entrance to the *trachea* is the *larynx*, which is made up of several cartilage segments. The vocal cords sit just within the opening.

The trachea is a tube, made up of rings of cartilage. It leads down to the lungs, where it divides into *bronchi*, which subdivide in their turn. Eventually, the air is led into the *alveoli* – small, membranous sacs with blood vessels in their walls. This is where the exchange of gases occurs, the blood taking in new oxygen and carbon dioxide being released.

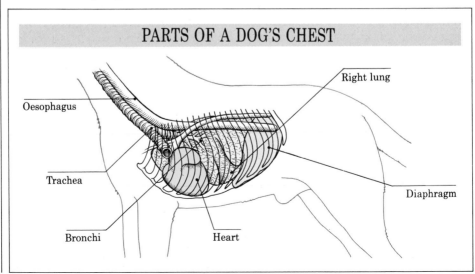

PARTS OF A DOG'S CHEST

Oesophagus

Right lung

Trachea

Diaphragm

Bronchi

Heart

The abdomen

Behind the dog's diaphragm is the body cavity called the abdomen. This is the home of several complex organs, concerned with internal maintenance, converting food into usable material, excreting waste, filtering and storing blood, and reproduction. The abdomen divides into three basic parts:
• The urogenital system, including the kidneys and the reproductive tract
• The spleen
• The digestive tract, including the intestine, liver and pancreas

The excretory system
The term "urogenital system" is used to cover two systems – excretory and reproductive. For a description of the reproductive system, see p.188.

The two kidneys hang from the roof of the dog's abdomen, close to the last of its ribs. Each kidney has a *cortex*, *medulla* and an area called the *pelvis*. The cortex and medulla form a complex filtration system, consisting of units called *nephrons*.

The function of the kidney
The kidneys filter the blood to remove unwanted and potentially toxic substances from the blood:
1 A clear fluid is produced from the blood by filtering out blood cells.
2 The fluid passes into ducts which remove sodium into the tissues.
3 This sodium draws out water from other parts of the duct, concentrating the urine.
4 Other waste products are excreted into the urine at various points.
5 The urine passes into collecting ducts, then into the kidney pelvis.

The most important and dangerous waste product in urine is *urea*, produced in the liver from the breakdown of excess amino acids. If urea builds up in the body, it causes serious problems, leading to death.

Each kidney has a *ureter* to carry the urine from the kidney to the bladder. Peristaltic waves (like those which move food in the intestine) carry the urine into the bladder.

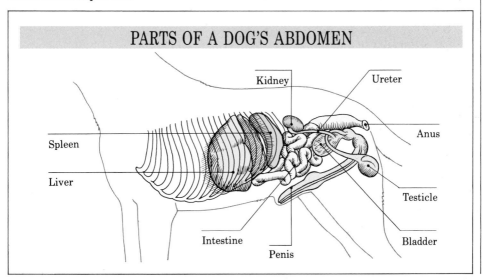

PARTS OF A DOG'S ABDOMEN

Kidney
Ureter
Anus
Spleen
Liver
Testicle
Intestine
Bladder
Penis

The digestive system

The simplest way to consider the dog's own complex "food processor" is via the component parts of the gut, each of which is a food-processing chamber with a specific job. These parts often have their own gland producing enzymes related to their job. The order of stages is:

1 Mouth and salivary glands
2 Oesophagus (gullet)
3 Stomach
4 Duodenum, small intestine and pancreas
5 Liver
6 Large intestine and rectum

The mouth

Once a dog is aware that food is available or that it soon will be, the gut swings into action. Saliva is produced in the mouth by the salivary glands to begin digestion of the impending meal. In many dogs' homes, the opening of a particular cupboard or the sound of the can opener is enough to trigger salivary secretion!

THE FUNCTIONS OF SALIVA

● Saliva acts as a binder to help hold together a bolus of food, and lubricates the oesophagus to ease its passage
● Saliva contains an enzyme which begins digesting starch in the mouth – this is secreted into the food and continues acting in the stomach
● Saliva also "cleans" the tongue
● The sense of taste is partly dependent on the action of saliva, which washes substances out of foods into the dog's taste buds
● Evaporation of saliva from the tongue is part of a dog's method of keeping cool (see p. 33)

From mouth to stomach

The dog takes food into its mouth and chews it using its powerful jaws. The tongue shapes the food into a "bolus", then moves it to the back of the mouth, lifts it through the pharynx, over the larynx and into the *oesophagus*, which opens to receive it and closes behind it.

PARTS OF A DOG'S DIGESTIVE SYSTEM

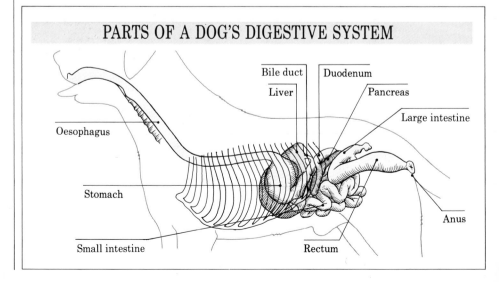

Bile duct
Liver
Duodenum
Pancreas
Large intestine
Oesophagus
Stomach
Anus
Small intestine
Rectum

This highly complex manoeuvre, involving dozens of tiny muscles and finely-tuned nervous control can be summed up in one word – swallowing.

In the oesophagus a muscular process called *peristalsis* squeezes food along the gut like toothpaste in a tube. The oesophagus has thicker walls and is more stretchy than the intestine, so dogs can swallow fairly large solid food items – bones, stones or small toys – although these may then stick in the stomach or small intestine (see p.246). The oesophagus moves the food through the chest into the stomach. A valve called the *cardiac sphincter* opens momentarily to let the bolus of food into the stomach then closes tightly behind it.

Digestion in the stomach
The wall of the dog's stomach is divided into two roughly equal areas – the fundic region and the pyloric region. The fundic region contains the fundic or gastric glands which produce acid, and an enzyme which produces pepsin for breaking down protein in the food. The pyloric region has glands which produce mucus to stop enzymes digesting the gut wall and to keep food moist.

The duodenum
After being held in the stomach for three to four hours, small amounts of food are moved into the *duodenum*. Glands in the duodenum produce a thick, alkaline secretion which begins neutralizing the acid food from the stomach and also protects the intestine from the acid. Other important digestive enzymes enter the duodenum from the *pancreas*.

By the time food has passed through the small intestine, the enzymes have completed their work and the food has been broken down into its component parts, the bulk of it being absorbed.

Much of the water present in the food is reabsorbed in the large intestine before it passes into the rectum and is finally voided as faeces.

The pancreas
This is a mass of tissue sitting in the loop of the duodenum, close to the stomach. The arrival of food in the duodenum promotes the secretion of pancreatic juices. Apart from digestive enzymes, it also produces *insulin*, to help store glucose. Lack of insulin causes *diabetes mellitus* (see p.245).

The liver
The largest single organ in the body of all animals, the liver is a very important "chemical factory". It performs several functions which are linked to the blood, food storage and the removal of toxins ("poisons").

GLANDS AND HORMONES

The many glands in the dog's body fall into two groups – Exocrine glands and Endocrine glands.

Exocrine glands secrete externally and include the salivary, sweat and mammary glands and glands of the stomach, mouth and oesophagus.

Endocrine glands These glands secrete internally. They send chemical "messengers" (hormones) via the bloodstream and include the pituitary, the thyroid, the ovaries and the testes.

A "feedback mechanism" The pituitary gland is a small bump on the underside of the brain. Sometimes called the "master gland", it controls most of the other glands by producing specific stimulating hormones, each of which stimulates one of the other glands to produce its hormone. The hormone produced by the "target gland" then acts on the pituitary to stop production of its stimulating hormone, shutting off the mechanism.

The skin and coat

A dog's skin consists of two basic layers – the *epidermis* (outer layer) and the *dermis* (inner layer).

The epidermis is not nearly so thick in a dog as in humans – the dog's coat performs the protective function for which man needs his thick skin.

The dermis contains blood vessels, skin glands (including the *sebaceous glands*, see below) and *hair follicles*, from which the hair grows up through the epidermis. In man, the dermis and epidermis are linked by interlocking ridges to give flexibility to the skin. The dog has very few of these ridges except on the thick skin of its nose and foot pads. Obviously a dog has far more hair follicles than a man, and these help fuse the two layers.

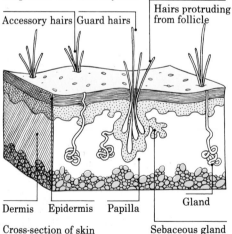

Cross-section of skin
Dermis Epidermis Papilla Gland
Accessory hairs Guard hairs Hairs protruding from follicle
Sebaceous gland

The dog's coat
Nearly all dogs (except some "hairless" breeds) are covered with a thick coat, made up of a mass of individual hairs, each of which grows from within a follicle. At the base of the follicle, a small *papilla* produces keratin – the substance of hair. Hairs grow from follicle complexes of several hairs, including one primary, or "guard" hair belonging to the coarser outer coat and several secondary hairs constituting the softer undercoat. Most of the follicles have a small muscle attached. Because of the acute angle of the attachment of this muscle, its contraction causes the dog's hair to "stand on end".

The sebaceous glands
Sebaceous glands are usually linked to a follicle and are responsible for the oil in a dog's coat. They produce sebum – a secretion which coats the hair to prevent excess wetting or drying and insulates the dog against temperature changes.

Special hairs
Certain sensitive hairs on the dog's body have deeper follicles, with an increased nerve and blood supply. These are the: ☐ *cilia* (eyelashes)
☐ *tragi* (hairs on the external ear)
☐ *vibrissae* (muzzle whiskers).

THE HAIR GROWTH CYCLE
The dog's hair is growing all the time and most dogs moult (see p. 174). The basic cycle of hair growth is divided into three phases: 1 Anagen, 2 Catagen and 3 Telogen.

Anagen is the stage of active hair growth from the papilla. Once a hair has reached its optimum length, it stops growing. The hair is still attached to the papilla – the Catagen stage. Eventually, the papilla contracts, loosening the hair before it begins growing a new hair. This is the Telogen stage and the hair is often finally lost and pushed out by a new hair. These phases of growth occur in various parts of the body at different times. The growth cycle often follows the path of the hair streams (see p.174).

Special features of the dog

Apart from all the various systems which keep it alive and healthy, there are certain aspects which make a dog unmistakably a dog! A mental picture of a dog conjures up a cheerful creature with a wagging tail, tongue perhaps hanging out, and giving the odd lively bark. These are not just ornamental features – they're all useful parts of the dog's way of life.

The dog's bark is one of its ways of signalling to people or to other dogs. There is a strong feeling against the surgical operation of de-barking (banned in the U.K.) – it robs a dog of a useful means of self-expression (see p.216). The dog's tail is another important "mood indicator". A wagging tail signifies pleasure; other positions of the tail show fear, submission or aggression (see pp.216–8). For why dogs pant, see below.

Other characteristics include the tactile whiskers (used for feeling in the dark) and the special anal sacs which allow the dog to scent-mark its territory. For more about how the dog uses these and other special physical endowments, see *Understanding Your Dog*, pp.210–25.

DOES A DOG SWEAT?

Dogs do sweat, but not for the same reasons as people. Dogs have apocrine sweat glands spread over the body which produce a secretion which when broken down by bacteria produces the characteristic "doggy" smell. However, these glands aren't involved in heat regulation at all. Dogs also have eccrine sweat glands in their paws. The secretion from these (mostly water) helps to keep the walking surface soft. Without it the continued friction on the pads would dry them out.

So how does a dog cope with heat regulation? Man has eccrine sweat glands all over his skin in vast numbers to aid the process. Dogs' coats give an insulating layer to reduce problems with overheating. The coat traps heat, and while it may feel hot to the touch, very little is conducted to the skin. Excess heat prompts a dog to produce more sweat from the glands in the paws, making it leave wet footprints!

In fact, most animals use evaporation through their respiratory tract to regulate heat. This is why dogs pant, particularly in hot weather. Panting aids heat loss by evaporation.

Interestingly, the mouse has a different method. Having no sweat glands, it licks itself all over when hot so as to lose heat by evaporation of saliva all over its body.

Dogs' large tongues provide a sizeable area for heat loss.

2

THE ORIGINS OF THE DOG

The dog is part of a family of similar animals which
includes not just dogs but also wolves, foxes, coyotes,
jackals and wild hunting dogs. All these animals have
points in common, the most important being their
indispensable and highly adaptable teeth. Long before
man met up with the dog on a domestic footing, its
ancestors were undergoing the process of evolution.
Although the exact origins of the domestic dog
remain uncertain, this evolution makes a fascinating
study and helps us to appreciate the more deeply
rooted aspects of anatomy and temperament.
Man's domestication of the dog has produced the
incredible variety we see today. The five and a half
million dogs kept as pets in Britain are a testimony to
the continuing success of the relationship.

Where does the dog come from?

The dog belongs to a family of dog-like animals called *Canidae* which are pack hunters. The domestic dog is known as *Canis familiaris*. Other members of the family are wolves, foxes, coyotes, jackals and wild hunting dogs. Some of these wild cousins of the dog are shown on pp.39–41. Some look like the dog, others are very different. They all have some things in common – long, narrow heads with long jaws and plentiful teeth. The cheek teeth are adapted partly for slicing and partly for grinding and can efficiently handle both carnivorous and vegetarian diets.

The dental structure of *Canidae* is one of the admirable qualities which has allowed them to spread so widely across the world and to survive in such a variety of habitats from arid deserts to the freezing Arctic, from tundra to jungle, and the mountain forests of Northern regions.

The evolution of the dog

Many different theories of the dog's evolution have been developed and explored. The wolf, fox and jackal have each been claimed as the dog's direct ancestor. In the 19th century, the great diversity of dog breeds led to the belief – championed by Darwin among others – that more than one wild ancestor had been involved. The jackal and the wolf, and perhaps even the coyote and hyaena, were supposed to have been independently domesticated and their progeny later crossed, so mixing up the genetic possibilities of several distinct species. We now know this is inaccurate and that the incredible variety of today's breeds of dog are the result of intense breeding of the early dogs by man, plus the effects of genetic mutation (see p.187).

Paleocene epoch
Sixty million years ago, a small, weasel-like animal with a long, flexible body, long tail and short legs lived in the forests. This was *Miacis*, the earliest ancestor not only of canids but also of other families – those of racoons, bears, weasels, civets, hyaenas and cats. It walked, like a modern bear, on the soles of its feet (not like modern dogs which walk on their "toes"). These feet had five well separated digits. *Miacis* had the distinctive teeth of the carnivore. Its brain was small but significantly bigger than those of the other primitive carnivores living at the time, the creodonts. These, though far more plentiful than *Miacis*, did not play a part in the evolution of the dog and finally became extinct about 20 million years ago, though most died out long before that.

PALEOCENE	EOCENE
60	55

Millions of years ago

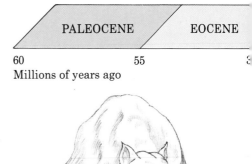

Amphicyon
A heavy bear-like dog with a long tail. It lived between 30 and 5 million years ago, becoming extinct late in the Miocene epoch.

Oligocene epoch

By the early Oligocene epoch, around 35 million years ago, *Miacis* had given rise to a variety of early canids. Over 40 varieties of primitive canids are known to science, some being bear-like dogs, others hyaena-like dogs, and others, the most curious of all, cat-like dogs. There were also dog-like dogs and these were the only ones destined to survive.

Miocene epoch

By the early Miocene epoch, 20 million years ago, a very basic dog-like dog was in existence. Named *Mesocyon*, it had shorter jaws than a modern dog, a long body and tail and stubby legs. The hind foot was still five-toed and spread, unlike the compact four-toed foot of modern canids. By the late Miocene, 10–15 million years ago, we find fossils of *Tomarctus*, a canid with longer jaws and a bigger brain. While not having the degree of intelligence of the dog, it possessed all its social instincts.

Pliocene epoch

The first true *Canis* made its appearance between five and seven million years ago. It was beginning to walk on four of its toes (the fifth was to become the dew claw) and had a more compact foot – ideal for chasing prey.

Quaternary period

By the beginning of the Quaternary period, one million years ago, an early wolf, the Etruscan, was to be found roaming Eurasia. Recent studies suggest that the Etruscan wolf may well have been a direct ancestor of the domestic dog as well as of the present-day wolves, including the small subspecies of the Middle East and India, *Canis lupus pallipes* – an animal closer to the dog than any other wolf subspecies.

The old idea that dogs evolved from jackals, foxes or jackal/wolf crosses has been abandoned. Now most people believe the direct ancestor is likely to have been an animal similar to today's grey wolf.

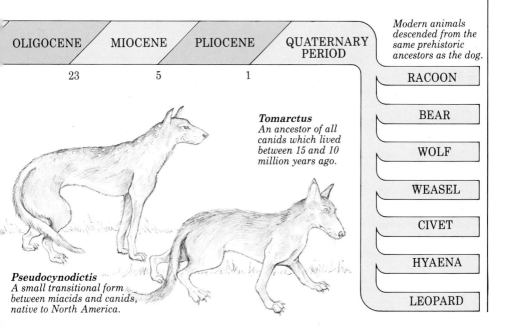

OLIGOCENE	MIOCENE	PLIOCENE	QUATERNARY PERIOD	Modern animals descended from the same prehistoric ancestors as the dog.
23	5	1		RACOON

BEAR

WOLF

WEASEL

CIVET

HYAENA

LEOPARD

Tomarctus
An ancestor of all canids which lived between 15 and 10 million years ago.

Pseudocynodictis
A small transitional form between miacids and canids, native to North America.

Early domestication of the dog

Recent fossil discoveries suggest that the first domestication of the dog took place in the Middle East at least 10,000 and perhaps as much as 35,000 years ago. Some scientists believe that the process of domestication began first with wolves scavenging in the middens of human habitation. Others think that the first contact between humans and wolves was when early man hunted the animals for food, killed the adults and took puppies away for fattening up. Subsequently, wandering bands of *Homo sapiens* brought the creature with them from the Middle East to Europe. Similar invasions may have occurred in Australia, with man importing an ancestor of the dingo.

Civilized man has always represented his dogs in his art and small sculptures of dogs with curled tails, dating from about 6500 B.C. have been discovered in Iraq. Domestic dog bones from an earlier period in the Stone Age (about 7500 B.C.) were excavated in Yorkshire and similar finds have been reported from 10,000 year-old cave sediments in Czechoslovakia. The oldest domestic dog remains unearthed in the U.S.A. came from Jaguar Cave, a Stone Age Indian site in the state of Idaho, dated at around 8300 B.C. Evidence of two kinds of dog – medium and large – was discovered.

The domestic dog spread rapidly all over the world except for Antarctica. Wherever they have lived, dogs have thrived because of their moderate specialization, great adaptability, high intelligence and use of social co-operation – the power of the pack.

Hound being walked in a Royal Park
Detail of a relief frieze from the North Palace at Nineveh, built by Ashurbanipal, circa 649 B.C. British Museum.

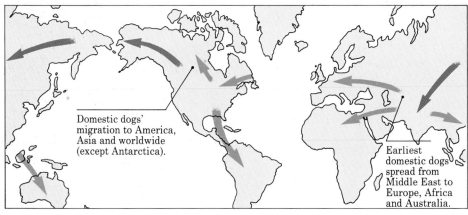

Domestic dogs' migration to America, Asia and worldwide (except Antarctica).

Earliest domestic dogs spread from Middle East to Europe, Africa and Australia.

Map showing the general directions of the worldwide spread of the domestic dog.

The wild cousins of the dog

The modern relatives of the domestic dog are numerous. All are descended from the same early canid stock (*Tomarctus*), but some are not true canids although they have dog-like features. These include the African wild hunting dog, the dhole, the bushdog and the racoon dog.

Grey wolf *(Canis lupus)*
The grey wolf occurs in North America, Europe, Asia and the Middle East, with up to 35 subspecies, including the Great Plains wolf that once followed the herds of American bison and the common wolf of European and Asian forests. It weighs 12–80 kg and its coat colour ranges from white through grey to red-brown or black. In the wild it lives up to 16 years; in captivity up to 20. It feeds on a wide variety of prey including moose, deer, hares, beaver and domestic animals. The wolf will also take carrion and vegetation.

Red wolf *(Canis rufus)*
The red wolf still occurs, hopefully, in South East America, but may well be extinct in the wild. It hybridized extensively with the coyote as the latter expanded eastwards. Weighing 15–30 kg, this animal is (or was) cinnamon or tawny-coloured with dark grey or black streaks.

Coyote *(Canis latrans)*
This canid is found in Canada and North America and weights 11–15 kg. Its coat colour is grey-buff with a black stripe down the middle of the back and black patches on the forelegs and tail. It feeds principally on rabbits and rodents but also takes antelope, deer and sheep. Occasionally, fruit and insects form part of its diet.

Part of a pack of European grey wolves (Canis lupus) *in a snowy forest.*

Jackal

There are four species of jackal, the golden (*Canis aureus*) from Africa, South East Europe and South Asia, the black-backed (*Canis mesomelas*) from East and South Africa, the simien (*Canis simensis*) from Ethiopia and the side-striped (*Canis adustus*) from Tropical Africa. The rarest is the simien, of which perhaps only four to five hundred now exist.

Jackals are slim, dog-like canids weighing 7–15 kg, with coats that vary from yellow and gold (the golden jackal), through russet with a brindle black and white back (the black-backed jackal) to grey with a white stripe on the sides (the side-striped jackal). They enjoy a varied diet including fruit, invertebrates, insects, amphibians, reptiles, small mammals, gazelles and carrion.

Black-backed jackals with their kill
Jackals are no longer considered a likely direct ancestor of dogs, whom they dislike.

Fox

There are four genera of foxes with 21 species. Foxes are one of the most widely distributed groups of mammal, being found in America, Europe, Asia and Africa. They live up to six years in the wild and up to 14 in captivity. The four genera of foxes (one of which is shown, right) are:

1 Vulpine foxes *(Vulpes)* These live in America, Asia and Africa. Species include the red fox and the swift fox.
2 South American foxes *(Dusicyon)* The species include the Argentine grey fox and the so-called small-eared dog, which is not a true dog.
3 Arctic fox *(Alopex lagopus)* This fox lives in the North Polar Region.
4 Bat-eared fox *(Otocyon megalotis)* A fox native to Africa.

Bat-eared fox
A distinctive member of the well-distributed fox family. Foxes live alone and hunt singly.

Dhole *(Cuon alpinus)*

This is the Asian wild dog, distributed throughout West Asia, China, India, Indochina and Indonesia. A secretive animal weighing 12–20 kg with a russet brown coat and black tail, the dhole is under threat from habitat destruction and persecution by man. It feeds on insects, reptiles, rodents and deer, and often kills by disembowelling its prey. Dholes go hunting in packs and are extremely savage.

Dhole and racoon dog
The foxy faces of the dhole (left) and the racoon dog (right). The latter, despite its resemblance to the racoon, is no relation.

Bushdog *(Spetheos venaticus)*
This is the least-known and most intriguing canid and comes from the forests of South America. It is a stocky, squat animal with a wedge-shaped face, stubby ears and a short tail. The coat colour is a rich brown. It weighs 5–7 kg. Very little is known about the life and habits of this elusive species which is endangered at the present time.

Racoon dog *(Nyctereutes procyonoides)*
This animal is native to Eastern Asia, the Far East, China, Japan and North Indochina, and has been introduced into parts of Europe. It looks very much like the racoon, but is not related to it. The racoon dog weighs up to 8 kg and has a long, brindled black and brown coat with black face and legs and black striped tail. It consumes a wide diet including fruit, insects, invertebrates and occasionally small mammals.

African wild hunting dog
(Lycaon pictus)
This fascinating animal inhabits Africa where it is found from the Sahara down to South Africa. It occurs in a variety of habitats but prefers savannah land. It weighs 20–30 kg and has a dark coat with a pattern of light or yellowish blotches unique to each individual. It lives nine to ten years in the wild. Hunting in packs, this species will prey on anything from rodents to zebra and large antelopes.

Maned wolf *(Chrysocyon brachyurus)*
This handsome South American canid weighs about 22 kg and has a red coat, black legs, muzzle and mane and white throat, inner surface of ears and tail tip. An endangered species, it is prone to disease, including kidney worms.

Dingo *(Canis dingo)*
This dog has inhabited Australia for at least eight thousand years. It also occurs in Malaysia, Thailand and Burma. It weighs around 20 kg and has a red/brown coat with white patches. It often attacks domestic animals such as sheep – a serious problem for farmers.

Dingoes at Ayers Rock
Native to Australia, this wild dog has constantly interbred with the domestic dog.

A pack of African wild hunting dogs in Botswana, with their "tortoise-shell" coats.

DOG BREEDS

Go to a dog show and you'll immediately be struck by the sight of so many diverse breeds assembled in one place – the huge, shaggy Pyrenean alongside the tiny Chihuahua, the tall, elegant Afghan beside the solid ugliness of the Bulldog, the wrinkled features of the Bloodhound contrasted with the smooth, egg-shaped face of the Bull Terrier. It seems unbelievable that all these could have been produced from one wolf-like ancestor, yet we know that the diversity of today's breeds is due to intensive selective breeding of the early dogs. Over the centuries, man has created dogs to aid him in the hunt in different ways, dogs to guard, dogs to herd and dogs to play with.

If you want to acquire a dog, use this chapter to find out about the breeds which interest you – their history and origins, their character and temperament, how they should look. Follow the advice given in *Choosing a Dog* (see pp.120–7), too.

The beginnings of breeding

Domestication of the dog is usually dated to between 10,000 and 35,000 years ago (see p.39), making it man's earliest animal companion. Breeding of dogs could have begun quite soon afterwards. One of the earliest objectives may have been to produce a dog that was quite distinct in appearance from a wolf, so that the two were unmistakable. Features such as small size, white coats and curly, upstanding tails were probably favoured in the ancient dog breeds for this reason.

Beyond this, dogs were undoubtedly bred for their usefulness. The first domesticated breeds may have been employed in hunting and defence, or even used as convenient sources of meat and fur – wolfskins were valued for warmth in the Ice-Age climate.

Hunting dogs in action
A section of the Bayeux tapestry, showing fierce hunting dogs with sharp-looking claws being employed with a falcon.

Hunting dogs

As time went on, dogs became more specialized and breeding shaped them for particular tasks. Hunting dogs were gradually developed into types.

Sight hounds

One of the earliest groups to emerge was a kind of hunting dog known as a "sight hound" or "gaze hound", best represented today by the Afghan (p.59), Saluki (p.67) and Greyhound (p.65). Dogs of this type are described in ancient Persian manuscripts and shown in Egyptian tomb paintings. They were of special value in open, treeless country where men armed with bows and arrows couldn't get close enough to their quarry. These swift, silent hounds ran it down, often aided by a trained falcon who would harry and distract the victim. From their Middle Eastern birthplace, gaze hounds were exported to produce such breeds as the Irish Wolfhound (p.66), Scottish Deerhound, Russian Borzoi (p.63) and even the Whippet (p.68).

Scent hounds

The other type of hound, the scent hound, was a much later invention and a distinctly European dog. Hunting in packs, it was a marathon runner rather than a sprinter, with the ability to follow a scent trail and the stamina to run the quarry to eventual exhaustion. Some scent hounds killed the prey; others were trained to keep it at bay then "give tongue", attracting the huntsman by baying. The Elkhound is a good example of this type.

Retrievers and pointers

With the invention of the gun, another major source of employment for hunting dogs was established. Dogs with sensitive noses could locate the targets for the hunter, others could flush the prey – usually birds – while a third group were needed to retrieve them once shot. New virtues were demanded of such dogs – a "soft mouth" in retrieving dogs to prevent damage to the birds, and restraint in the case of pointers which had to freeze when they caught a scent.

The hunters began with dogs that had long been used for hunting with nets, principally a now-extinct breed known as the Spanish Pointer (p.50). By intensive breeding, they established the required qualities, producing dogs of unsurpassed loyalty and intelligence.

The early terriers

Many centuries earlier, another type of hunting dog of a very different build and temperament had been developed to tackle burrowing animals – foxes, badgers, rats and rabbits. These dogs were, for some reason, largely produced in Britain and were established here very early. The Roman troops noticed them and described them as *terrarii*, from which the name "terrier" comes. Short legs, and a fiery, tenacious spirit are their principal attributes. The British terriers were for centuries a rag-bag mixture of tough, working dogs, but in the late 18th and 19th centuries they became very popular, particularly among the working classes of the new industrial centres. A great variety of distinctive types were developed.

Guards, herders and playthings

Hunting was only one of the ways in which dogs could assist man. Once other animals such as sheep and goats had been domesticated, the dog's usefulness as a herder probably became apparent. The sort of tactics which a wolf uses to separate its intended victim from the herd, were exploited in the sheepdog.

Other dogs were developed over the centuries as guard-dogs, dogs of war, sledge-dogs and beasts of burden. As man's activities diversified, different roles opened up. Dogs could rescue people from drowning, guide them through snowy mountains, alert them to intruders, run alongside carriages, track down criminals, sniff out explosives, and guide the blind.

In contrast to these hard-working dogs, there was a tradition of completely idle "toy" breeds, which provided companionship, affection and amusement. These breeds go back at least 2,000 years, and were independently developed in Europe and the Far East. Miniaturization was an important feature, though in many, the extremes of size were only achieved quite recently. Once the preserve of the aristocracy, toys are now kept in enormous numbers by people in all walks of life.

Extinct breeds
Illustrations from Thomas Bewick's "General History of Quadrupeds", 1790, showing a Mastiff type (top) and a Ban-Dog (bottom).

Breed families of today

The usage of dogs – whether for gun-work or coursing, as watch-dogs, sheep-herders or toys – is the basis for the group system used in dog shows today. But cutting across these classifications reveals the remnants of ancient family relationships. Mastiffs (p.77), for example, have a recognized physique: burly, short-necked with a massive head and wrinkled face. Most such dogs are large and used as guard-dogs, but one toy breed, the Pug (p.117), shows the same sort of family characteristics. Most of the toy dogs are related to larger breeds in other groups – terriers, spaniels and coursing dogs – with very different roles. The Pomeranian (p.116), for example, bears all the marks of a Spitz dog, undoubtedly the most distinctive of the family groups.

The Spitz breeds

The Spitz dogs are a distinctive group that all have an erect tail which curls over the back, a sharply pointed, wolf-like face, short erect ears, a sturdy, four-square stance, and a ruff of thicker fur around the neck. Examples are the Finnish Spitz, the Samoyed (p.83), the Akita (right) and the Keeshond (p.47). There are dozens of Spitz breeds and they all originate from the far North, once being the only type of dog found in sub-Arctic regions. They were used by the Eskimos and their Siberian counterparts for herding, sledge-pulling and other strenuous work. How such a distinctive group could have arisen and been maintained is a matter for speculation, but it seems clear that the isolation of the North's cold regions was instrumental in preserving their distinctive appearance.

Other distinctive dogs

In other parts of the world isolation has again been a factor in producing singular breeds. The barren steppes of Mongolia produced the Chow Chow (p.104), whose black tongue and stiff,

Rhodesian Ridgeback
A breed originally from South Africa. The distinctive line of hair running along the back and forming the shape of a dagger, is unique.

Akita
The Japanese Akita is a strong, Spitz-type dog, and the most popular of the three breeds native to Japan. It is gradually becoming more widespread in other countries.

straight legs mark it out from other dogs. Also out of Asia came the extraordinary sheepdogs of Hungary, the Komondor and Puli, whose long, profuse coat will, with a little persuasion, fall into cords which look exactly like Rastafarian "dreadlocks".

Farther east, China engendered the strangely wrinkled Shar Pei and the bizarre Crested Dog – completely bald, but for a plume of long, silky hair on its head. The African continent also boasts two unusual dogs, the Rhodesian Ridgeback, whose name refers to a peculiar line of black hair running the length of the spine, and the odd little barkless Basenji, from Central Africa, whose voice is a soft, yodelling howl.

The influence of the dog show
Dog shows became popular in the second half of the nineteenth century. Breeders' conflicting ideas about how a breed should look led to the establishment of clubs which set a standard for each breed.

The introduction of these standardized "ideals" heralded a fundamental change in attitude to breeds of dog. From then on, appearance was all-important, and the usefulness of dogs, which had previously been the breeder's guiding light, took second place.

The problem of inbreeding
At the same time, the idea of pure-breeding (crossing only with dogs of the same breed) automatically took hold. This resulted in different breeds becoming largely isolated in a genetic sense, so that the same, rather limited set of genes became endlessly mixed and remixed down the pedigree lines. The dogs that won shows were in demand as parents, while those that didn't conform to the ideal were discarded by the breeders. The inevitable consequence of all this was a certain amount of inbreeding – the crossing of dogs already related. This

Keeshond (above)
A typical Spitz breed from Holland with a wonderfully full coat.
Basenji (right)
Native to Africa, this dog doesn't bark.

has resulted in some genetic defects and, in certain types, loss of vigour.

Some defects may not be all that obvious, or may not manifest themselves until the dog is seven or eight years old, allowing the victim to reproduce and so pass on these characters to the next generation. Other defects may be corrected by surgery, as in the Shar Pei, which often has a congenital defect known as entropion (see p.256), where the eyelids turn inwards, digging into the eyes and causing immense pain. A simple operation can rectify this in an individual, but can't change its genes, and its progeny are likely to be victims of the same disability.

Responsible breeders try to weed out weak, ailing or temperamentally unsound animals, but others are tempted to breed from a dog with outstanding "show characters", whatever its defects. When fashion dictates that a certain breed is in demand, there's a tendency for some breeders to cash in and sell "production-line" puppies. These may conform in appearance to a breed, but often have genetic faults.

The Shar Pei
An ancient Chinese breed which has been rescued from near-extinction. Despite its strange appearance, it is quite an attraction at shows.

THE BREED STANDARDS

The world of the dog show (see *Dog Shows*, pp.198–209), can be rather difficult to understand at first. At the major shows, seemingly identical dogs parade in front of a judge who inspects each closely, looks in their mouths, watches them run round the ring, and then, mysteriously, pronounces one the winner. The casual onlooker is unlikely to understand how that particular dog differed from all the others.

The basis for the judge's decision is the "breed standard" – a description of the ideal to which that breed should aspire. The "Key Characteristics" given for every breed shown in this chapter are derived from the official standard for that breed. The standard is drawn up by the breed club and revised or refined from time to time. It is detailed and often very lengthy, but entirely verbal – no sketches or photographs accompany it.

Consequently the words are open to individual interpretation, and each judge makes of the breed standard what he or she will. Some might favour one dog, while another would award the prize to a different individual, although they would probably agree if asked to pick the outright losers.

It is this element of variability that keeps dog shows going. Without it, they might well fall victim to their own essential illogic: on the one hand they are trying to get dogs to conform to an ideal, but on the other, judging one to be better than another.

The breed categories

This chapter groups breeds in the following categories:

Gundogs pp.50–8

Hounds pp.59–68

Working Dogs pp.69–87

Terriers pp.88–101

Special Dogs pp. 102–9

Toy Dogs pp.110–19

In general, the breed categories are the same in the U.K. and the U.S.A. In the original shows, all dogs were judged together. Later came a division into sporting and non-sporting, then the sporting category was further divided into three groups: Gundogs (still called "Sporting Dogs" in the U.S.A.), Hounds and Terriers. The non-sporting dogs proved more difficult to classify. The Toys were separated out, then the Working Dogs, leaving a miscellaneous collection known as "Utility" in the U.K., but as "Non-sporting Dogs" in the U.S.A. Most of its members are highly distinctive dogs, so the name "Special Dogs" has been given to it here.

Four dogs in the "Special" group of this chapter belong in different categories in the U.S.A. They are:
- Miniature Schnauzer (Terriers)
- Giant Schnauzer (Working Dogs)
- Shih Tzu (Toys)
- Toy Poodle (Toys).

The Bichon Frisé (Toys) belongs to the Non-sporting group of the U.S.A.

ASPECTS OF APPEARANCE

Some breeds need very little preparation for the show-ring. For the majority, however, hours of brushing, clipping, and shampooing are necessary preliminaries. In dogs like this, the skilful treatment of the coat is an essential part of the breed "look". (For how to groom various coat types, see p.176.)

Ear cropping Another integral aspect of a dog's appearance may be cropped ears. The practice is illegal in the U.K. With those breeds which either may or must have cropped ears in the U.S.A., a note is included to this effect on the relevant breeds pages.

Tail docking This is a fairly common feature of many breeds and some breeds are required to have it done for the show-ring. Tail docking is normally carried out at a few days old (see p.131).

Dobermanns with cropped and uncropped ears
Cropped ears stand erect. In some countries, ear cropping is thought essential for some breeds; in the U.K. it is banned.

Pointer

A breed where appearance takes second place to working abilities. An extremely professional show-dog.

History Originally used to locate hares, which were then coursed by greyhounds, the Pointer came into its own with the advent of the gun, since it could pinpoint game accurately. The oldest breed, the Spanish Pointer, goes back 300 years or more. The English Pointer was bred from Spanish stock and emerged as a distinct breed in the last century, a faster and more enterprising animal than earlier pointers.

Temperament Once a rather fierce breed, the introduction of setter blood has made the Pointer an easily managed dog.

Requirements A Pointer can become a good, affectionate pet, but its heart is really in its work, and it needs to hunt regularly.

German Shorthaired Pointer
A hardy gundog combining the skills of a pointer and a retriever. The short tail, produced by docking, should be carried down or horizontally.

KEY CHARACTERISTICS *Pointer*

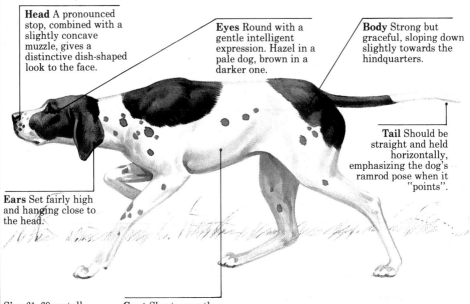

Head A pronounced stop, combined with a slightly concave muzzle, gives a distinctive dish-shaped look to the face.

Eyes Round with a gentle intelligent expression. Hazel in a pale dog, brown in a darker one.

Body Strong but graceful, sloping down slightly towards the hindquarters.

Tail Should be straight and held horizontally, emphasizing the dog's ramrod pose when it "points".

Ears Set fairly high and hanging close to the head.

Size 61–69 cm tall.

Coat Short, smooth and variable in colour. Lemon, orange, liver and black are all seen, usually mixed with white.

The "point" The dog freezes in this characteristic pose when it catches a scent, and remains still until told to move forward.

Golden Retriever

A dog which has seen a meteoric rise in popularity since its recognition as a distinct breed in 1913. Though still a gundog at heart, the Golden Retriever makes an excellent family pet.

History Like the Flat-coated Retrievers from which they were derived, Golden Retrievers are intelligent, hardworking dogs that can withstand extremely cold, wet conditions. Both breeds were designed specifically for wild-fowl hunting, and in creating them various setters and spaniels were crossed with the St John's Newfoundland. Water-spaniel blood was added later. Like its ancestors, the Golden Retriever loves swimming.

Temperament The gentle, good-humoured face of this dog reveals its personality. It is also obedient and highly intelligent.

Requirements Plenty of exercise is essential, and a cold climate suits this breed best. It needs regular grooming.

KEY CHARACTERISTICS *Golden Retriever*

Eyes Set wide apart, dark in colour, with dark rims.

Tail Sitting horizontally for preference, not upstanding or curled at the end.

Ears Set high on the head, but not too large.

Head A good broad head with powerful muzzle and black nose.

Body Deep-chested and well-balanced.

Coat Wavy or flat with generous feathering, in gold or cream, without white patches.

Size 51–56 cm tall for a bitch, 56–61 cm tall for a dog.

Flat-coated Retriever
The Golden Retriever was bred from a glossy dark-coloured breed known as the Flat-coated Retriever. Its coat can be black or liver-coloured. It remains a popular gundog and is an excellent show-dog but is only now becoming widely accepted as a pet.

Labrador Retriever

A breed that combines many virtues, being a first-class gundog and an ideal family pet.

History The Labrador's career has had three distinct phases. It began as a fisherman's dog in Newfoundland, trained to bring in the nets through perilous, icy waters. This was probably the breed known as the St John's Newfoundland.

Newfoundland fishermen, bringing fish across to England, also sold off their dogs, and in its new home the breed was developed as a gundog. The name "Labrador" was coined in 1887, by an early devotee of the breed, the Earl of Malmesbury. More recently the Labrador has become one of the best-known companion dogs in the world and the dog most favoured as a guide for the blind.

Temperament The main reason for the Labrador's success as a pet is its personality: good tempered, amiable, loyal and utterly reliable with children, but not so placid as to fail to defend properly.

Requirements Because these dogs are so easy-going there is a tendency to think that they can adapt to almost any lifestyle. But they aren't well suited to a completely sedentary suburban existence and do need a fair amount of exercise to stay in trim. They should be allowed to swim regularly, for their love of water is an inescapable part of their past.

KEY CHARACTERISTICS *Labrador Retriever*

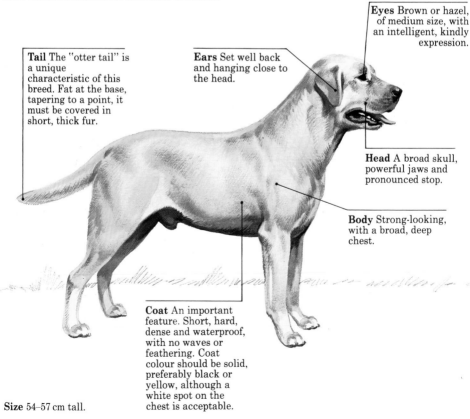

Eyes Brown or hazel, of medium size, with an intelligent, kindly expression.

Tail The "otter tail" is a unique characteristic of this breed. Fat at the base, tapering to a point, it must be covered in short, thick fur.

Ears Set well back and hanging close to the head.

Head A broad skull, powerful jaws and pronounced stop.

Body Strong-looking, with a broad, deep chest.

Coat An important feature. Short, hard, dense and waterproof, with no waves or feathering. Coat colour should be solid, preferably black or yellow, although a white spot on the chest is acceptable.

Size 54–57 cm tall.

Irish Red Setter

Often known simply as the "Red Setter", this is the raciest of the gundogs.

History Spaniels, other setters and the Spanish pointers may all have played a part in this breed's ancestry. Once a red-and-white dog, the pure red form appeared in the 19th century and became increasingly popular. Setters were originally used for locating game which was then caught in a net. They freeze like a pointer on scenting their quarry, but then drop to the ground, or "set".

Temperament Irish Setters have great charm – lively, affectionate, excitable and mischievous, they need firm handling and thorough obedience training.

Requirements Wide open spaces, where they can work off their superabundant energy and high spirits, are essential.

English Setter
The smallest of the setters, the English has a silky, wavy coat, always partially white. It is exceptionally affectionate and friendly, so much so that it makes a useless guard-dog. The Irish Setter is better in this respect.

KEY CHARACTERISTICS *Irish Red Setter*

Size Balance and proportion are more important than height. Average height is 68.5 cm.

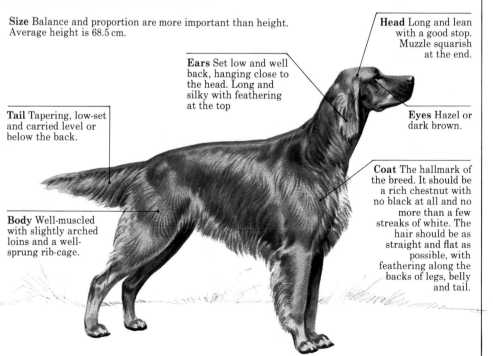

Head Long and lean with a good stop. Muzzle squarish at the end.

Ears Set low and well back, hanging close to the head. Long and silky with feathering at the top

Tail Tapering, low-set and carried level or below the back.

Eyes Hazel or dark brown.

Body Well-muscled with slightly arched loins and a well-sprung rib-cage.

Coat The hallmark of the breed. It should be a rich chestnut with no black at all and no more than a few streaks of white. The hair should be as straight and flat as possible, with feathering along the backs of legs, belly and tail.

Brittany Spaniel

An all-round gundog that is very popular in France and America. It has not yet been awarded championship status by the British Kennel Club.

History The name "spaniel" is probably derived from "Espanol" and recalls the fact that many gundogs – setters and pointers, as well as spaniels – trace their forebears back to the ancient sporting dogs of Spain. In general, spaniels are used to flush birds for the guns, whereas pointers and setters are primarily concerned with locating game. But the Brittany Spaniel is an exception in that it points, as well as putting up the quarry for the guns, and retrieving it afterwards. This versatile dog also displays a lean, leggy physique that has more in common with the setters than with other spaniels. Within the last century, English Pointer blood was added to the breed which undoubtedly accentuated these characteristics. The Brittany remains very much a working dog, and any decorative features, such as feathering of the coat that might hamper it in dense undergrowth, are discouraged.

Temperament As with most gundogs, the long working partnership with man has produced an affable, intelligent, cooperative and willing breed. They are fairly suspicious of strangers.

Requirements Regular long walks are a must, and the Brittany will be happiest if allowed to work.

KEY CHARACTERISTICS *Brittany Spaniel*

Ears Short, leafy and set above the eye-level.

Head Wedge-shaped, with a medium stop. Nose wide with good nostrils, colour to tone with the darkest body colour.

Coat Dense, wavy or flat, but not curly or silky. The colour is a deep orange and white, or liver and white, with no black.

Tail No more than a stump, maximum length 10 cm. This may be a natural feature, or one produced by docking.

Eyes Amber or brown, not protuberant, and well protected by the brow.

Body A short, straight back and muscular, sloping shoulders.

Size 44.5–52 cm tall.

Springer Spaniel

A sturdy gundog, with a good-natured vitality that makes it an excellent companion.

History When the old and diverse group of dogs known as "land spaniels" were separated into two distinct groups, the larger types acquired the name of Springer Spaniels, since they were used primarily to "spring" game for falconers. To be successful at this work, great stamina and endurance were required, plus a keen nose and an inexhaustible interest in flushing birds. With the introduction of the gun, the breed's role changed, as it was also required to retrieve birds.

Temperament Willing and affectionate.

Requirements This is essentially a country dog, although it can adapt to urban life if adequate exercise is allowed for. The coat needs regular grooming.

Welsh Springer Spaniel
A little smaller and more lightly built than the English Springer Spaniel, this breed is always red and white in colour.

KEY CHARACTERISTICS *Springer Spaniel*

Eyes Dark hazel with an alert, kindly expression. The haws (third eyelids) should not be visible.

Tail Set low, well feathered and carried level. It is usually docked.

Head Fairly broad, with a pronounced stop, divided by a fluting between the eyes.

Ears Set in line with the eyes and close to the head.

Coat Close and weather-resistant, but not coarse. Liver and white or black and white are the preferred colours, with or without tan markings.

Body Strong-looking, with muscular thighs. The chest should have a good depth.

Size About 51 cm tall.

American Cocker Spaniel

Like the English Cocker Spaniel from which it was derived, this breed has largely relinquished its sporting past to become an enormously popular pet.

History Around 1880, the first English Cocker Spaniels were introduced in America. A distinct type soon emerged from the original, as a selective breeding programme got underway to produce a dog better adapted to the needs of American sportsmen. The game-birds tended to be smaller than in England, and the dog decreased in size correspondingly. Other changes accompanied this, and by the 1930s the differences warranted separation of the English and American Cockers. Both are now officially recognized in each country. The younger breed was the favourite dog in its native home in the years after the Second World War, and it is one of the more common spaniels in Britain.

Temperament Breeding for the show has not affected this spaniel's intelligent and sporty nature.

Requirements Regular trimming and grooming of the coat plus plenty of exercise are needed.

KEY CHARACTERISTICS *American Cocker Spaniel*

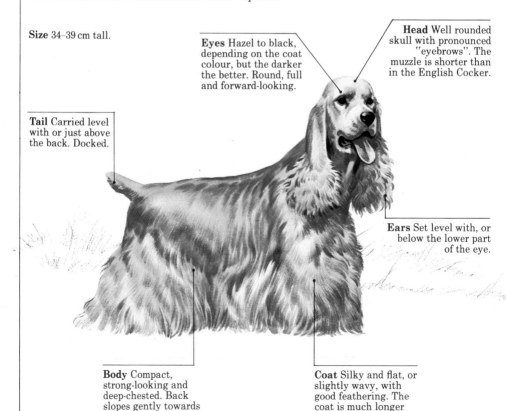

Size 34–39 cm tall.

Eyes Hazel to black, depending on the coat colour, but the darker the better. Round, full and forward-looking.

Head Well rounded skull with pronounced "eyebrows". The muzzle is shorter than in the English Cocker.

Tail Carried level with or just above the back. Docked.

Ears Set level with, or below the lower part of the eye.

Body Compact, strong-looking and deep-chested. Back slopes gently towards the tail.

Coat Silky and flat, or slightly wavy, with good feathering. The coat is much longer than in English Cockers. Colours very variable.

Cocker Spaniel

The family of breeds known as spaniels dates back at least to the 14th century, when Chaucer wrote of "Spanyels", in his Canterbury Tales.

History As the ancient spaniel family diversified, its representatives became specialized for different types of work. By the early 19th century there was a group identified as the "cockers", and these were the forebears of today's breed. Their name may have come from the old word "cock" – to flush game – but it could also have derived from the use of this breed in hunting woodcock. The Cocker's development was centred around Wales and southern England, but as more colour varieties evolved, adding roans, black and white, and red, for example, to the original black, the Cocker gained more widespread admiration. It was Britain's most popular breed by the mid-1930s, and is reasonably common in America.

Temperament Cheerful, loving and intelligent, the Cocker makes a perfect companion.

Requirements The coat needs regular brushing, and some trimming on the feet and ears. Plenty of exercise is a must, too, so this isn't a suitable breed for busy families with little spare time.

KEY CHARACTERISTICS *Cocker Spaniel*

Eyes Dark brown, never pale, full but not prominent.

Head Handsomely chiselled, with a distinct stop at the halfway mark. Muzzle square and nose wide.

Body Very strong and compact. Topline sloping gradually towards the tail.

Tail Carried level and docked.

Ears Set level with the eyes.

Coat Silky and flat, with some feathering. Colours are very variable.

Size 38–41 cm tall.

Weimaraner

The "grey ghost dog" of Germany, this is a "purpose-built" breed with a wide range of hunting skills.

History Some dogs emerge gradually over the centuries, others are deliberately put together by breeders with a clear objective in mind. There's a bit of both in the Weimaraner, for grey hunting dogs have been known in Germany since at least the 1630s, but it was only in the 19th century that the sporting noblemen of Weimar took charge of the breed and moulded it to their own specifications. The result was a superb, all-round gundog, capable of tackling both large and small game. Until 1929, it was rigorously controlled by the Weimaraner club, and breeding was not allowed outside Germany. But eventually an American enthusiast succeeded in introducing the dog in America where it soon became a highly popular sporting dog.

Temperament With good breeding stock and careful handling, the Weimaraner can become a reliable family dog. But it is an intelligent and wilful animal, for whom a thorough course of training is recommended. Undue fierceness has at times been a problem; it is vital to obtain puppies from a reputable source.

Requirements A Weimaraner needs plentiful exercise every day.

KEY CHARACTERISTICS *Weimaraner*

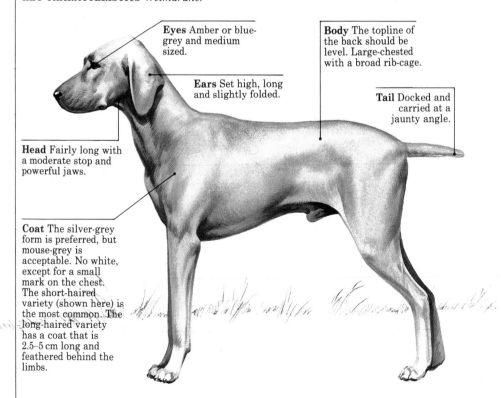

Eyes Amber or blue-grey and medium sized.

Ears Set high, long and slightly folded.

Body The topline of the back should be level. Large-chested with a broad rib-cage.

Tail Docked and carried at a jaunty angle.

Head Fairly long with a moderate stop and powerful jaws.

Coat The silver-grey form is preferred, but mouse-grey is acceptable. No white, except for a small mark on the chest. The short-haired variety (shown here) is the most common. The long-haired variety has a coat that is 2.5–5 cm long and feathered behind the limbs.

Size 56–63.3 cm tall for a bitch, 61–68.5 cm tall for a dog.

Afghan Hound

A supremely elegant dog which, according to Afghan legend, travelled on the Ark with Noah.

History The ancestors of the Afghan are believed to have come from Egypt, where references to a dog of this type date back to 3,000 B.C. Trade routes between the Middle East and Far East probably carried this valuable hound up into the Afghan mountains, where the length of its coat was increased as a protection against extreme winter cold. For centuries it remained a dog of the nobility, hunting gazelles, antelope, wolves and foxes. The first British import arrived in 1886, but the breed did not reach America until 1926.

Temperament Pleasant and good natured, but with an independent streak that can cause trouble if not dealt with firmly. Its urge to chase and kill is very strong. The appearance of aloofness, however, is deceptive: Afghans need kindness and attention and will pine if treated as nothing more than four-legged ornaments.

Requirements Definitely a dog for those with plenty of spare time and money. It needs generous amounts of exercise, grooming and food.

KEY CHARACTERISTICS *Afghan Hound*

Head Long, but not too narrow. The nose black, or liver-coloured in a pale dog.

Eyes Dark or golden, almost triangular, with an Oriental slant.

Tail Set low, but raised when the dog moves. Ringed at the end and sparsely feathered.

Body Moderate length, level, muscular back. A reasonably deep chest.

Ears Set low and well back. Carried close to the head and covered by silky hair.

Coat Very long and fine except along the back and on the foreface. Pasterns can be bare.

Size 61–68 cm tall for a bitch. 68.5–73.5 cm tall for a dog.

Basset Hound

With its nose inevitably close to the ground, the Basset is among the finest of the scent hounds.

History This sturdy, short-legged hound originated in France in the late 16th century. The shape of its head and the sharpness of its scenting powers suggest a close relationship with the Bloodhound, and it may have arisen through a mutation in that breed, producing dwarfism. In the early 19th century, Bassets came into their own, being most useful to those hunting on foot. Though slow-moving, they trundle through seemingly impenetrable undergrowth with ease, and can be used for hunting hares, rabbits and pheasants.

Temperament Appearances can be misleading. Behind the Basset's doleful expression lies an exceptionally merry, lively dog, affectionate and good with children. Generally obedient, it becomes oblivious to everything when on to a scent.

Requirements The Basset's ponderous gait doesn't mean that it can do without exercise – a sedentary dog quickly becomes overweight.

KEY CHARACTERISTICS *Basset Hound*

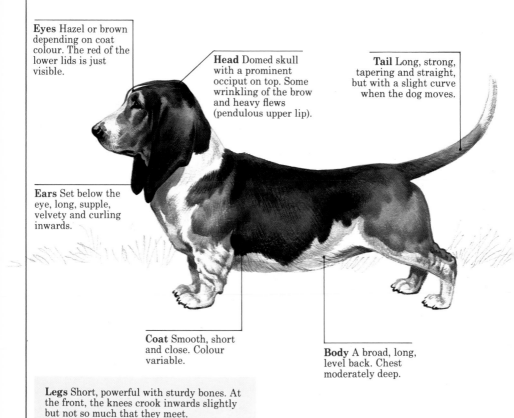

Eyes Hazel or brown depending on coat colour. The red of the lower lids is just visible.

Head Domed skull with a prominent occiput on top. Some wrinkling of the brow and heavy flews (pendulous upper lip).

Tail Long, strong, tapering and straight, but with a slight curve when the dog moves.

Ears Set below the eye, long, supple, velvety and curling inwards.

Coat Smooth, short and close. Colour variable.

Body A broad, long, level back. Chest moderately deep.

Legs Short, powerful with sturdy bones. At the front, the knees crook inwards slightly but not so much that they meet.

Size 33–38 cm tall.

Beagle

Like its larger cousin, the Foxhound, the Beagle is a sturdy intelligent dog with a long, well-documented history.

History Beagles have a 500-year tradition of hunting hares, using their fine noses to keep track of their quarry, and running them down by sheer persistence. The smallest dogs, standing less than 25 cm tall and known as "Pocket Beagles", could be carried to the start of the chase on horseback, in the capacious pocket of a hunting coat. But Beagles were also useful to hunters on foot, and the smaller ones, in particular, were used for hunting rabbits.

Temperament Cheerful and friendly, but with a tendency to wilfulness typical of pack dogs. Obedience training and firm handling are essential.

Requirements Beagles should be exercised every day, and they cannot be left alone for too long.

American Foxhound
Descended from English foxhounds, first brought to the New World in 1650, the American Foxhound is a large dog, standing 53–63.5 cm tall.

KEY CHARACTERISTICS *Beagle*

Head Divided halfway by a definite stop. Squarish muzzle with moderate flews (upper lip) and a broad nose.

Eyes Dark brown or hazel, neither bulging nor deeply set.

Tail Sturdy and set high. Carried gaily, but not curling over the dog's back.

Ears Long and low-set, with a fine texture.

Coat Short, dense and waterproof.

Body A deep chest, powerful loins, and a straight, level back.

Size 33–40 cm tall.

Bloodhound

A large hound whose formidable sense of smell is legendary.

History This is an ancient breed, at least two thousand years old. In France, Switzerland and Belgium they are known as St Hubert Hounds, after the patron saint of hunting, who kept a pack of large, black Bloodhounds at his abbey. The breed has had many royal enthusiasts in the past, and its name may reflect its aristocratic connections and long bloodlines as much as its hunting prowess. Certainly it does not refer to any ferocity, the Bloodhound being one of the gentlest of dogs. It regards hunting as something of a game: having found its quarry it is completely satisfied and will probably lick it energetically or simply wag its tail.

Temperament The Bloodhound isn't everyone's ideal pet. It is generally a solemn and reserved dog, although affectionate with its family. Sniffing things out is a lifelong obsession, and Bloodhounds are difficult to recall once they are on the trail.

Requirements Carefully regulated feeding and plenty of vigorous exercise are essential.

KEY CHARACTERISTICS *Bloodhound*

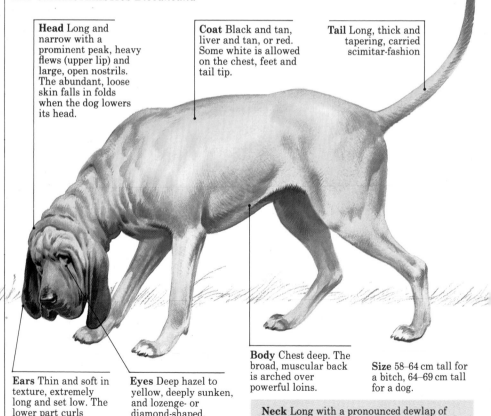

Head Long and narrow with a prominent peak, heavy flews (upper lip) and large, open nostrils. The abundant, loose skin falls in folds when the dog lowers its head.

Coat Black and tan, liver and tan, or red. Some white is allowed on the chest, feet and tail tip.

Tail Long, thick and tapering, carried scimitar-fashion

Ears Thin and soft in texture, extremely long and set low. The lower part curls inwards and backwards.

Eyes Deep hazel to yellow, deeply sunken, and lozenge- or diamond-shaped.

Body Chest deep. The broad, muscular back is arched over powerful loins.

Size 58–64 cm tall for a bitch, 64–69 cm tall for a dog.

Neck Long with a pronounced dewlap of loose skin.

Borzoi

Like the Afghan, the Borzoi is a gaze hound – a fast-running dog that hunts by sight.

History The Borzoi is said to have the same Middle Eastern ancestors as the Saluki and Afghan, but these ancient coursing dogs were unable to survive the severe winters further north. Crossing with a long-legged Russian collie type introduced the necessary hardiness and a thick, curly coat. Borzois were kept in packs by the Russian nobility and used for the ritualistic hunting of wolves. A present from the Czar to Queen Victoria introduced the breed to Britain in 1842, and Borzois arrived in America in 1889.

Temperament Generally calm and affectionate, although it should be remembered that they are a hunting breed. As always, it is best to obtain puppies from a recognized breeder. The size, power and speed of the animal makes obedience training essential.

Requirements This is not a dog to be taken on lightly. Its appetite, both for food and exercise, is huge, the coat needs regular grooming, and its personality requires firm and consistent management.

KEY CHARACTERISTICS *Borzoi*

Eyes Dark, alert and almond-shaped, with dark rims.

Body The back should be gently arched. Chest deep but rather narrow.

Ears Small, fine and mobile.

Head Long and lean with almost no stop, giving the distinctive narrow wedge-shape. Nose black.

Coat Long and preferably curly, but wavy or flat coats are acceptable. On the head, ears and front legs it should be short and smooth. Any colour, but white usually predominates.

Tail Long, low and thickly feathered, straight or sickle-shaped, but not curled.

Size 68 cm or more tall for a bitch, 73 cm or more tall for a dog.

Dachshunds

Small, short-legged dogs that were wrongly classified through a misunderstanding: the German name "dachshund" means "badger-dog", but the "hund" was translated as "hound".

History Dachshunds were bred to hunt foxes and rabbits as well as badgers, their small size allowing them to pursue the animals underground. The original dogs were of standard size, but towards the end of the 19th century smaller Dachshunds were developed. Miniatures are now the most popular.

Temperament All Dachshunds are very lively, particularly the smooth-haired breed. They also make good watch-dogs.

Requirements A romp in a large garden usually provides enough exercise.

KEY CHARACTERISTICS *Standard Smooth-haired Dachshund*

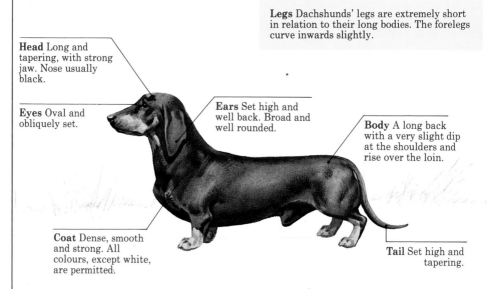

Legs Dachshunds' legs are extremely short in relation to their long bodies. The forelegs curve inwards slightly.

Head Long and tapering, with strong jaw. Nose usually black.

Eyes Oval and obliquely set.

Ears Set high and well back. Broad and well rounded.

Body A long back with a very slight dip at the shoulders and rise over the loin.

Coat Dense, smooth and strong. All colours, except white, are permitted.

Tail Set high and tapering.

Size Standard: up to 10.4 kg for a bitch, 11.3 kg for a dog. Miniature: up to 5 kg.

Long-haired and Wire-haired Dachshunds
Although similar in most respects, Long-haired Dachshunds are generally more calm and reserved than the smooth-haired breed. The wire- *haired type shows traces of the terrier blood used to introduce its coat and has an affectionate, energetic and sporty temperament. Both varieties also come in Miniature.*

Greyhound

The fastest-running of all dogs, with a speed of almost 40 mph. Three basic types have been developed – the track dog, the show-dog and the coursing dog.

History The origin of the name "Greyhound" is a matter for debate, but it may be a corruption of "gaze hound", a collective name for dogs that hunt by sight. Like other gaze hounds, the Greyhound originated in the Middle East and is thought to be as much as 6,000 years old. It is unusual among long-established breeds in having changed remarkably little over the centuries.

Temperament Gentle, affectionate and loyal. It is extremely biddable and well behaved, so makes an excellent show-dog.

Requirements Plenty of exercise and food.

Italian Greyhound
A miniature version of the Greyhound, the Italian weighs only 2.5 to 3.5 kg. Its slender bones and petite build put it in the toy dog category.

KEY CHARACTERISTICS *Greyhound*

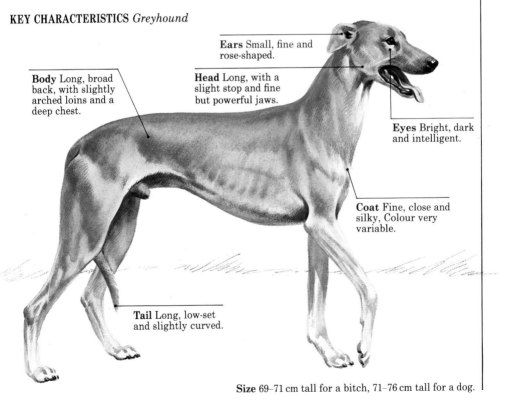

Ears Small, fine and rose-shaped.

Body Long, broad back, with slightly arched loins and a deep chest.

Head Long, with a slight stop and fine but powerful jaws.

Eyes Bright, dark and intelligent.

Coat Fine, close and silky, Colour very variable.

Tail Long, low-set and slightly curved.

Size 69–71 cm tall for a bitch, 71–76 cm tall for a dog.

Irish Wolfhound

Centuries of Celtic legend surround this huge, dignified hound, the hunting companion of Ireland's ancient kings and queens.

History As far back as Roman times, Ireland was known for its exceptional hounds – dogs of dramatic size and versatile hunting abilities. These qualities made them popular additions to the households of the European nobility. Although their main duty was to hunt the wolves which then roamed the Irish forests, they could also be used in the pursuit of other large game, including deer and wild boar. But the fate of the Wolfhound was linked with its main quarry, and its popularity waned as the last wolves were killed in the 18th century. It required concerted efforts and input from other breeds (including the Scottish Deerhound) to resurrect the Irish Wolfhound in the late 19th century.

Temperament A "gentle giant", this hound is reliable, intelligent and companionable. Despite its immense power and abilities as a guard-dog, it can be trusted with children.

Requirements A Wolfhound's owners must allow it the space it needs, and take its appetites for food and exercise seriously.

KEY CHARACTERISTICS *Irish Wolfhound*

Tail Long and slightly curved. Moderately thick and covered with hair.

Head Long, but not too broad, with a long, slightly pointed muzzle.

Eyes Dark.

Ears Small and lying flat.

Coat Wiry and rough. Colour very variable, including grey and black.

Body Back preferably long. Belly drawn up and loins arched, with good depth to the chest.

Size At least 71 cm tall for a bitch, 79 cm tall for a dog.

Saluki

The Saluki, or Gazelle Hound, combines an exotic, graceful appearance with exceptional speed and stamina.

History The Saluki is a relative of the Afghan Hound (see p.59), but its Middle Eastern history is perhaps even older. Its fine features are recognizable in dogs portrayed in a pharoah's tomb over 3,000 years ago. The hound's popularity endured and it became the favourite of the Persians and Arabs, who used it in conjunction with falcons to hunt gazelles. There are feathered and smooth-haired varieties, and while they share similar origins, one type is often preferred in a particular part of this hound's wide range, which encompasses most of the Middle East. In the late 19th century the first attempts to popularize the breed in Britain were made, most notably by Lady Amherst. After a slower start in America the Saluki is now well established.

Temperament Although friendly, responsive and loyal to its owner, this dog requires obedience training. Salukis have a sensitive nature and should be handled gently.

Requirements Definitely a dog for the open country where it can use its incredible speed to full effect. It needs to be groomed fairly often.

KEY CHARACTERISTICS *Saluki*

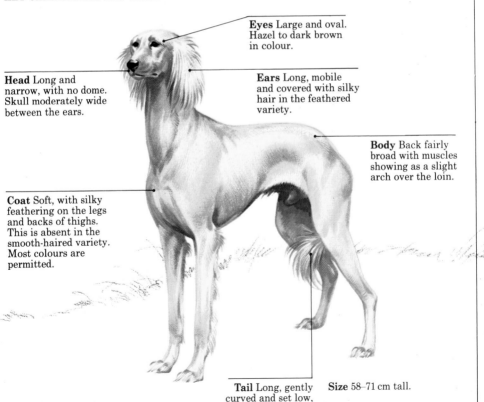

Eyes Large and oval. Hazel to dark brown in colour.

Head Long and narrow, with no dome. Skull moderately wide between the ears.

Ears Long, mobile and covered with silky hair in the feathered variety.

Body Back fairly broad with muscles showing as a slight arch over the loin.

Coat Soft, with silky feathering on the legs and backs of thighs. This is absent in the smooth-haired variety. Most colours are permitted.

Tail Long, gently curved and set low, with feathering on the underside.

Size 58–71 cm tall.

Whippet

A small gaze hound that can match the Greyhound for speed and grace.

History The Whippet's story is one of "riches to rags". Its main ancestor, the Greyhound (see p.65), was a dog of kings and noblemen, dating back to the pharoahs of Egypt. More recently, in the industrialized areas of north-east England, this aristocratic breed was crossed with local terriers to produce "rag dogs", which were trained to run at top speed towards their masters when they waved a piece of cloth. In this way the dogs could be raced against each other for Sunday entertainment. Whippets, whose name probably comes from an old English word for small dogs, were also used for catching rabbits. The original breed included rough-coated dogs, but these fell out of favour once the Whippet began to take part in shows.

Temperament Gentle, friendly and obedient.

Requirements A chance to run regularly is needed, but not too far or too long for most owners to cope with quite easily. A clean dog, with a small appetite, the Whippet is a remarkably undemanding pet. The habit of shivering conveys an impression of delicacy which is misleading, but some protection against cold weather is a good idea.

KEY CHARACTERISTICS *Whippet*

Size 44–47 cm tall.

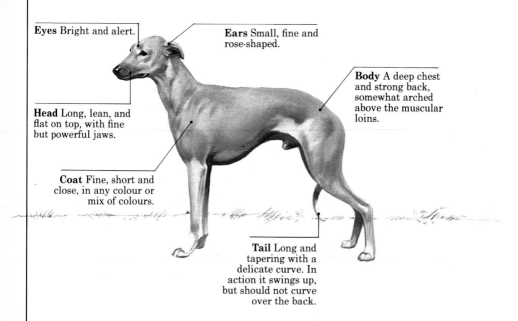

Eyes Bright and alert.

Ears Small, fine and rose-shaped.

Body A deep chest and strong back, somewhat arched above the muscular loins.

Head Long, lean, and flat on top, with fine but powerful jaws.

Coat Fine, short and close, in any colour or mix of colours.

Tail Long and tapering with a delicate curve. In action it swings up, but should not curve over the back.

Bernese Mountain Dog

A charming and very beautiful dog that is becoming increasingly popular.

History Unusually for a dog, the Bernese was bred to pull carts. It was the "work-horse" of weavers and cheesemakers in the canton of Berne, while similar, related breeds were favoured in other parts of Switzerland. Legend has it that they first arrived there with the Roman legions, for whom they acted as guard-dogs. This may be fact or fantasy, but whatever the early history of the breed, there's no doubt that it was in serious decline at the end of the 19th century. Then a prominent citizen of Berne stepped in, sought out the best specimens and bred from them to produce the sturdy, attractive dogs we see today. The Bernese Mountain Dog retains its working instincts and enjoys pulling carts, often being used to give rides to children at fêtes and shows.

Temperament Good-natured, peaceable, cheerful and affectionate.

Requirements Plenty of exercise, an ample diet and regular grooming are needed. The Bernese makes an excellent family pet for those who can afford a fairly large dog.

KEY CHARACTERISTICS *Bernese Mountain Dog*

Coat Long, soft and silky with a slight wave. The markings are characteristic: jet black, with patches of rich tan on all legs, part of the chest and over each eye. A white blaze and white chest are essential, and white paws and tail-tip desirable.

Head A flat skull with a well defined stop, slight furrow between the eyes and strong muzzle.

Ears Triangular, medium-sized and lying flat.

Eyes Dark brown and almond-shaped.

Body Compact, with a deep chest and a straight back.

Tail Bushy and reaching just below the hocks.

Size 58–66 cm tall for a bitch, 63.5–70 cm tall for a dog.

Boxer

A sturdy, energetic dog that's always full of high spirits and makes an excellent guard.

History The Boxer probably has its origins in German dogs of the mastiff type, used for bull-baiting in medieval times. But the breed as we know it only came into being in the 19th century, when German breeders crossed these ancient dogs with other breeds, notably the Bulldog, and selected for particular traits. They were intent on developing the perfect police dog: ferocious and fearless, but also intelligent and controllable, powerful and robust, but not so heavy as to be unable to jump a high wall, or pursue a criminal at speed. The Boxer is thus a made-to-measure breed, and in its native land it is still valued for police work. Elsewhere in the world it has become important as a guard-dog and family pet.

Temperament A lively, often boisterous dog. Despite its fierce background, the Boxer is generally trustworthy, but it is important to get puppies from a reputable breeder.

Requirements Exercise, and lots of it, is a must for this breed.

KEY CHARACTERISTICS *Boxer*

Special note The ears may be cropped (and thus stand erect) in other countries, but not in Britain.

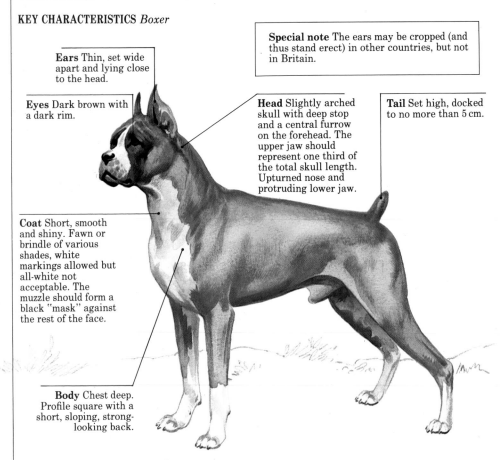

Ears Thin, set wide apart and lying close to the head.

Eyes Dark brown with a dark rim.

Head Slightly arched skull with deep stop and a central furrow on the forehead. The upper jaw should represent one third of the total skull length. Upturned nose and protruding lower jaw.

Tail Set high, docked to no more than 5 cm.

Coat Short, smooth and shiny. Fawn or brindle of various shades, white markings allowed but all-white not acceptable. The muzzle should form a black "mask" against the rest of the face.

Body Chest deep. Profile square with a short, sloping, strong-looking back.

Size 53–58.5 cm tall for a bitch, 56–61 cm tall for a dog.

Bearded Collie

Worked as a shepherding dog for centuries in Britain, this energetic, cheerful collie makes an excellent companion.

History Its origin is uncertain but one story has it that Magyar dogs, brought to Scotland by Polish traders in the Middle Ages, were its main ancestors. These animals may also have been the forebears of the Old English Sheepdog, which shows many similarities to this breed. The numbers of the Bearded Collie, (once known as the Highland Collie) declined rapidly during and between the wars. The breed was virtually extinct when, in 1944, it was resurrected from one breeding pair.

Temperament A very friendly dog.

Requirements The long coat requires weekly brushing, more so in the first two years of life. This dog is accustomed to hard work and needs regular exercise.

KEY CHARACTERISTICS *Bearded Collie*

Size 51–53 cm tall for a bitch, 53–56 cm tall for a dog.

Eyes Large and set quite wide apart. Colour to tone with coat. Not obscured by the arched eyebrows.

Ears Set high, hanging, with a covering of long hair.

Bearded Collie puppies
Bearded Collie puppies are slow to mature, and require extra brushing for the first two years of life, while the coat develops.

Head Broad, with a moderately long foreface and slight stop.

Tail Quite long and set low with a slight curve at the tip when at rest.

Body Long, with a straight front, level back and deep chest.

Coat Double, with soft undercoat and hard, straight outer coat. Variable colouring, including black, shades of grey and sandy.

Border Collie

An invaluable assistant to shepherds all over the world, the Border Collie is now gaining popularity away from the farm.

History The strong herding instinct of this collie was originally developed in the Scottish border country. It has been bred for trainability and intelligence rather than for looks, and is shown at sheepdog trials more often than in the ring. For years the International Sheepdog Society has imposed standards of working ability on the breed, but only in 1976 was it adopted by the British Kennel Club. Official recognition usually changes the emphasis in breeding, to attain a standardized appearance, but livestock farmers' strong interests in the dog will probably ensure that its usefulness is not impaired.

Temperament Rather excitable, but with their tendency to "herd" children, these loyal, obedient dogs make good family pets.

Requirements Plenty of exercise.

KEY CHARACTERISTICS *Border Collie*

Eyes Oval and set wide apart. Dark brown except for merles (mixed colourings), where some blue is permitted.

Head Rather broad skull, with a short muzzle tapering to a black nose. Distinct stop.

Coat The two varieties are moderately long- and smooth-coated. In the former, there should be a mane, bushy tail and breeching. A range of colours is permissible, but not predominant white.

Ears Medium-sized and set well apart. Semi-erect and mobile.

Tail Curving gracefully down at least to the hock. Never carried over the back.

Body Wide, deep chest. Strong, broad back over slightly arched, muscular loins.

Size About 53 cm tall.

Border Collie
The breed makes an outstanding sheepdog. The Border Collie has to be sensitive to its master's every gesture, call or whistle in the delicate task of herding sheep.

Rough Collie

A good representative of this breed is one of the most beautiful of all dogs.

History Although its exact origins are uncertain, the Rough Collie's ancestors were Scottish herding dogs, and despite recent breeding for the show, it displays the intelligence and patience required for its original purpose. When Queen Victoria encountered them during a visit to Balmoral, she was entranced and acquired several for the Windsor kennels. This sparked off more general popularity, both in Britain and America.

Temperament Combining a sense of fun with great intelligence, these collies make excellent companions.

Requirements The good looks of this dog carry the price of frequent grooming and exercise.

Smooth Collie
This breed and the Rough Collie are so similar in all but coat length that they are judged by the same standard in the U.S.A., and were only recently separated in Britain. The Smooth Collie may have helped to drive sheep to market.

KEY CHARACTERISTICS *Rough Collie*

Body Rather long in proportion to height, with a deep chest. Back slightly arched over loins.

Ears Small and set reasonably high on the skull. Semi-erect, with the top third tipping over when alert.

Eyes Almond-shaped and set rather obliquely. Dark brown, but merle (mixed-coloured) dogs can have one blue eye, or partially blue eyes.

Tail Long, reaching down at least to the hocks, with a slight upward turn at the tip.

Head Clean-cut profile tapering smoothly from the flat skull to a blunt, well-rounded muzzle. A slight stop. Nose must be black.

Coat Long and dense with abundant tail covering, mane, and feathering. Recognized colours are sable and white, tricolour (black, white, and tan) and blue merle.

Size 51–56 cm tall for a bitch, 56–61 cm tall for a dog.

Dobermann Pinscher

This excellent guard-dog owes its combination of agility and toughness to one man's dedication to its breeding programme.

History Louis Dobermann spent the last decades of the 19th century in pursuit of his ideal breed. Although we have no precise knowledge of its stock, the Dobermann's forebears included the Manchester Terrier (now a fairly rare breed), the Rottweiler (see p. 81) and probably the shepherd dogs of its native Thuringia. The earliest Dobermanns were reputedly very fierce, but subsequent breeding has produced dogs of greater stability. These have retained the adaptability of the breed, and apart from guarding, the "Dobe" can be trained for many other jobs, including tracking, working sheep and retrieving.

Temperament Any sign of nervousness should be avoided when choosing a puppy, but a dog from good stock can be very loyal, and even affectionate with its family.

Requirements Careful training and a reasonable amount of exercise.

KEY CHARACTERISTICS *Dobermann Pinscher*

Special note The ears are usually cropped in America, but never in Britain.

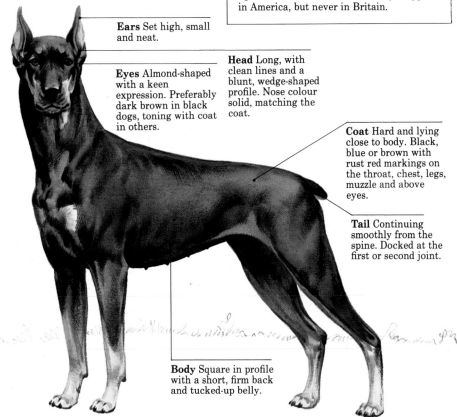

Ears Set high, small and neat.

Eyes Almond-shaped with a keen expression. Preferably dark brown in black dogs, toning with coat in others.

Head Long, with clean lines and a blunt, wedge-shaped profile. Nose colour solid, matching the coat.

Coat Hard and lying close to body. Black, blue or brown with rust red markings on the throat, chest, legs, muzzle and above eyes.

Tail Continuing smoothly from the spine. Docked at the first or second joint.

Body Square in profile with a short, firm back and tucked-up belly.

Size 65 cm tall for a bitch, 68.5 cm tall for a dog.

German Shepherd Dog

The grace, strength and intelligence of the German Shepherd Dog, or Alsatian, have ensured that it is one of the most popular breeds, much valued as a guard-dog, and for military and police work.

History Although now well established, this excellent working dog is the outcome of a breeding programme started only at the very end of the last century. In producing it, several different European pastoral dogs were used. Invaluable to the Germans in the First World War, the breed was introduced to Britain and America by soldiers returning home.

Temperament Dependable and intelligent in a good example of the breed. Mass-production has resulted in some undue fierceness, or nervousness, so obtain a puppy from a reputable breeder.

Requirements Plenty of exercise and some brushing. These dogs respond particularly well to training.

Belgian Shepherd Dog: Groenendael
The Groenendael is the best known of the three breeds of Belgian Shepherd Dog. Although otherwise very similar, the Tervueren has a reddish-fawn coat with black overlay. The Malinois has a shorter coat, giving it a close resemblance to the German Shepherd Dog.

KEY CHARACTERISTICS *German Shepherd Dog*

Ears Set high, broad at base with erect, pointed tips.

Body Muscular and deep-chested with a broad, straight back.

Eyes Almond-shaped, dark and intelligent.

Tail Hanging at least to the hock with a slight curve.

Head Quite broad and tapering cleanly to a sharp muzzle. Nose should be black.

Coat Smooth and double, with a thick undercoat and flat outer coat, both lying close to the body. Colour unimportant, but all-white dogs are not favoured.

Size 56–61 cm tall for a bitch, 61–66 cm tall for a dog.

Great Dane

An aristocratic breed, combining huge stature with great elegance.

History The ancestors of these noble dogs were to be found in royal households throughout Europe during the Middle Ages. Then, as now, they were very much a status symbol, but their practical value was in the wild-boar hunt. Despite the name "Great Dane", Germany, rather than Denmark, has been the centre of this breed's development. It was a favourite of Bismarck, who kept several as guards.

Temperament A gentlemanly dog that is well aware of its own strength.

Requirements The amounts of food, exercise and obedience training this dog needs correspond to its immense size, and ownership is a heavy responsibility.

KEY CHARACTERISTICS *Great Dane*

Head A generally clean-cut outline is desirable. The flat skull has a slight central indentation and pronounced "eyebrows". The nose should be black, except in merles and harlequins.

Ears Small, set high and carried erect, with only the tips falling forward.

Harlequin Great Dane
In the 18th century, these dogs were favoured by the aristocracy, who liked their carriages to be flanked by these distinctive outriders.

Tail Thick at base and tapering to just below the hocks.

Eyes Medium-sized and set deep. Dark in all but harlequins, in which light blue and odd colouring is allowed.

Coat Sleek and short. Colour varieties are yellow to orange striped with brindle, fawn, blue, black and harlequin (black marks on white).

Body Very deep chest with a well tucked-up belly. Strong back over muscular loins.

Size 71 cm tall for a bitch, 76 cm tall for a dog.

Special note The ears are usually cropped in America, but never in Britain.

Mastiff

Once England's dog of war, the bulky but dignified Mastiff is now an amiable family member.

History As for many breeds with a long history, colourful stories about the origins and feats of the Mastiff abound. Its deeds are recorded in accounts of battle, from the Roman invasion of Britain, to Agincourt and beyond. Less heroic was its use in dog-fighting and bear-baiting in Medieval England. From the 17th century the Mastiff's popularity waned and, were it not for the work of American breeders, it might be extinct today.

Temperament Gentle, obedient, loyal and tolerant of children. Despite its huge size, the Mastiff is one of the most affectionate dogs, and fiercely protective of its owner's property.

Requirements Large amounts of meat and regular walks.

Bullmastiff
The product of a cross between Bulldogs and Mastiffs, the Bullmastiff was only taken in hand as a breed in the mid-19th century.

KEY CHARACTERISTICS *Mastiff*

Eyes Small and set wide apart.

Head Forehead smooth, except for a central depression running upwards from between the eyes and general wrinkling when dog is alert. Nose black. Muzzle short and broad.

Coat Short and flat. Colours are apricot, silver, fawn or dark fawn brindle. Ears, muzzle and eye-surrounds should be black.

Size Great height combined with proportionate bulk is desirable.

Ears Set high. Small, thin and lying flat.

Tail Set high and tapering down to the hocks. Slightly curved when excited.

Body Broad, deep chest. Wide, muscular back and loins.

Newfoundland

Life on a gale-swept Atlantic island has produced a dog with remarkable gifts.
History Although the breed certainly evolved on Newfoundland, there are conflicting reports of the stock from which it arose. Some say its ancestors were dogs brought over by early Viking settlers, others look to the Pyrenean mountain dogs of French fishermen who emigrated to the island in the 17th century. Whatever its forebears, the Newfoundland developed into an invaluable assistant to these sea-going people. The reputation of these stoical, good-natured dogs spread; in the 18th century they were brought to Britain.
Temperament Hard to fault. Very placid with a reassuring, serene expression.
Requirements They should, if possible

have access to a pond, a river, or the sea. The coat needs thorough grooming at least once a week. A substantial amount of meat is essential to its well-being.

Newfoundland swimming
Water is an obsession with these dogs. Many people owe their lives to its extraordinary aptitude for swimming and water rescue.

KEY CHARACTERISTICS *Newfoundland*

Head Broad and massive with a short, square muzzle.

Ears Small, set well back and lying close to the head.

Eyes Small, deep-set and quite wide apart. Dark brown in colour.

Tail Quick thick and reaching just below the hocks, carried up when moving.

Body Deep, broad chest and wide back, over muscular loins.

Coat Water-resistant, flat and dense. Colours are black, deep chocolate brown, bronze-brown, or white with black markings (known as a "Landseer").

Size 66 cm tall for a bitch, 71 cm tall for a dog

Old English Sheepdog

Despite the glamorous appearance conferred by its long fluffy coat, the Old English Sheepdog's origins are very much in the working tradition.

History The Bearded Collie (see p.71) is thought to have had common ancestors with the Old English Sheepdog, or "bobtail". It was bred no more than a couple of centuries ago in south-west England as a drover and herder, being used to take sheep and cattle to market, and at other times to guard the flock.

Temperament Any puppy from a reputable dealer can grow up to be amiable and obedient, if given attention and careful training.

Requirements The long coat will grow matted and dirty unless brushed frequently. Confinement may spoil the dog's character, and plenty of exercise is a necessity.

Old English Sheepdog puppy
The fluffy, appealing looks of these puppies make it easy to forget that they soon turn into huge dogs, requiring plenty of space and food.

KEY CHARACTERISTICS *Old English Sheepdog*

Head Large, square skull, well arched over the eyes. Strong jaw and well-defined stop. Nose large and black.

Ears Small and lying flat.

Eyes Dark brown or wall eyes.

Tail Docked in the week after birth if present.

Coat Abundant and shaggy with no curl. Colours are grey, grizzle, blue or blue merle, with or without white markings.

Body Compact and short with a deep chest. Loins slightly arched.

Size 66 cm tall for a bitch, 71 cm tall for a dog.

Pyrenean Mountain Dog

This is probably the strongest of all dogs, but its gentle nature has made it very popular.

History This sturdy mountain dog's forebears came originally from Asia over a thousand years ago, but for centuries they were confined to the Pyrenees, where they were used as sheepdogs. Protecting the flocks from the depredations of wolves and bears in the harsh mountain climate required great endurance and vigilance. The same qualities were later valued when examples of the breed were taken further afield, notably to the court of Louis XIV. They became guards for many *chateaux*. At one time they were also taken to battle. For these roles spiked iron collars were sometimes fitted.

Temperament Sensible, loyal and responsive to commands.

Requirements The longish coat requires frequent brushing. Regular walks are essential and romps across open country desirable. The Pyrenean has an enormous appetite and is therefore an expensive undertaking.

KEY CHARACTERISTICS *Pyrenean Mountain Dog*

Mouth The lips and roof of the mouth are black or marked with black.

Ears Small and triangular with rounded tips. Usually lying flat against the head.

Eyes Almond-shaped and dark amber-brown. The eyelids should be edged with black.

Head Strong-looking, but not too heavy. Should have a V-shaped outline when viewed from the top. Black nose.

Tail Should reach below the hocks, and be well-covered with hair.

Coat Abundant on the neck, shoulders and on the back of the thighs. Colours are white, white patched with badger, wolf-grey or pale yellow.

Body Wide, deep chest and broad, strong back.

Size 66 cm tall for a bitch, 71 cm tall for a dog.

Rottweiler

A rugged cattle dog of southern Germany which is today used by police, and as a household guard.

History Although it takes its name from the small German town of Rottweil, the forebears of this muscular breed are believed to have crossed the Alps from Italy with the Romans. The meat for the soldiers was transported "on the hoof" for hundreds of miles, which required particularly skilful cattle dogs. Some of these were left behind as the legions retreated, and by the Middle Ages the local people were using the "Rottweiler Metzgerhund" (Rottweil butcher's dog) for driving cattle to market. In the 19th century this role was usurped by the railway, and the breed only avoided extinction by the timely efforts of its admirers around 1900. Since then much has been done to improve the Rottweiler, and the reward is a strong, yet friendly dog.

Temperament Aggressive towards intruders, but affectionate with its family.

Requirements Obedience training and frequent exercise are needed.

KEY CHARACTERISTICS *Rottweiler*

Size 58.5–63.5 cm tall for a bitch, 63.5–68.5 cm tall for a dog.

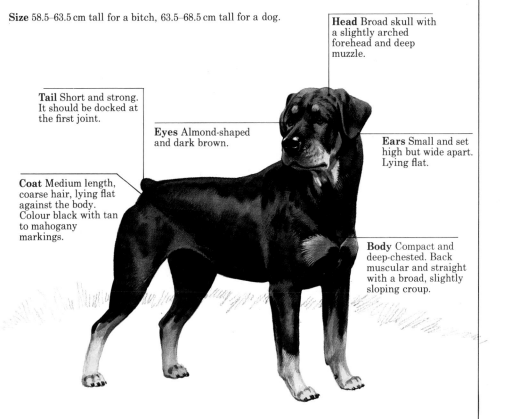

Head Broad skull with a slightly arched forehead and deep muzzle.

Tail Short and strong. It should be docked at the first joint.

Eyes Almond-shaped and dark brown.

Ears Small and set high but wide apart. Lying flat.

Coat Medium length, coarse hair, lying flat against the body. Colour black with tan to mahogany markings.

Body Compact and deep-chested. Back muscular and straight with a broad, slightly sloping croup.

St Bernard

A working dog bred for a particularly dangerous task, this huge dog has adapted well to domestic life.

History In common with the other European mastiff-like dogs, the ancestors of the St Bernard probably originated in Asia. It takes its name from the *Hospice du Grand Saint Bernard*, a refuge for travellers on the main alpine pass between Switzerland and Italy. The first records of large dogs at the hospice date from the early 18th century, and the breed was developed by the monks to guide people along tortuous, snow-covered paths and to assist in mountain rescue. It is hard to separate fact from fiction in St Bernard stories, but it is certain that the dogs excelled in endurance, tenacity and sense of smell. They saved many lives, often by locating people buried deeply in snow after an avalanche. It is thought that the original St Bernards had a coat of intermediate length. Subsequent cross-breeding, involving Newfoundlands, for example, has produced the two modern varieties, rough- and smooth-haired.

Temperament A quiet, intelligent and friendly nature.

Requirements A giant among dogs, needing spacious living quarters and plentiful amounts of meat. Without adequate exercise the tendency to weakness in the hindquarters may become a problem.

KEY CHARACTERISTICS *St Bernard*

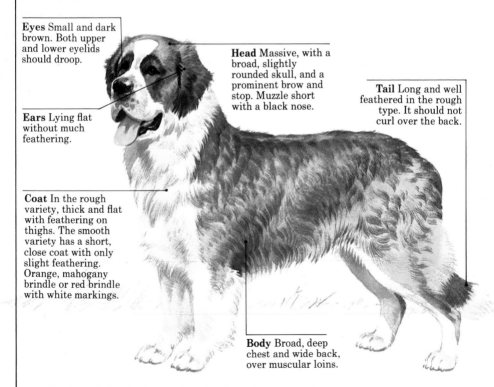

Eyes Small and dark brown. Both upper and lower eyelids should droop.

Head Massive, with a broad, slightly rounded skull, and a prominent brow and stop. Muzzle short with a black nose.

Tail Long and well feathered in the rough type. It should not curl over the back.

Ears Lying flat without much feathering.

Coat In the rough variety, thick and flat with feathering on thighs. The smooth variety has a short, close coat with only slight feathering. Orange, mahogany brindle or red brindle with white markings.

Body Broad, deep chest and wide back, over muscular loins.

Size Great size desirable when combined with good proportion.

Samoyed

This Spitz breed is named after its first masters, the Samoyed tribesmen of Siberia.

History Samoyeds were originally used to herd and guard reindeer, and to pull sledges when harnessed in packs. However, it was the dog's luxurious good looks, rather than hardiness or strength, that won it admiration when fur traders brought back the first specimens to Europe and America. In the 19th century the numbers kept as pets increased rapidly, and they were included on polar expeditions. Although sometimes still competing in sledge races, the qualities for which the Samoyed was originally bred have been largely eclipsed by the characteristics of a show and companion breed. The darker coat colours of some of the early introductions are excluded from the breed standards of today.

Temperament The Samoyed's expression falls naturally into a smile. This reflects its good-natured approach to people, including other animals and, unfortunately, intruders.

Requirements The long coat sheds easily, and must be brushed at least twice a week. This dog needs daily exercise and loves romping through snow.

KEY CHARACTERISTICS *Samoyed*

Ears Set wide apart and held erect in adult dogs. Well covered with hair, inside and out.

Tail Long and curled over back when alert, in the usual Spitz style.

Head Wedge-shaped with a wide skull. Foreface tapers to a preferably black nose.

Eyes Almond-shaped and set well apart. Mid- to dark-brown in colour.

Coat Long outer coat growing through soft, close-lying undercoat. Colours are white, white and biscuit, or cream.

Body A deep, wide chest and broad, muscular back.

Size 46–51 cm tall for a bitch, 51–56 cm tall for a dog.

Shetland Sheepdog

Sometimes mistaken for a miniature Rough Collie, the "Sheltie" is a breed in its own right, though it undoubtedly shares some ancestors with the larger breed and was once known as the Miniature Collie.

History Despite its small size and refined good looks, the Shetland has a well-deserved place among the working dogs. The thick coat once protected its forebears from the harsh climate of the Shetland Isles, where the dogs were used to herd sheep. Their diminutive stature was no handicap, as all animals on these islands are smaller than their mainland counterparts. Improvements to the breed's appearance were made early this century, but the Shetland retains its trainability and taste for work. Its cheerful nature makes it a good show-dog.

Temperament Shyness with strangers makes the Shetland an excellent guard, if rather too persistent with the warning bark. The dog is a loyal companion to its family.

Requirements The long coat requires frequent grooming; beneath the tough outer coat is a thick, soft undercoat. Although the Shetland is compact and can live in confined spaces, a long walk each day is desirable.

KEY CHARACTERISTICS *Shetland Sheepdog*

Ears Small, set high and quite close together. Semi-erect when alert.

Eyes Almond-shaped and set obliquely. Dark brown, although blue is acceptable in merles.

Body Well proportioned with a deep chest, level back and gradually sloping croup.

Head A long, blunt wedge, tapering cleanly to the black nose. A slight stop divides the rounded muzzle from the flat skull.

Tail Set low and reaching at least to hock with a slight upward curve.

Coat Harsh, long outer coat forms abundant mane and frill. Colours include tricolour (black, white and tan), sable and blue merle (blue and grey mixed with black).

Size 35.5 cm tall for a bitch, 37 cm tall for a dog.

Siberian Husky

A hard-working and strikingly beautiful member of the Spitz group.

History Although "husky" is now a general name for all sledge-pulling dogs, the Siberian is the only official Husky. As with the Samoyed (see p.83), the name derives from its first owners – the Chukchis, a nomadic tribe of eastern Siberia. The care they invested in breeding the dogs has been rewarded by the incredible stamina Huskies display.

Temperament Despite its rather wolf-like appearance, the Husky is remarkably calm and gentle with people, so much so that it cannot be expected to guard property. It rarely barks, but howls instead.

Requirements The call of the wild easily conquers any human attachment, and most Huskies must be kept on a lead all the time.

Alaskan Malamute
A very powerful sledge dog, generally able to pull heavier loads than the Siberian Husky, and also used to carry packs. It was a valued companion of early Arctic explorers.

KEY CHARACTERISTICS *Siberian Husky*

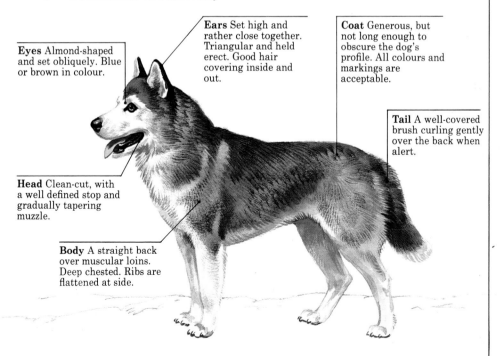

Ears Set high and rather close together. Triangular and held erect. Good hair covering inside and out.

Eyes Almond-shaped and set obliquely. Blue or brown in colour.

Coat Generous, but not long enough to obscure the dog's profile. All colours and markings are acceptable.

Tail A well-covered brush curling gently over the back when alert.

Head Clean-cut, with a well defined stop and gradually tapering muzzle.

Body A straight back over muscular loins. Deep chested. Ribs are flattened at side.

Size 51–56 cm tall for a bitch, 53–60 cm tall for a dog.

Cardigan Welsh Corgi

The Cardiganshire breed is believed to be the older of the two Corgis, whose name is derived from the Celtic word for dog.

History Although notable for their absence from historical documents, Corgis are thought to have been used as cattle herders in Wales for centuries. They were in the group of dogs known as "heelers", because they ran nimbly between the cattle, nipping the heels of those which strayed out of line. Their short legs allowed them to move quickly in among the herd and escape kicks. Despite being eclipsed in popularity by the Pembroke, adherents of the Cardigan Corgi maintain that it was the original heeler. Although numbers of the breed have remained low, it has undergone a recent revival, notably in Australia.

Temperament The Cardigan tends to be slightly less outgoing than the Pembroke, but is very loyal to its master.

Requirements Despite adapting well to town life, Corgis need frequent long walks. They tend to lose a large amount of hair, so frequent grooming is desirable.

KEY CHARACTERISTICS *Cardigan Welsh Corgi*

Head "Fox-like" in appearance, with the muzzle tapering moderately to a black, rather pointed nose.

Ears Large and set well back. Held erect with a rounded tip.

Size 30.5 cm tall.

Eyes Of medium size, and rather widely set. Preferably dark in colour, or blending with the coat. Blue is permissible in merles (mixed colouring).

Tail Set low. Falls close to the ground like a fox's brush.

Coat Any colour except all-white. White markings are permissible.

Body Quite long with a broad, deep chest and a clearly defined waist.

Pembroke Welsh Corgi

These Corgis make very cheerful companions, approaching life with immense verve and charm.

History As with the Cardigan Corgi, the past of the Pembrokeshire breed is largely uncharted, but some say that it arrived in Wales with Flemish weavers who settled there in the 12th century. However, the many similarities between the two Corgis point to a shared ancestry, and make this story rather unlikely. Whatever its origins, the Pembroke Corgi, like its cousin, worked as a cattle dog on the Welsh hills, the sturdy, muscular body, combined with surprising speed, fitting it well for the work. This century has seen a huge upsurge in the Pembroke's popularity as a pet and show-dog, largely because of royal enthusiasm for the breed.

Temperament The lively, intelligent and willing Pembroke makes an excellent family pet.

Requirements Regular exercise is needed, as these small dogs easily become overweight. Frequent grooming is desirable.

KEY CHARACTERISTICS *Pembroke Welsh Corgi*

Ears Held erect with a slightly pointed tip.

Eyes Medium-sized, round, and hazel in colour.

Head "Fox-like" with a slightly tapering muzzle and a black nose.

Body Rather long with a deep chest. The back should have a level topline.

Size 25.5–30.5 cm tall.

Coat Dense and of medium length. Colours are fawn, red, sable, or black and tan, with or without white markings.

Tail Preferred naturally short, but otherwise docked.

Airedale Terrier

The "king of terriers", the Airedale acted as guard and messenger in the First War.

History Although the size of the Airedale prevents it from pursuing its quarry underground, in other respects it is an archetypal terrier. Its history begins in the mid-19th century, when sportsmen in Yorkshire crossed the now-extinct Black-and-Tan Terrier with the Otter Hound, to produce a dog which was large enough for use in both badger and otter hunts.

Temperament Although an aggressive hunter, the Airedale can be an affectionate family member, and makes a good guard.

Requirements Daily walks of a few miles. One of the Airedale's virtues is that it doesn't shed much hair.

Welsh Terrier
Although of earlier origin than the Airedale and much smaller, the Welsh Terrier shares its Black-and-Tan Terrier ancestry.

KEY CHARACTERISTICS *Airedale Terrier*

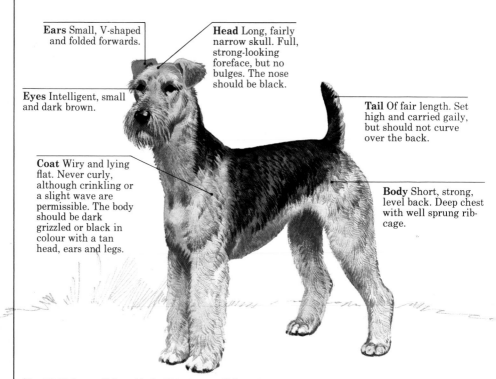

Ears Small, V-shaped and folded forwards.

Head Long, fairly narrow skull. Full, strong-looking foreface, but no bulges. The nose should be black.

Eyes Intelligent, small and dark brown.

Tail Of fair length. Set high and carried gaily, but should not curve over the back.

Coat Wiry and lying flat. Never curly, although crinkling or a slight wave are permissible. The body should be dark grizzled or black in colour with a tan head, ears and legs.

Body Short, strong, level back. Deep chest with well sprung rib-cage.

Size 56–58.5 cm tall for a bitch, 58.5–61 cm tall for a dog.

Australian Terrier

The Australian is one of the very few terriers to have been bred outside Britain.

History Working dogs were an essential part of the luggage taken to Australia by early settlers, and several types of terrier were introduced. Breeding between these produced a variety of broken-coated dogs, and in the 19th century these were further crossed with several British terriers, including the Skye (see p.99), Dandie Dinmont (see p.93), Cairn (see p.92) and Yorkshire (see p.119). The Australian breed produced from this "melting pot" of terriers proved itself to be an excellent guard, and kept down those less welcome immigrants, the rats and rabbits. The tough little hybrid dog also proved itself in contests with Australia's many poisonous snakes – a new adversary for terriers. The breed remains popular in its country of origin, but has gained favour only slowly in Britain and America.

Temperament The Australian has charm and a bright personality, making it an excellent pet as well as a good guard.

Requirements Although an energetic breed, its needs are remarkably modest. This adaptable terrier is ideal for a city flat.

KEY CHARACTERISTICS *Australian Terrier*

Ears Small, pointed and erect.

Eyes Small, with a keen expression. Dark brown in colour.

Body Long and strong-looking with a moderately deep chest.

Tail Docked and set high.

Head Long, with a powerful muzzle and slight stop. The flat skull bears a silky topknot.

Coat Long, harsh outer coat on the body only. Shorter hair elsewhere. Colours include all-red, and blue with tan markings.

Size 25.5 cm tall.

Border Terrier

This rugged, compact terrier was bred for hunting over the rainswept hillsides of the Scottish border country.

History The demands made by the border huntsmen on their terriers were particularly stringent. The terrain was steep and rocky, the rain relentless, and long distances had to be covered. Once it had followed a fox to earth for miles, the dog then needed the courage and strength to defend itself underground. Small wonder that the Border Terrier is very hardy, despite subsequent breeding for the pet market. In the 1920s the reputation of the breed spread to England, where it came to be valued as a pet and in the hunt.

Temperament Early obedience training is desirable. Otherwise loyal and friendly.

Requirements This is a very active dog which must be allowed to use up its energy on long walks.

Bedlington Terrier
Also from the Border Country, although unlike the Border Terrier in most other respects, the Bedlington was bred by Northumberland miners and steelworkers in the last century. Its lamb-like appearance (which is produced by careful clipping) is deceptive, for it is a true terrier, originally being used to catch rats and rabbits.

KEY CHARACTERISTICS *Border Terrier*

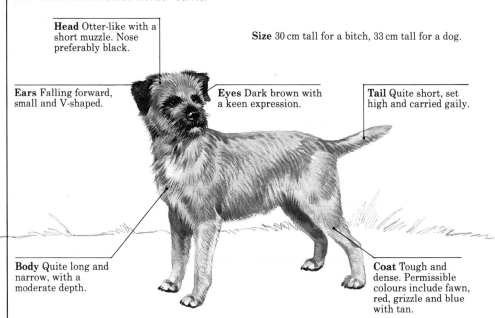

Head Otter-like with a short muzzle. Nose preferably black.

Size 30 cm tall for a bitch, 33 cm tall for a dog.

Ears Falling forward, small and V-shaped.

Eyes Dark brown with a keen expression.

Tail Quite short, set high and carried gaily.

Body Quite long and narrow, with a moderate depth.

Coat Tough and dense. Permissible colours include fawn, red, grizzle and blue with tan.

Bull Terrier

A strong, compact dog, characterized by its egg-shaped head.

History Although now regarded as rather a smart breed, the Bull Terrier has its origins among the fighting dogs of the 19th century. Around 1860, a Birmingham dog dealer, James Hinks, engineered a refinement of the original Staffordshire Bull Terriers, incorporating qualities of the English White Terrier and, possibly, the Dalmatian and Pointer. The result was a white, well-muscled dog which was sufficiently urbane in appearance for the show-ring, but retained the strength and tenacity of its fighting relatives. Its tolerance of tropical climates later made it a favourite with the British Civil Service in Africa and India. Because all-white Bull Terriers often suffer from deafness, some additional coat colour was introduced into the breed in the 1920s.

Temperament The dog has a very strong character, and forms lasting relationships with people. However, it is relentlessly aggressive towards other dogs. Bitches tend to be more peaceable.

Requirements A firm training, lively environment and long walks.

Miniature Bull Terrier
By selecting and mating small Bull Terriers, a miniature version has been produced, identical to the standard in all but size.

KEY CHARACTERISTICS *Bull Terrier*

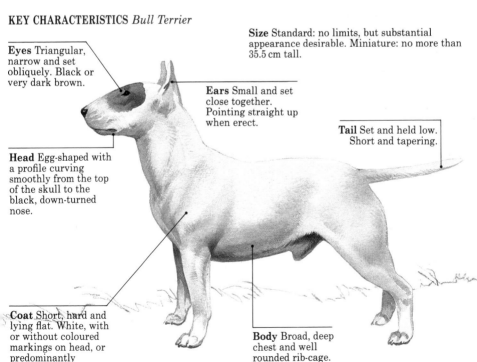

Eyes Triangular, narrow and set obliquely. Black or very dark brown.

Ears Small and set close together. Pointing straight up when erect.

Head Egg-shaped with a profile curving smoothly from the top of the skull to the black, down-turned nose.

Tail Set and held low. Short and tapering.

Size Standard: no limits, but substantial appearance desirable. Miniature: no more than 35.5 cm tall.

Coat Short, hard and lying flat. White, with or without coloured markings on head, or predominantly coloured.

Body Broad, deep chest and well rounded rib-cage. Short, strong back.

Cairn Terrier

A plucky, lively little terrier which has accompanied huntsmen over the rugged Highland terrain for centuries.

History Originally bred on Skye, the identity of the Cairn Terrier was at first confused with the island's other native dog (see p.99). But whereas the luxurious long coat of the Skye Terrier led to early popularity as a pet, and breeding to further enhance its appearance, the Cairn Terrier retained its rather shaggy and unkempt looks. It was named after the piles of stones left to mark ancient burial sites on Skye, as the little dog was adept at following a fox if it took refuge among these mounds. Although not officially recognized until this century, today the breed has overtaken the Skye Terrier in popularity, both in Britain and America.

Temperament Lively, intelligent, loyal, pugnacious and voluble – this is not a dog for those seeking serene and quiet companionship.

Requirements A little grooming and a moderate amount of exercise keep the Cairn Terrier quite happy.

KEY CHARACTERISTICS *Cairn Terrier*

Head The skull is broad and the jaw powerful. The nose should be dark.

Coat Hard, weather-resistant outer coat and soft undercoat. Hair abundant on head. Colours include red, grey, sandy and brindle, often with darker muzzle and ears.

Ears Set quite far apart. Small, erect and pointed.

Eyes Deep set with full eyebrows. Dark hazel in colour.

Tail Short and carried erect.

Body Compact, with an appearance of strength. Rib-cage well sprung and deep.

Size 23 cm tall for a bitch, 24 cm tall for a dog.

Dandie Dinmont Terrier

The only dog breed to be named after a fictional character: Dandie Dinmont featured in a Walter Scott novel, as a breeder of small terriers on the Scottish border.

History The ancestors of this long-bodied dog were probably rough-coated terriers, from which the Dandie Dinmont emerged as a distinct type in the early 18th century. Its original role in fox, badger and otter hunting has been abandoned and it is now a popular show-dog and pet.

Temperament The soulful expression of its dark eyes belies the typical terrier nature of the Dandie Dinmont, though it is calmer and quieter than many terriers.

Requirements The long coat must be groomed and plucked fairly frequently. The fluffy topknot is an important feature in show-dogs, and is maintained by grooming.

Sealyham
There is thought to be Dandie Dinmont blood in this plucky little terrier. It was developed during the second half of the 19th century in Wales, and used in hunting badgers, otters and foxes.

KEY CHARACTERISTICS *Dandie Dinmont Terrier*

Ears Set far apart and towards the back of the skull. Long and hanging close to the cheek.

Eyes Set quite wide apart and low on the head. Dark hazel in colour.

Tail Quite short and carried high.

Head Quite large with a broad skull, domed forehead and muscular jaws. The muzzle is deep, with a bare patch behind the black nose.

Size 20.5 cm to 28 cm tall.

Body Strong-looking with the long back slightly arched over the loins. Chest is deep.

Coat Quite long. The body has a mixture of hard and soft hair. Colours are black to pale grey (termed pepper) or reddish-brown to fawn (termed mustard). A white mark on the chest is permissible.

Legs The front legs are short and very well muscled. The hind legs are longer.

Wire Fox Terrier

A particularly spruce and handsome breed.
History The Fox Terriers are thought to
have descended from dogs used in fox-
hunting in the early 19th century. Some
were crossed with the Wire-haired Terrier
to produce the Wire Fox Terrier, and
others with the Old English White Terrier
to give the smooth variety. Early
interbreeding between wire- and smooth-
haired types introduced white into the coat
of the former. After the First World War
the Wire Fox Terrier became fashionable as
a pet and show-dog, and is still popular.
Temperament The energy and hunting
instincts of Fox Terriers are irrepressible,
but with firm handling they make
affectionate and protective family pets.
Requirements Plenty of activity and long
walks. The coat needs regular grooming
and trimming to keep a smart appearance.

Smooth Fox Terrier
*Although the heyday of this dog's popularity is
long past, it was well established as a show-dog
before its wire-haired cousin, and still wins
respect as an unpretentious, solid breed, with
many loyal admirers.*

KEY CHARACTERISTICS *Wire Fox Terrier*

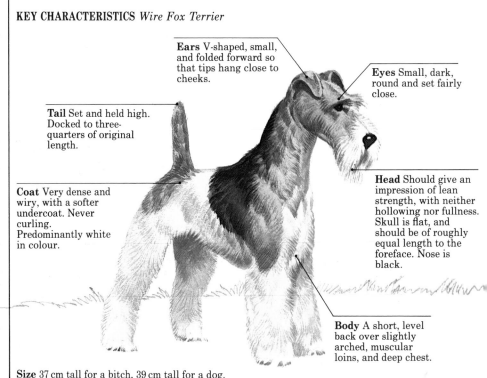

Ears V-shaped, small,
and folded forward so
that tips hang close to
cheeks.

Eyes Small, dark,
round and set fairly
close.

Tail Set and held high.
Docked to three-
quarters of original
length.

Coat Very dense and
wiry, with a softer
undercoat. Never
curling.
Predominantly white
in colour.

Head Should give an
impression of lean
strength, with neither
hollowing nor fullness.
Skull is flat, and
should be of roughly
equal length to the
foreface. Nose is
black.

Body A short, level
back over slightly
arched, muscular
loins, and deep chest.

Size 37 cm tall for a bitch, 39 cm tall for a dog.

Jack Russell Terrier

One of the ironies of the dog-show world is that these immensely popular little terriers are never seen in the ring, since they remain unrecognized by the Kennel Club.

History The first dogs to be called Jack Russells were bred from Wire Fox Terriers by a Devon clergyman in the early 19th century. The Reverend John Russell required of his terriers only that they should possess speed in following the hounds and tenacity in confronting the fox underground. At other times Jack Russells were useful in keeping vermin down. The emphasis in breeding has continued to be the terrier's temperament, so much so that its appearance is highly variable. A Jack Russell may differ considerably from the dog shown here, and the "Key Characteristics" are not based on an established Breed Standard, as with other breeds in the book. Nevertheless, the Jack Russell is unmistakable, with its characteristic knowing expression, its bouncy gait, inimitable bark, and unmatched enthusiasm for running and rabbiting.

Temperament Energetic, excitable, intelligent and game for anything (including chasing much larger dogs). They are also loyal and amusing pets, and make excellent guards.

Requirements Like many small dogs, Jack Russells tend to obesity if not allowed regular exercise.

KEY CHARACTERISTICS *Jack Russell Terrier*

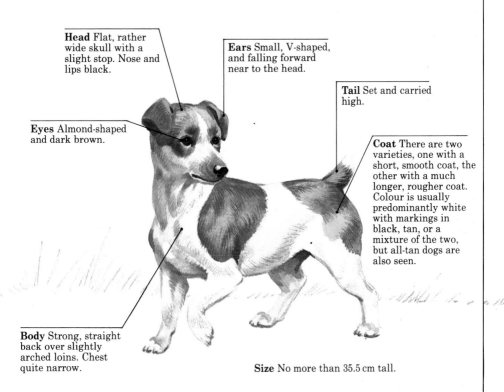

Head Flat, rather wide skull with a slight stop. Nose and lips black.

Ears Small, V-shaped, and falling forward near to the head.

Tail Set and carried high.

Eyes Almond-shaped and dark brown.

Coat There are two varieties, one with a short, smooth coat, the other with a much longer, rougher coat. Colour is usually predominantly white with markings in black, tan, or a mixture of the two, but all-tan dogs are also seen.

Body Strong, straight back over slightly arched loins. Chest quite narrow.

Size No more than 35.5 cm tall.

Norfolk Terrier

A relatively new name for an old type of terrier, previously classed as a Norwich. **History** When the Norwich Terrier (see p. 97) was recognized as a breed in the 1930s, its standard permitted both prick- and drop-ears. The two varieties had both evolved from old terrier breeds, and for a long time were interbred. In the 1930s, breeders began to distinguish between the two types. Breeders took pride in their particular type, maintaining that the ears were only the "tip of the iceberg", and that there were many other distinctions between the Norfolk and Norwich Terriers. Controversy surrounded their classification until the 1960s, when the drop-eared type was renamed the Norfolk Terrier and given a new standard.

Temperament Lively and alert, with a typical terrier assertiveness. The breed's ability to guard is enhanced by its acute hearing.

Requirements Plenty of walks are needed to satisfy its incredible capacity for lively exercise. The coat requires the minimum of care to keep it looking tidy and trim.

KEY CHARACTERISTICS *Norfolk Terrier*

Size 25.5 cm tall.

Ears Medium-sized and V-shaped. Folding forwards to hang next to the cheeks.

Body Back is short. General impression should be of compact strength.

Eyes Deeply-set, oval and dark brown or black in colour.

Tail Docked to half its length.

Head A powerful, wedge-shaped muzzle and a broad skull.

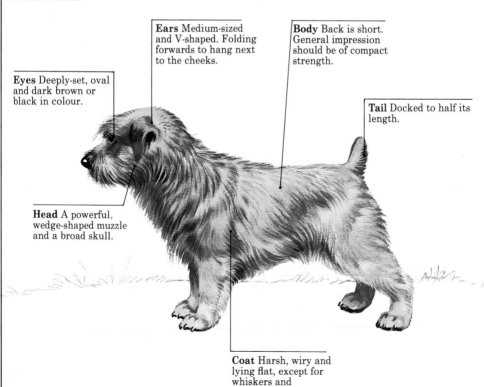

Coat Harsh, wiry and lying flat, except for whiskers and eyebrows.

Norwich Terrier

Small terriers, that once followed the fox and badger to earth in the East Anglian countryside.

History Although it is clear that these terriers have been bred for hunting, little is known about their origin. The issue is confused by the different names used for them in the past, including the Jones Terrier and Cantab Terrier. The latter reflects the popularity of the Norwich among Cambridge undergraduates in the late 19th century. These diminutive terriers were lively companions, useful in hunting vermin, but at the same time small enough to be kept in college rooms. The first specimens were taken to America early this century, where many were used in their original role, running with the hounds in fox-hunts.

Temperament Small dogs with a large interest in what goes on around them. They make very good watch-dogs.

Requirements Like the Norfolk, these are clean dogs needing little grooming apart from routine removal of dead hair. They should be walked frequently.

KEY CHARACTERISTICS *Norwich Terrier*

Size 25.5 cm tall.

Ears Set wide apart, and erect with pointed tips.

Body Compact with a short, level back.

Eyes Oval-shaped, small and dark.

Tail Docked to half the original length.

Head Wide skull with a well-defined stop. Muzzle a strong-looking wedge.

Coat Straight, wiry and close-lying. More abundant on the neck, muzzle and over the eyes. Shades of red, wheaten, grizzle or black and tan are permissible.

Scottish Terrier

Once known as the Aberdeen Terrier, this proud little dog commands a respect disproportionate to its size.

History Originally bred to chase the fox and badger, the "Scottie" combines compact strength and bravery. It was only one of several types of dog shown as "Scottish Terriers" in the 1870s. Confusion and controversy inevitably surrounded the choice of one of these as the national breed, but by the late 19th century the matter was settled, and a breed standard drawn up. Although black dogs are the most popular, the Scottie has several colour varieties, including brindled shades. At the turn of the century, the breed was the favourite terrier in Britain, and held this place for many years.

Temperament Generally a one-man-dog, this terrier is aloof with strangers. The Scottie maintains an air of self-possession and a strong individuality, but it does make a good household pet.

Requirements Early obedience training is desirable to prevent this terrier from becoming over-protective of its family. To keep in condition it must be allowed plenty of exercise.

KEY CHARACTERISTICS *Scottish Terrier*

Size 25 cm tall for a bitch, 28 cm tall for a dog.

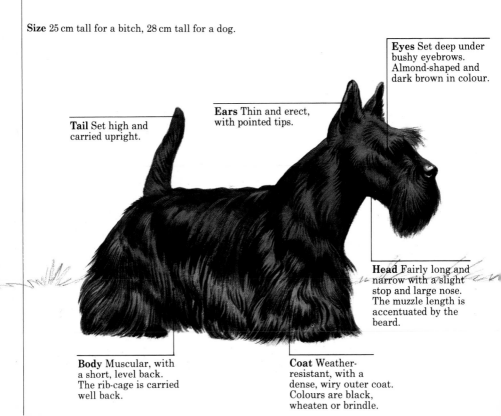

Eyes Set deep under bushy eyebrows. Almond-shaped and dark brown in colour.

Ears Thin and erect, with pointed tips.

Tail Set high and carried upright.

Head Fairly long and narrow with a slight stop and large nose. The muzzle length is accentuated by the beard.

Body Muscular, with a short, level back. The rib-cage is carried well back.

Coat Weather-resistant, with a dense, wiry outer coat. Colours are black, wheaten or brindle.

Skye Terrier

A dog with a distinctive appearance and rather serious demeanour.

History There is a legend that these little terriers swam ashore in 1590, after ships of the Spanish Armada were wrecked near Skye. Sadly this romantic tale is untrue, for the first dog book to be published in English, which predated the Armada by twenty years, described dogs which were almost certainly the Skye's ancestors. Like the other Scottish terriers, to which it is clearly related, the Skye Terrier was used to hunt foxes and badgers, and a protective coat and strong jaws were favoured by breeders. After a period of great popularity in the late 19th century, this breed has now been largely overtaken by other terriers.

Temperament A "one-man dog", intensely loyal to its master, and usually wary of strangers. Without affection, the Skye can become rather dour.

Requirements The abundant coat needs frequent grooming, and regular walks are essential.

KEY CHARACTERISTICS *Skye Terrier*

Size 23 cm tall for a bitch, 25 cm tall for a dog.

Ears Prick or drop. The inner edges of the former should be inclined towards each other. Drop ears should be larger and hang straight.

Coat A short, soft undercoat and long, straight, hard outer coat. Profuse hair hangs over the ears. The many permissible colours include fawn and grey. Ears are black.

Head Long, with powerful jaws and a black nose.

Tail The raised tail is held level with the back. When hanging, the end curls upwards.

Body Long and low with a level back.

Eyes Hazel in colour and set close together.

Staffordshire Bull Terrier

The courage and kindness of these dogs have endeared them to many, despite their somewhat murky past.

History In the early 19th century bull-baiting was made illegal and dog-fighting took over as "entertainment" for the more blood-thirsty sector of society. The best sport was to be had if the contenders were both bulky and tenacious, so Bulldogs were crossed with terriers. The products were ugly, pugnacious dogs, ideal for fights, as well as being good ratters. Dog-fighting was in turn outlawed, but the Staffordshire Bull Terrier's benevolence and amiability towards humans made it such a good pet that it was saved from extinction.

Temperament Very loyal to its owner and good with children.

Requirements Firm obedience training and plenty of exercise, to avoid obesity.

American Staffordshire Terrier
From Staffordshire Bull Terriers taken across the Atlantic in the 19th century, rather larger and fiercer dogs were selected. Despite its instinctive courage, it is very gentle with people.

KEY CHARACTERISTICS *Staffordshire Bull Terrier*

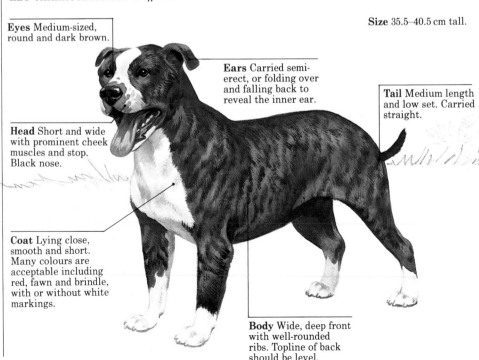

Eyes Medium-sized, round and dark brown.

Size 35.5–40.5 cm tall.

Ears Carried semi-erect, or folding over and falling back to reveal the inner ear.

Tail Medium length and low set. Carried straight.

Head Short and wide with prominent cheek muscles and stop. Black nose.

Coat Lying close, smooth and short. Many colours are acceptable including red, fawn and brindle, with or without white markings.

Body Wide, deep front with well-rounded ribs. Topline of back should be level.

West Highland White Terrier

The endearing looks of these jaunty terriers disguise a tenacious, fiery spirit.

History The similarity of many of the Scottish Terriers suggests that they have all evolved from a common ancestral type. In the mid-19th century, white dogs from the Highlands were selected to produce a pure-breeding white terrier. At first these dogs were named after their place of origin, Poltalloch in Argyll. In those days, dogs were seldom bred for appearance alone, and the West Highland White Terrier, as the breed later became known, was tough and tireless in its pursuit of the fox over rocky terrain. Now the handsome little dog is a favourite in the show-ring, and a popular pet both in America and in Europe.

Temperament A self-confident and affectionate dog with an engaging sense of fun. Its acute hearing and great courage make it an effective watch-dog.

Requirements The "Westie" thrives on attention and should not be deprived of it. Regular grooming and removal of shed hair are desirable.

KEY CHARACTERISTICS *West Highland White Terrier*

Size About 28 cm tall.

Coat A hard outer coat and short, soft undercoat. Colour must be pure white.

Head Skull slightly domed with a distinct stop. Jaws are strong. Nose should be black.

Ears Small, erect and pointed, with a covering of short hair.

Tail Quite short and carried straight.

Eyes Set wide apart, and dark brown in colour.

Body Strongly built and compact. Back is level and chest deep.

Boston Terrier

Despite its name, the Boston Terrier has never been used to follow vermin to earth, but excels as a companion and house dog.

History The first Boston Terriers were products of a Bulldog (see p.103) and a White English Terrier, crossed in Massachussetts in the mid-19th century. Subsequent refinement, using French Bulldog blood, resulted in a compact, well-muscled breed with distinctive, neat markings. The affectionate nature and modest requirements of the breed, combined with its attractive appearance, quickly established it as a favourite pet in North America. Its popularity has endured in spite of the fact that a Caesarian section is required for many births, making breeding expensive.

After a rather slow start, the Boston Terrier is now well established in Britain.

Temperament Very affectionate, lively and intelligent: an ideal pet that also makes an outstanding show-dog.

Requirements The breed does not have a working past, and although regular exercise is desirable, the Boston does not need long, strenuous walks. The coat requires very little attention.

KEY CHARACTERISTICS *Boston Terrier*

Size There are three weight classes: lightweight under 6.8 kg; middleweight 6.8–9.1 kg; heavyweight 9.1–11.4 kg.

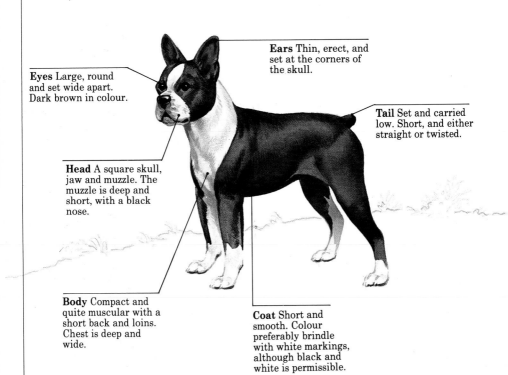

Ears Thin, erect, and set at the corners of the skull.

Eyes Large, round and set wide apart. Dark brown in colour.

Tail Set and carried low. Short, and either straight or twisted.

Head A square skull, jaw and muzzle. The muzzle is deep and short, with a black nose.

Body Compact and quite muscular with a short back and loins. Chest is deep and wide.

Coat Short and smooth. Colour preferably brindle with white markings, although black and white is permissible.

Bulldog

Despite its forbidding appearance, Britain's national dog is an amiable and affectionate companion.

History For centuries bull-baiting was a common sight on the village greens of England, where a bull would be tied up and dogs encouraged to attack it. A type of dog particularly well adapted to the "sport" – short in the leg, ferocious and with strong jaws – was developed from Mastiff stock. Bull-baiting became illegal in 1835, and over the years breeding has taken the rough edges from the dog's character, and exaggerated its stocky build and pushed-in face. The Bulldog came to symbolize something peculiarly British, and today it has no shortage of admirers.

Temperament Surprisingly gentle and very reliable with children. Their reactions to animals are unpredictable however, and care should be taken with other pets. They make good watch-dogs.

Requirements Very little grooming and only a moderate amount of exercise. Bulldogs can suffer very badly in heat.

French Bulldog
Controversy surrounds the origin of this small breed. The smaller varieties of Bulldog were probably among its forebears.

KEY CHARACTERISTICS *Bulldog*

Size 22.7 kg for a bitch, 25 kg for a dog.

Tail Set and carried low. Tapers rapidly to a point from a wide base.

Body Thick-set, with broad, deep chest and short back, arched over narrow loins and hindquarters.

Ears Small, thin in texture, and folded over. Set high and wide apart.

Eyes Set far apart and rather low. Round and very dark brown.

Head Very large, with a "pushed-in", muscular appearance and wrinkled skin. The flews (upper lip) hang low over the sides of the lower jaw, the front of which is prominent and upturned.

Coat Short, soft and close-lying. Colours include fawn and brindles, with or without a black mask or muzzle.

Legs The front legs are bowed in outline and short in proportion to the back legs.

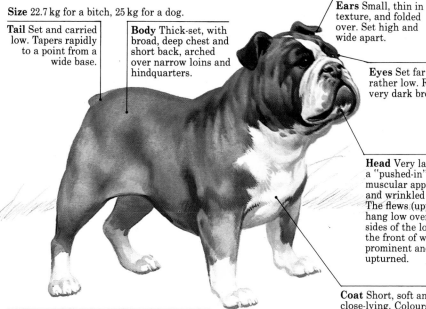

Chow Chow

The Chow Chow is an exceptional breed in having not one but two unique features. The first is the black mouth and tongue, while the second is the stiff, awkward-looking gait, that results from its completely straight hind legs.

History The Chow Chow is a Spitz type, first brought to England from China in the 18th century, and often said to be a Chinese breed, kept for its fur and meat. But its original homeland was probably Mongolia where massive, black-mouthed dogs were used in war as long as 3,000 years ago. The Chow Chow remained a ferocious hunting breed for most of its history, and only in more recent centuries did the Chinese begin to use it, along with other types of dog, as a source of food.

Temperament A rather self-contained, aloof dog, but it can be affectionate with its owner. Although the fierceness of their ancestors is no longer evident, Chows do not take kindly to collars and leads, and have a rather scornful attitude to obedience training. They can only be trusted with children they know well.

Requirements The Chow's nutritional requirements differ from those of other dogs, and too much fresh meat can have ill-effects. The thick coat needs a quick brush every day, and, as with all large dogs, exercise is essential.

KEY CHARACTERISTICS *Chow Chow*

Head Flat, broad skull with a square muzzle. Nose black, or paler in a light coloured dog.

Ears Small, thick and erect. Set well forward over the eyes, they contribute to the typical Chow "scowl".

Eyes Small, dark and almond-shaped for preference, but paler colours are allowed in dogs with light coats.

Tail Curling upwards over the back in typical Spitz style.

Coat A thick double coat standing out from the body. Show dogs must have solid colours, with cream, fawn, blue-grey, red or black all being permissible.

Body Compact, solid and well-proportioned, with a deep, broad chest.

Size 46–51 cm tall.

Black tongue A distinctive feature of the Chow Chow is the blue-black tongue.
Hindquarters The muscular legs are perfectly straight.

Dalmatian

A breed with an interesting past, that makes an ideal companion and family pet.

History The idea that this breed originated in Dalmatia, Yugoslavia is now known to be wrong, but the name has stuck. A very old European breed, its exact origins are obscure, but the Pointer (see p.50) was certainly among its ancestors. In the 19th century it became a fashionable carriage dog, which would race along beside, or even between, the huge wheels. Dalmatians still show the urge to run with vehicles, and often have a great affinity with horses, another legacy of their past.

Temperament An intelligent, cheerful, lively dog, good with children and easily trained.

Requirements Not a dog for the Sunday stroller. In its carriage days the Dalmatian happily ran up to 30 miles a day, so it needs plenty of exercise. Being used to human company, it will pine if left alone for long.

Dalmatian puppies
At birth the puppies are pure white. They soon develop the faint smudges which become spots.

KEY CHARACTERISTICS *Dalmatian*

Head Long, powerful muzzle and moderate stop. The nose should be brown or black, matching the spots.

Ears Set high and preferably spotted, not solid black or brown.

Tail Fairly long, reaching to the hocks, and spotted for preference. A slight upward curve is good but curliness is not.

Eyes Black spotted dogs should have dark eyes and black markings right around both eyes. For brown dogs the eyes must be amber and the "mascara" brown.

Coat Short, dense and sleek. The spots should be brown or black (never both), round and regular in size.

Body A sleek, muscular dog, not unlike a Pointer.

Size 56–61 cm tall.

Lhasa Apso

This is the most popular of the small dogs that have been introduced from Tibet, and is named after its capital city, Lhasa.

History The Lhasa Apso was bred by holy men in Tibet's many Buddhist temples and monasteries. These were often at high altitude in the Himalayas, where the breed's thick coat would have been invaluable. Some say that the second part of its name derives from "rapso", meaning "goat" in Tibetan, as the dog's wiry coat is similar to goat hair. Lhasa Apsos performed tasks around the monasteries, acting as watch-dogs, and were believed to bring good fortune to their owners. It was impossible to buy the dogs – instead they were given as gifts in appreciation of services rendered.

The first Apsos to arrive in Britain came from Bhutan, to be followed by other specimens from the Lhasa area. The two types were combined and Apsos were sometimes seen at British shows in the first half of this century. Now the Lhasa Apso is a highly successful show-dog and a very popular family pet worldwide.

Temperament A very friendly little dog with an assertive manner.

Requirements Plenty of affection. The long coat needs grooming daily.

KEY CHARACTERISTICS *Lhasa Apso*

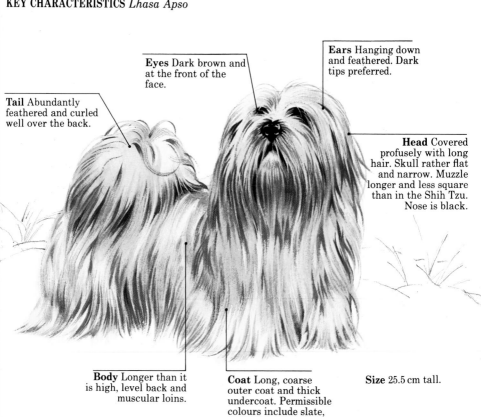

Eyes Dark brown and at the front of the face.

Ears Hanging down and feathered. Dark tips preferred.

Tail Abundantly feathered and curled well over the back.

Head Covered profusely with long hair. Skull rather flat and narrow. Muzzle longer and less square than in the Shih Tzu. Nose is black.

Body Longer than it is high, level back and muscular loins.

Coat Long, coarse outer coat and thick undercoat. Permissible colours include slate, sandy, brown, and white.

Size 25.5 cm tall.

Poodles

Poodles – Standard, Miniature and Toy – are the most popular dogs in many countries, including the United States.

History These dogs have had a very varied past, descending originally from German gundogs, known as *pudels*, which were used to retrieve game from water. In the 19th century, the appealing looks and trainability of poodles made them a useful addition to the entourage of French circuses. Later, they emerged from the entertainment business to become the world's most popular pets. The Poodle's long coat has always been trimmed in some way, and today there are several patterns.

Temperament Generally friendly, intelligent and loyal.

Requirements The hair grows indefinitely and isn't shed, so needs regular clipping.

Toy and Standard Poodles
The standards for the three Poodle breeds are identical in all but size. Toys should not exceed 28 cm; Standard Poodles must be at least 38 cm.

KEY CHARACTERISTICS *Miniature Poodle*

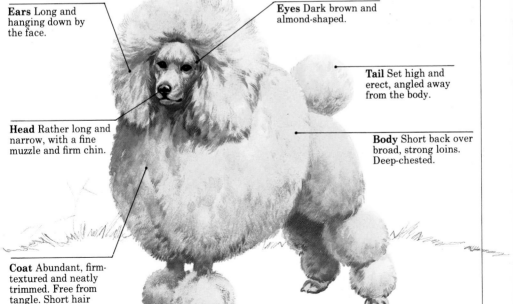

Ears Long and hanging down by the face.

Eyes Dark brown and almond-shaped.

Tail Set high and erect, angled away from the body.

Head Rather long and narrow, with a fine muzzle and firm chin.

Body Short back over broad, strong loins. Deep-chested.

Coat Abundant, firm-textured and neatly trimmed. Free from tangle. Short hair should curl close to the body. All solid colours are permissible.

Size 28–38 cm tall.

Miniature Schnauzer

This jaunty, intelligent little dog has won more admirers than either of the other Schnauzers, the Standard and Giant.

History All three Schnauzer breeds originated in the cattle and sheep farming areas of southern Germany. Records of a Schnauzer-type dog date back to the early 16th century. Their ancestors are thought to include the wire-haired German *Pinscher* and the *Schafer Pudel*, and the first Schnauzers were probably similar to today's Standard breed. They were all-purpose dogs, being good ratters and excellent guards. Breeders used the *Affenpinscher* – a tiny, monkey-like, wire-haired breed – to produce smaller dogs. Subsequent refinement resulted in the Miniature Schnauzer, also known as the *Zwergschnauzer*.

Temperament Full of good-natured energy, and very friendly towards children.

Requirements Long walks and regular, careful grooming of the coarse coat.

Giant Schnauzer
This highly intelligent breed was also developed from the Standard Schnauzer, and was originally used as a drover's dog in Bavaria.

KEY CHARACTERISTICS *Miniature Schnauzer*

Ears Set high, V-shaped and falling forward.

Eyes Dark brown and oval, under full eyebrows.

Special note In America the ears are generally cropped to a point.

Head Strong-looking with a gradual taper from the ears to the black nose. Muzzle powerful with abundant whiskers and moustache.

Tail Set high and docked.

Coat Hard and wiry. Long on legs and head but short elsewhere. Colours are black or "pepper and salt" – a mix of light and dark grey.

Body Back sloping gradually towards the hindquarters. Quite a deep chest with a visible breast bone.

Size 33 cm tall for a bitch, 35.5 cm tall for a dog.

Shih Tzu

This attractive small dog was kept as a companion and watch-dog in the Chinese imperial courts.

History The Shih Tzu is named after a curious animal featured in Chinese mythology – the Lion Dog. Buddhists in China revered the lion, and the little dogs were given similar respect. The ancestors of the breed originated in Tibet, and may have been related to the Lhasa Apso (see p.106). These found their way to China centuries ago, as gifts of goodwill from the Tibetan monasteries to the Chinese emperors. The Shih Tzu was introduced to Britain and America in the 1930s, and for a short time was classed with the Lhasa Apsos. Since its recognition as a separate breed, more and more people have become aware of this delightful dog.

Temperament Bred primarily as a pet, the Shih Tzu has great charm and vitality.

Requirements The long coat demands daily care to keep its good looks. However, the breed needs only moderate exercise.

KEY CHARACTERISTICS *Shih Tzu*

Ears Large and pendant. Hidden by a thick covering of long hair.

Eyes Dark brown, rounded and quite large.

Head Broad, with abundant long hair on crown and muzzle. Muzzle short and square, but not wrinkled. Nose black.

Tail Set high and curled over back.

Coat Very long and thick. All colours permissible, but those with white markings on the forehead and tail tip are particularly favoured.

Body Long, level back and wide chest.

Size 26.5 cm tall.

Bichon Frisé

A very lively little dog, and one that is much more sturdy and playful than many toy breeds.

History The Bichon Frisé is regarded as a French breed, but its exact origins are unknown. It is probably descended from an early water spaniel, but some think that sailors brought it back to the Mediterranean from the Canary Islands in the 14th century. Similarity with the Maltese (see p.113) suggests that the two breeds shared some of their forebears. For centuries, Bichon Frisés were companion dogs in the European courts, where they enjoyed a pampered existence. In the 19th century, however, the breed fell from grace, and, like the Poodle (see p.107), was draughted into circus troupes. The robust, cheerful nature of the modern Bichon is probably a legacy of its days as a hard-working entertainer. In the 20th century, the breed has found popularity as a pet in America, and the time seems ripe for it to become fashionable in Britain.

Temperament A good-natured companion, amusing, affectionate, and well-behaved with both children and other dogs.

Requirements The "powder puff" appearance of show-dogs is the result of much washing, trimming, brushing and talcum powder. Without this intensive treatment, the dog has an agreeable curly coat, but it must be groomed regularly. Strenuous exercise isn't needed.

KEY CHARACTERISTICS *Bichon Frisé*

Head Carried high. Nose is a round, black, shiny button on a rather short muzzle. Beneath the rounded growth of hair, the skull is flat.

Eyes Medium-sized and round, or nearly so. Dark brown with dark rims.

Tail Set quite low. Curled, but not tightly, over the back.

Ears Long and fine, with a good covering of hair. Hanging close to the skull.

Coat Delicate, silky, white curls. Length is from 7 to 10 cm.

Size Up to 30 cm tall.

Body A deep chest. Loins are muscular with a slight arch.

Cavalier King Charles Spaniel

Although now well established, this attractive dog was the product of a breeding programme started only this century. It is significantly larger than its cousin, the King Charles.

History Small spaniels, bred for companionship rather than the field, were depicted at the feet of European royalty in tapestries and paintings from the 15th century onwards. In England the type of toy spaniel held in special favour by King Charles II endured into this century. But many people felt that breeding during the 19th century, possibly involving Pugs, had

resulted in a dog rather removed from the original type. In the 1920s, a detailed "formula" for the Cavalier King Charles Spaniel was produced, to direct the efforts of breeders. They selected for a larger dog with a longer muzzle and flat skull. The Cavalier King Charles was a winner, and quickly gained popularity in Britain and, to a lesser extent in America.

Temperament Very companionable and level-headed.

Requirements Plenty of exercise and daily grooming to bring out the best in the breed's silky coat.

KEY CHARACTERISTICS *Cavalier King Charles Spaniel*

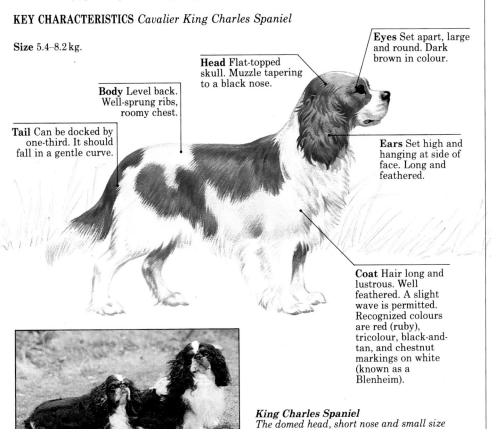

Size 5.4–8.2 kg.

Eyes Set apart, large and round. Dark brown in colour.

Head Flat-topped skull. Muzzle tapering to a black nose.

Body Level back. Well-sprung ribs, roomy chest.

Tail Can be docked by one-third. It should fall in a gentle curve.

Ears Set high and hanging at side of face. Long and feathered.

Coat Hair long and lustrous. Well feathered. A slight wave is permitted. Recognized colours are red (ruby), tricolour, black-and-tan, and chestnut markings on white (known as a Blenheim).

King Charles Spaniel
The domed head, short nose and small size distinguish this dog from the Cavalier King Charles. It is very good-natured, and friendly towards children.

Chihuahua

Some members of this breed weigh under a kilogram, making them the smallest dogs in the world.

History Although named after a Mexican city and strongly associated with South America, there is disagreement about the Chihuahua's exact origin, though most say that it was reared by the Aztecs or Incas.

Pottery dog figurines found in Mexico certainly show dogs of this type. One theory is that such small dogs were fattened up and used for food; another that they had some religious significance; yet another that similar dogs lived wild in the Mexican mountains. Whatever its origin, it still maintains several unique characteristics.

The first specimens reached America in the late 19th century, and these are the ancestors of almost all Chihuahuas there, and in Britain, today. The Chihuahua makes an excellent show-dog.

Temperament A good companion which loves attention, but is happier when not with other breeds.

Requirements The Chihuahua's appetites for exercise and food are predictably small; it can be quite particular about its diet.

KEY CHARACTERISTICS *Long-coat Chihuahua*

Tail Carried up or over the back and quite long.

Body Topline of back is level. Chest is deep.

Size Up to 2.7 kg.

Ears Large and forming rather a wide angle with the top of the skull.

Eyes Round, large and set well apart.

Head Domed skull, which may in a few cases be incomplete, the gap being termed a *molera*. Stop is distinct. The muzzle is short and pointed.

Coat Long, soft and straight, flat or with only a slight wave. Hair more abundant in places, forming a ruff, plumed tail, and feathering.

Smooth-coat Chihuahua
For a long time the Smooth-coat Chihuahua was much more common than the long-coated version, but the balance is now tipping. The two varieties are identical in all but coat length.

Maltese

Although superficially similar to the toy dogs from the East, the Maltese is very much a Mediterranean breed.

History There are conflicting accounts of this dog's precise place of origin. Most believe that a pure-breeding line was first established on the island of Malta, while others think of Sicily as its home. All are agreed, however, that the type is centuries old, and royal portraits which include lapdogs suggest that its appearance has not changed much over the years. The Maltese has never had to work for its living, but was kept as a companion dog by the European nobility. The first specimens arrived in Britain during the reign of Henry VIII, and it enjoyed consistent popularity until the introduction of the Eastern toy breeds at the end of the 19th century. Although eclipsed by these, the Maltese has never been in danger of disappearing, and today it is well known both in Britain and America.

Temperament An affectionate and lively little dog, which provides its owner with loyal companionship, but is suspicious of strangers.

Requirements The long coat must be groomed carefully each day, and washed frequently. A small amount of exercise is needed, although the Maltese should not be taken out in severe cold or heavy rain.

KEY CHARACTERISTICS *Maltese*

Size Up to 25.5 cm tall.

Head Of medium size with a distinct stop. The nose is black.

Ears Long and pendant with an abundant covering of long hair.

Eyes Dark brown and oval-shaped.

Tail Curling over the back with abundant covering of hair.

Body Compact and short, with a level back.

Coat White, straight, long and silky.

Papillon

The "butterfly" dog of France, whose face, with its central white blaze and large, wing-like ears, was the inspiration for its beautiful name. The silky hair covering the ears adds to the effect.

History The Papillon is another of the small companion dogs that once seemed an essential part of the household for Europe's aristocracy. Legend has it that Marie Antoinette was a keen admirer of the breed. It was common for dogs to be included in portraits of their owners, and Papillons were subjects for Rubens and Rembrandt, among others. The drop-eared version of the breed, seen much less often, is called a Phalène, the French for "moth". Belgium and France are thought to have contributed most to the Papillon's development, but in America and Britain, selective breeding this century has produced slightly smaller dogs.

Temperament A lively intelligence and an affectionate nature make this breed excellent company.

Requirements Although small, the Papillon isn't too frail, and likes exercise and fresh air. The coat needs frequent grooming.

KEY CHARACTERISTICS *Papillon*

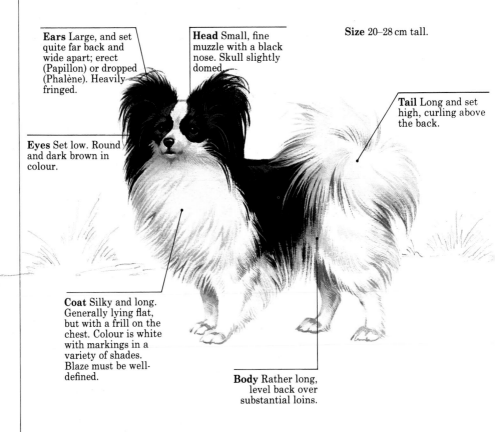

Ears Large, and set quite far back and wide apart; erect (Papillon) or dropped (Phalène). Heavily fringed.

Head Small, fine muzzle with a black nose. Skull slightly domed.

Size 20–28 cm tall.

Tail Long and set high, curling above the back.

Eyes Set low. Round and dark brown in colour.

Coat Silky and long. Generally lying flat, but with a frill on the chest. Colour is white with markings in a variety of shades. Blaze must be well-defined.

Body Rather long, level back over substantial loins.

Pekingese

What was once an exclusively palace breed in China is now regarded as an ideal pet for smaller homes.

History The dogs of the Chinese imperial court were held in far greater esteem than the companion dogs of European royalty. Pekingese were regarded as sacred, and no effort was spared in ensuring that pure breeding lines were maintained. Responsibility for the dogs' well-being fell to palace eunuchs, and they adhered to a strict breed standard, set out in words and pictures over the centuries. The first "Pekes" to reach the West were seized by the British when the imperial palace was looted in 1860. They were an immediate success, and the breed rapidly became very popular in Britain and America.

Temperament A surprisingly assertive little dog, which makes a good watch-dog.

Requirements Plenty of attention. The long coat needs daily grooming. Pekes have a tendency to develop breathing problems, and this should be watched for.

Japanese Chin
Like the Pekingese, this dog originated in China, and the dogs' ancestries probably have much in common. The Japanese Chin was once the court dog of Japan. Specimens were brought to the West in the late 19th century.

KEY CHARACTERISTICS *Pekingese*

Head Large and broad with a flat, wide, wrinkled muzzle. Nose is black with wide nostrils.

Eyes Set wide apart. Large, round and prominent. Dark brown in colour.

Tail Set high, slightly curved over back to either side, with profuse feathering.

Ears Heart-shaped and hanging close to the skull. Abundant, long hair accentuates the length.

Body Short, but quite substantial. Deep chest and level back.

Coat Very long and profuse, with abundant feathering. The outer coat is rather coarse. Many colours and markings are permitted.

Size Up to 5.5 kg for a bitch, 5 kg for a dog.

Pomeranian

The smallest of the Spitz group (see p.46), this dainty, picturesque toy seems far removed from its sledge-pulling cousins.

History In Pomerania, on the German Baltic sea coast, a distinct type evolved from northern Spitz dogs, such as the Samoyed (see p.83). The original Pomeranians were fairly ordinary dogs, mostly white in colour and much larger than the breed recognized today. They offered little that was new, either as pets or working dogs, and it wasn't until breeders selected for a smaller type that the breed became common outside Germany. A greater variety of coat colours was encouraged at the same time, including a warm, gingery orange, now the most popular colour. This selective breeding occurred towards the end of the last century. Since then, decreasing stature has brought increasing popularity, and Pomeranians are now common in both Britain and America.

Temperament Great loyalty, and a wariness of intruders, makes the Pomeranian an excellent watch-dog, but in general it is a quiet and well-behaved dog.

Requirements The luxuriant coat benefits from regular brushing. Pomeranians need little exercise.

KEY CHARACTERISTICS *Pomeranian*

Feet Very small. They move quickly, giving the dog a light, twinkling gait.

Ears Small and carried erect.

Tail Lies flat and straight over the back. Profusely covered with hair.

Head Foxy-looking, with a flatish, wide skull and fine muzzle.

Eyes Oval-shaped, and of medium size. Dark brown in colour.

Body Compact, with a short back and well-rounded rib-cage.

Coat Hard-textured, straight and long, forming a ball of fur from which the head and legs protrude. The face and legs have shorter, softer hair. Colours include orange, white, brown and black.

Size 2–2.5 kg for a bitch, 1.8–2 kg for a dog.

Pomeranian puppies
These fluffy bundles, looking like childrens' soft toys, will grow into dainty, elegant adults.

Pug

A charmingly compact breed, with a good temper and dignified manner. Such beauty as it has lies in the pattern of wrinkles on its forehead, and the smooth, firm texture of its coat. Its tightly curled tail and flattened face give the Pug an amusing appearance.

History While some think that the Pug's ancestors were short-haired versions of the Pekingese, others contend that the well-muscled little dog is a scaled-down mastiff. The first dogs to arrive in Europe were those brought back from the East by Dutch traders, and specimens reached Britain by the 17th century. The solidity and unabashed inelegance of the dogs appealed to Victorian tastes, and from the mid- to late 19th century, Pugs were in great demand as pets. This popularity later declined, but today numbers are rising, both in Britain and America.

Temperament Very affectionate, with a desire to become part of the family. Amenable to training.

Requirements Only a little time need be spent on coat care and exercising. Like other companion dogs, the breed does like plenty of attention.

KEY CHARACTERISTICS *Pug*

Size 6.4–8.2 kg.

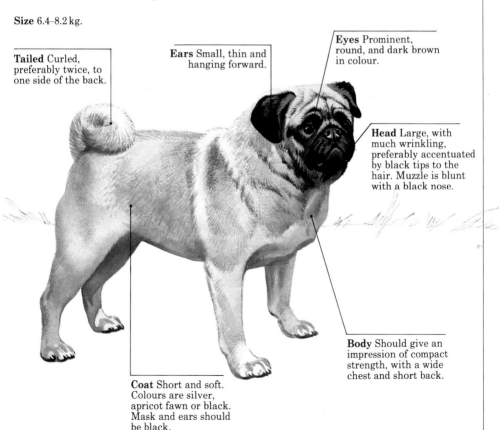

Tailed Curled, preferably twice, to one side of the back.

Ears Small, thin and hanging forward.

Eyes Prominent, round, and dark brown in colour.

Head Large, with much wrinkling, preferably accentuated by black tips to the hair. Muzzle is blunt with a black nose.

Body Should give an impression of compact strength, with a wide chest and short back.

Coat Short and soft. Colours are silver, apricot fawn or black. Mask and ears should be black.

Silky Terrier

Australia's toy terrier is full of drive and energy, and makes a rewarding pet.

History This breed has inherited a roughly equal measure of characters from its two main ancestors, the Australian and Yorkshire Terriers (see pp.89 and 119). The cross was first made in the mid-19th century, and during the following decades, when toy dogs were increasingly in vogue, the type became established. Its development was centred around Sydney, and the breed was first known as the "Sydney Silky", becoming the Australian Silky Terrier on official recognition. As with the Norwich Terrier (see p.97), both prick- and drop-eared varieties existed.

However, the latter is excluded from the breed standard, and, unlike the Norfolk Terrier (see p.96), hasn't received separate recognition. Although a welcome member of a great many Australian homes, the Silky Terrier only gained a foothold in America after the Second World War, and in Britain it is still uncommon.

Temperament The breed's strong character and liveliness demand a great deal of its owner's attention.

Requirements A Silky Terrier rarely sits still, and, unlike many of the other toy breeds, needs regular exercise. The long coat must be groomed regularly to avoid it falling into mats.

KEY CHARACTERISTICS *Silky Terrier*

Size About 23 cm tall.

Ears Set high. Small, V-shaped and pricked.

Tail Docked and held erect.

Eyes Small, dark and round, with a keen expression.

Head Quite long and broad, with a flat skull bearing a silky topknot. Nose is black.

Coat All hair is fine and silky. The body hair should be from 13 to 15 cm long. Colours are blue or grey-blue, both with tan markings.

Body Quite long, with a level back over strong loins. A deep chest.

Yorkshire Terrier

A toy version of the terrier breeds, but with a strength of character to match its larger relatives.

History Yorkshire Terriers originated in the mid-19th century around the industrial heartlands of northern England. They were bred by working men, for whom a large dog would have been difficult to keep, but who wanted a lively companion. Their probable forebears are the old Black-and-Tan Terriers, the Maltese (see p.113), and the now-extinct Clydesdale Terrier. From each litter the smallest dogs were selected for breeding, and the Yorkshire Terrier gradually "shrank" to the proportions we see today. The first dogs were shown in Britain in 1860, and the breed reached America in 1880. The Yorkshire Terrier now has a well-established place among the favourite breeds in many countries of the world.

Temperament Surprisingly domineering for its size, and a very good watch-dog.

Requirements Frequent grooming of the long, silky coat is necessary to prevent knots and tangles from forming.

KEY CHARACTERISTICS *Yorkshire Terrier*

Size Up to 3.2 kg.

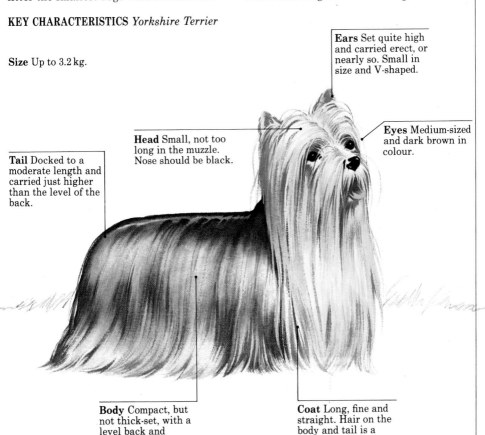

Ears Set quite high and carried erect, or nearly so. Small in size and V-shaped.

Eyes Medium-sized and dark brown in colour.

Head Small, not too long in the muzzle. Nose should be black.

Tail Docked to a moderate length and carried just higher than the level of the back.

Body Compact, but not thick-set, with a level back and muscular loins.

Coat Long, fine and straight. Hair on the body and tail is a dark, steely blue; elsewhere it is tan.

4

CHOOSING A DOG

A look through the breeds section of this book shows
you the incredible variety of shapes, sizes and
temperaments of dogs available. Finding the dog
that's just right for you needs care and forethought.
You'll have to decide whether to choose a puppy or an
adult dog, a dog or a bitch, a large or small dog,
pedigree or mongrel. Perhaps you're after a guard-
dog, a gundog, or even a show-dog? Maybe you're
looking for a companion for an elderly member of the
family or a playmate for the children. You may like
the look of a particular breed, but can you cope with
its needs in terms of exercise, feeding and grooming?
Taking on a dog means you're making a commitment
to the animal for its lifetime. So choosing a dog that
fits your lifestyle makes good sense. For further
guidelines, consult *Dog Breeds* (see pp.42–119),
Housing, Handling and Training (see pp.142–59), and
Grooming (see pp.172–83).

Making the right choice

Man has a long-standing link with dogs – an extension of the basic attachment that maintains contact between people. Human relationships are based on "social signals" – facial expression, eye and voice contact, time spent together, mutual dependancy and responsibility, the reassurance of touch. These behavioural signals are also seen between people and pets.

Why have a dog?

Dogs seek out people and take obvious pleasure in their company. They often fulfil a childlike role and are dependent on their owners throughout their life. This dependancy works both ways. The psychological value of stroking a dog is well-known to doctors – it reduces stress and lowers blood pressure. Your dog is part of your family – friend, protector, companion, comforter, entertainer. You'll wonder how you ever managed without it.

What kind of dog?

It makes sense to try to match your lifestyle and preferences to the temperament and needs of the dog. One of the main considerations is the dog's personality – see pp.50–119 for guidelines on the character of different breeds. You may be looking for a dog with behavioural characteristics like ability to guard, herd, retrieve or "point". Other questions you'll have to ask yourself are: What age? What size? What sex? Mongrel or pedigree?

What age of dog?

This is one of the first decisions you should make. Of course, a puppy is delightful, especially if you've got children in the house, but there may be reasons why an older dog is more appropriate.

If you're looking for a good companion and you'd like to take it out and about with you right from the

Pedigree dogs come in all shapes, sizes and colours, as this happy, healthy collection shows.

start, a young adult dog may suit you best. Elderly people can find a boisterous puppy a strain, but may be able to give a good home to a displaced older dog.

Puppies

If you choose a puppy, there should be someone at home all day, or periodically throughout the day. You must spend time with a puppy, both to develop a good relationship with it and to give it the chance to become properly house-trained. Taking a young puppy away from its mother is quite a serious upset; frequent or long separations from you, its new "parents", can cause problems.

Older dogs

If you choose an older dog, make sure it is house-trained – a dog that has been kennelled for a long time may not be. Find out exactly why the dog needs a home – it could be nervous, aggressive or dirty around the house. You must be prepared to be patient with the dog. Again, don't leave it alone for too long.

A special relationship
Your new puppy will soon come to rely on you, not just for food, but also for affection and companionship – things it can give you, too.

What size of dog?

Size is an important consideration. Large dogs may be good intruder deterrents, but could lead to a visit from the bank manager instead! Large breeds are expensive both to buy and to feed. Once grown up, they need a great deal of exercise. Obviously, they aren't suited to city centres, particularly houses or flats with small gardens. Walking a dog late at night can be risky in a city and your initial resolve to take it out regularly could weaken.

Small children can be knocked over by big, bouncy puppies, and elderly people often find large breeds a handful. But most of the giant breeds are as gentle as they are large and, once adult, usually careful with children.

Small and toy breeds need far less exercise – they'll virtually exercise themselves in a garden, particularly if two are kept together. Take care with young children – toy dogs' bones are fine and fragile and children can accidentally hurt them seriously.

Lifespan

Large breeds tend to age quicker than small breeds, which normally live longer. Great Danes, for instance, are fairly old at eight or nine years and few live beyond 11–12 years of age. Few Labradors last more than 14 years, but some terriers may reach 20! Toy breeds tend to have shorter lifespans than "regular" small dogs.

The problem of waste

There's no getting away from the problem of faecal waste; it causes considerable public concern. Large dogs eat a lot of food and produce a proportional amount of waste. This can be burned or buried in your garden, but clearing it from elsewhere is difficult. Think about this when deciding on the size of your dog.

A dog or a bitch?

Deciding what sex of dog you want can be difficult. Most dog owners have their own views on this subject, but both sexes have their pros and cons. Bitches are often considered more demanding of attention than dogs: they are easier to train and more likely to form a solid attachment to their owner, so they make better guide dogs.

One drawback of bitches is their twice-yearly reproductive cycle. During her "heat" a bitch is attractive to dogs and may make desperate attempts to escape. The discharge can be messy and some bitches are prone to false pregnancy (see pp.189 and 261). The solution is surgical neutering which adds quite a significant cost. But if you're keen to breed from your pet and you'd like to give children the fun of a litter of puppies at home, choose a bitch.

Fans of dogs maintain that they're more consistent in temperament than bitches. A dog will certainly roam in search of bitches if one is on heat in the area, which can cause problems for the owners of both dog and bitch. Their more dominant nature can make dogs more difficult to train and perhaps more likely to challenge human authority. Dogs are said to have more character; this is partly true – it's part of their independence and they enjoy strutting around like turkey cocks!

A dog may become so aggressive or wander so much that neutering is called for – this may or may not be successful and can change a dog's character. Neutering should never be carried out just for convenience – make sure there's a valid reason.

Mongrel or pedigree?

The term "mongrel" is unfortunate. It carries mental pictures of scavenging curs or the pathetic half-starved creatures seen in the streets of some cities. In fact, the word simply means a dog of unidentifiable breeding or mixed parentage – a "cross-breed". Mongrels have many points in their favour – they're much less afflicted by inherited diseases than pedigree dogs, and seem to avoid some of the more common ailments. They're just as susceptible to serious diseases though, and need the same amount of care and attention as the most expensive of pedigree animals.

Understandably, mongrels aren't as predictable as other dogs in terms of temperament and adult looks. If possible, visit the mother and her litter to get some idea of how your puppy might turn out. Try enquiring tactfully about the father. Even if the pregnancy was a mistake, he may well be known to the bitch's owners.

There are breeders who carry out intentional cross-breeding, usually between pedigree dogs. Such matings can also happen by accident – some pedigree bitches seem to delight in escaping to be mated by any breed except their own! The offspring of such

A cross-breed
A cheerful mongrel like this bright-eyed specimen makes an excellent pet, although you won't be able to enter it at an official show.

couplings are classed, perhaps unfairly, as mongrels, even though their parentage is known. These "first crosses" may escape hereditary disorders while still being fairly predictable in looks and temperament. These factors aren't always forseeable though, and cross-breeding has produced terrible results, with puppies inheriting the worst aspects of both parents. Like the pedigree stock that produced them, mongrels can be aggressive.

Border Collie crosses and Labrador crosses are among the most commonly seen mongrels. These are usually attractive, happy dogs and very energetic in their young years.

The case for pedigree dogs is easy to make. These dogs have been selected to fit certain specifications. Once you know which breed you want, choosing a pedigree dog means you know approximately how big it will grow,

what its temperament will be like, and its likely requirements in terms of food, exercise, work and grooming.

Apart from mongrels and pedigree dogs, there are the "type" dogs – the classics being the Jack Russell Terrier, the Heeler and the Lurcher. These aren't internationally recognized as breeds but they're recognizable types which breed true.

A boy and his dog
A child and a dog in high spirits together is a delightful sight. Fast-running Lurchers (not a recognized breed) are a well-established type.

CHOOSING AND BUYING A PEDIGREE DOG

This is where you have to combine personal taste with an appreciation of the practicalities. Don't just base your choice on a picture of a breed in this or any other book. Look into the special needs of the breed and consider your ability to fulfil them. Try to assess the amount of grooming involved. Long-haired breeds are likely to need a lot of grooming; even some short-haired breeds have their drawbacks. For instance, Labradors often have long moults and a black one kept in a house with pale carpets could cause problems!

Don't ignore the hereditary defects to which some breeds are prone. These vary and you should be informed about them in order to make a balanced decision and ask breeders the right questions. Ask local vets about any particular problems in local strains. A breeder stating that all his dogs are X-rayed for hip dysplasia, isn't quite the same as one stating they are free of it. Ask to see disorder clearance certificates where there are approved schemes in existence. If these aren't forthcoming, ask the breeder if he minds you

contacting his vet. Without his client's permission, a vet won't tell you anything about a breeder, although a general enquiry about a source of a particular breed might turn up trumps by elimination! Try to make as many enquiries as possible before seeing a litter of puppies. One look at their appealing eyes can be irresistible, particularly to any children accompanying you. You need to be as sure as possible that your chosen puppy doesn't suffer from congenital diseases or defects.

Choosing a puppy

Once your researches have led you to a breeder willing to sell you a puppy of the right breed and sex, you'll need to arrange to view the litter in order to pick out a puppy. Many good breeders will want to interview you, too! You'll rarely be allowed to see puppies younger than four weeks old – you'll certainly not be allowed to handle them for fear of upsetting the bitch.

Watch the puppies playing. See how they interact and how they react to you. Remember that the one curled up fast asleep may well have been rushing around shortly before. Puppies are very active for short periods, but they tire quickly. Their individual personalities will shine through, so look for the one that fits your needs. Is it the quiet puppy that seeks you out to be nursed that appeals to you, or the "go-getter" that leaps out of the box to see what is happening?

Unless you're very experienced with the guard breeds or sure of your ability to control them, avoid the bolder puppies of these breeds. They may challenge you for superiority later. Try to avoid the "shrinking violets" of guard breeds, too – once grown, their nervousness can lead to mistrust and aggression. A quiet but confident bitch is a good choice for a breed such as a German Shepherd or Dobermann in a fairly inexperienced pet household.

Buying a puppy for show
Although the occasional Crufts winner was bought as a pet which "made good", you usually get what you pay for. To obtain a guaranteed show-dog (not necessarily a winner, but good enough to be worth serious showing), you'll need to pay considerably more than for a pet dog. You may have to wait until the puppy is six months old

FINDING A PUPPY

You want a dog, you've chosen a breed, decided what sex, and opted for a puppy rather than an adult ... what next?
● Find out all you can about the breed and any hereditary diseases that may occur in it
● Write to the relevant breed society for information on organized schemes to eradicate these problems. Ask for lists of participating breeders and those with certified free stock
● Buy dog magazines (these can be ordered from

your newsagent). They give details of dog shows and names of breeders to give you a starting point
● Consult agencies which put people in touch with breeders who have puppies, and the special directories which list a number of breeders
● Call at your local vet's to see if they have any suggestions
● Go to shows locally – and further afield if you're interested in showing. Try to get a feeling for the breed, talk to the breeders and discuss the problems

● Avoid pet shops and puppy dealers. Usually, the puppies they've bought come from many different sources, often unlicensed breeders keeping too many bitches in unsuitable conditions. The puppies have often travelled long distances and may already be poorly
● Above all, don't buy on impulse. If you follow these guidelines, your chosen dog will be a companion and part of your family for at least the next ten years – well worth all the effort!

before you can have it, and when you've found a breeder willing to part with a good show specimen at six months, you'll have to pay for the privilege.

It can be difficult even for an experienced breeder to pick out winners from young puppies. Many breeders say that three weeks is a good age to get a correct notion of a puppy's worth. After this, puppies have a growth spurt and look comparatively unattractive until around 12 weeks. An otherwise perfect dog may be spoiled for show at four or five months because its teeth have grown badly and its "bite" is incorrect. This problem may conflict with when a breeder wants to sell puppies. (For the best age to acquire a puppy, see p.138.) Most breeds adapt best to a new home at about six to seven weeks, but if you do buy a show-dog at this age, you're gambling on your judgement and the judgement and honesty of the breeder. The breeder's experience is very

important and you can only really rely on someone who has been successful with your chosen breed.

If you're contemplating breeding from your show-dog, buy a bitch. You should expect to pay more for her because of her breeding potential. Relatively few males are used for stud – these need to be really good.

Jack Russell puppies in a pen
When choosing a puppy, spend a little time watching the litter playing together. Puppies' antics reveal their different personalities.

WHAT IS A HEALTHY PUPPY?

When you've found a suitable puppy, there are several basic points to check:
● The eyes should be bright and alert, with no discharges or cataracts
● The skin and ears should be clean and smell pleasant
● Check that faeces in the pen are well-formed
● Are the puppy's teeth correctly aligned and has it the right number for its age?
● If it is a male puppy, does it have two testicles? (see *Breeding*, p. 189)
● Is the body well-proportioned? It helps to have seen adults of the breed so you can differentiate between spindly and simply gangly puppies
● A healthy puppy is often heavier than it looks, but shouldn't be fat

FINDING A YOUNG ADULT DOG

If you've decided that a young adult dog fits your needs best, there are several potential sources:
● Local vets. If they have kennel space, vets occasionally house a dog – perhaps a stray that has been treated after a road accident, or a dog no longer wanted by a client
● Local animal welfare groups. Find out about these through local vets
● Breeders sometimes have young dogs which they have kept with a view to showing, but which didn't turn out quite as they hoped
● Breeders may also wish to find homes for older bitches after they have finished breeding
● Breed societies usually run a rescue service for dogs of their own breed

PUPPY-CARE

From the moment of birth, a puppy is changing and developing day by day, week by week, in many different ways. Whether you're caring for a litter of puppies born to your own bitch, or you're the new owner of a diminutive canine pet, this is a delightful period. Many dogs exhibit "puppy-like" behaviour all their life, but strictly speaking, puppyhood ends at 12 months. It's the time when a dog is at its most appealing – discovering new experiences, making friends, learning to play, bark, explore, eat solid foods. This chapter gives you practical advice on all aspects of caring for and feeding puppies. Welcoming a puppy into your home is particularly exciting. Make sure you're prepared and that both house and garden are safe. Toilet and obedience training are dealt with in *Housing, Handling and Training* (see pp.142–59), problem behaviour in *Understanding Your Dog* (see pp.210–25).

The newborn puppy

In a normal, healthy litter, each newborn puppy finds its way to the source of milk shortly after birth. During the first one or two days of its life, a puppy absorbs from its mother's first milk (*colostrum*) the protective antibodies necessary to see it through its first six to ten weeks. Most puppies feed from their mother for the first few weeks of their life (make sure the whole litter is suckling properly). After this you should decide on the best time to introduce solid foods and begin weaning (see p.132). The bitch keeps the puppies clean and also cleans up their faeces, although you should change the newspaper in the whelping box regularly.

Puppies are both blind and deaf at birth. Their eyes open at around 10–14 days, although it is another seven before they can focus properly. Their hearing starts to function as the ear canals open when they are between 13 and 17 days old.

Nail trimming
You may need to trim the puppies' nails at 14–21 days. The "kneading" movements they make while feeding can scratch the bitch's underside. Use baby nail scissors.

Sleep and rest
Just like babies, puppies have an amazing capacity for sleep. Well-fed puppies do little other than sleep and suckle for the first week of their life. After this, their activities increase until, by three weeks, they are wobbling around, exploring the whelping box. Up to the age of 12–14 weeks, you'll notice that periods of incredible activity are interspersed with periods of coma-like sleep – you'll be glad of these at times!

Keeping the puppies warm
Temperature is something you need to watch carefully and in which you'll need to play an active part. Puppies develop within the uterus at 38.5°C and, despite a drop in the bitch's body temperature just before whelping, their wet arrival into the world comes as a shock. Wet puppies chill easily but may not show any signs for up to 48

The whelping box
Although the bitch needs to leave the box periodically for feeding and relieving herself, the puppies should stay in the box for at least the first four weeks. When they're ready to venture out of it, they'll find their own way! At this stage, you should provide a pen around the box. If the weather is fine and warm, box and pen can be placed in the garden for a short while.

WAYS OF PROVIDING HEAT

For the room
- Radiators or fan heaters

For the bed
- Well-wrapped hot-water bottles
- Proprietary heater pads placed under bedding
- Infra-red or dull emitting bulb lamps

Warning
- Don't let puppies come into direct contact with heater pads – they may get burned.
- Don't place infra-red lamps too close to puppies – they can cause localized overheating or even burns.

Keeping a newborn puppy warm
Hot-water bottles are an economical way of providing warmth for new puppies. Refill them regularly and wrap them well.

hours, by which time an infection may occur which they are unable to resist.

Newborn puppies can't shiver properly and until they are seven to ten days old, are unable to make their hair stand on end in order to trap an insulating layer of air. So puppies' heat regulation is very poor, and their body temperatures tend to rise and fall with that of their surroundings. After six or seven days, they develop some control over heat regulation but it isn't particularly efficient until four weeks of age. This is why you should provide supplementary heat for at least the first two weeks, even if the puppies are in the bitch's box, and longer if they aren't (orphan, rejected or some hand-reared puppies).

Keep the room temperature at around 30–3°C (puppies can tolerate slight variations on this for short periods). An alternative plan is to keep the room temperature at a minimum of 21°C and to provide extra heat for the actual bed. The room temperature can be allowed to drop by 3°C each fortnight until the normal ambient temperature is reached. It's important to take great care over how the supplementary heat is provided. As a puppy's heat regulation is so inefficient, direct heat applied to one area of its body isn't properly dissipated and can damage the skin.

Detecting a weak puppy

Healthy puppies feel dry, warm and full, with "normal" skin tension. When you pick them up, they respond by wriggling. Weak puppies often feel damp and limp. Their skin is non-elastic and "tents" when you pick up a fold. A happy, healthy litter makes a gentle murmuring sound, punctuated with squeaks and sharp cries when they are hungry or during feeding. Weak puppies don't settle – they crawl around, wasting energy and emitting thin, plaintive wails, Eventually, they'll lie passively in a corner of the whelping box. Be on the lookout for puppies which aren't getting any milk. It's possible for a puppy to miss out on several feeds until it's too weak to feed at all. A puppy like this needs special attention and will probably have to be removed from the box and hand-reared (see p.134). If in doubt, consult your veterinary surgeon.

Feeding and weaning

If all goes well, a litter of puppies should feed happily from their mother until around three to five weeks of age. Sometime during this period, while they are still taking plenty of milk from the bitch, you can start supplementing the bitch's milk, so that the puppies learn to lap from a saucer. This avoids any "check" in the puppies' growth due to a reduction in food, and also promotes a natural reduction in the amount of milk the bitch produces, as the puppies make less demands on her.

Weaning puppies off the bitch
The first step towards weaning is to make up a sloppy mixture of baby cereal and warmed cow's milk and put a little of this into each puppy's mouth with your finger or the handle end of a teaspoon. After introducing the mixture this way, put it in the puppy pen in saucers twice daily. For the first week or so the puppies will crawl through their meals and will need wiping down after feeding. Any milk or

feed left on the skin can cause dermatitis or hair loss. The bitch is usually excluded during feeds to avoid her interfering too much. As the puppies learn to lap properly and take plenty from their dish they can be given food three or four times a day; at this stage you can introduce meat.

The traditional first solid food of scraped best stewing steak isn't ideal since it is low in calcium. If you want to use fresh meat, you should supplement the calcium with bone flour. To scrape meat, lay a piece of stewing steak out flat and draw the blade of a sharp knife firmly across it, gathering a kind of "meat paste". If the puppies are over three weeks old, you can give them raw minced beef straight away, with bone flour.

Alternatively use a specially formulated tinned puppy food. Even canned all-meat adult dog foods are better balanced than fresh meat, although you should add a little bone flour to these too. Whatever you choose, it must be finely ground. To

First steps to weaning
Start by offering the puppies a little milk and baby cereal in saucers, twice a day. This isn't usually done earlier than the middle of their third week. They'll probably continue feeding partially from their mother for a few weeks.
*   It's important to clean any feed off the puppies after every meal. When all the puppies are lapping milk and cereal properly, introduce some meat and rusk feeds as well.*

make canned meat easier for puppies to eat, pour on a small amount (less than 10 percent volume for volume) of hot water and crush it with a knife.

As the milk supply from the bitch dwindles, give the puppies more feeds yourself. Puppies need feeding more frequently than adult dogs for the same reasons that human babies require frequent feeds – for rapid growth and development. The calorific requirements of a puppy, on a weight for weight basis, are up to four times those of an adult dog.

Don't be in too much of a hurry to wean a litter of puppies if feeding is going well and their mother still has sufficient milk to nourish them. But if puppies aren't weaned by five weeks, start this in earnest, beginning with meat (see left). In general, puppies should be taking very little – if anything – from the bitch by six weeks of age.

DAILY FEED TIMETABLE (7–12 WEEKS)

Milk and cereal	Morning
Meat and rusk	Mid-day
Meat and rusk	Afternoon
Milk and cereal	Evening

Developing adult eating habits

At around twelve weeks of age, a puppy usually loses interest in one of the feeds of its own accord, so drop one of the milk meals. Three feeds a day are usually continued until six months, then two feeds a day until nine months. Whether you continue to feed your dog twice daily or cut down to once depends partly on circumstances and partly on the dog. In general, the smaller toy dogs fare better on two meals a day.

The right approach to feeding

Don't give any of the puppies the opportunity to become a fussy feeder. When you put down a meal for a puppy, introduce it to the food and leave it quietly. Don't just put the food down and expect the puppy to find it. Allow 20–30 minutes for the meal to be eaten then pick it up again. Leftovers can sometimes be covered, refrigerated, and re-offered at the next meal, perhaps with a little gravy or stock. Again, pick the meal up after 20–30 minutes or it will become dry and tasteless. For more on feeding techniques, see pp.170–1.

WEANING BOTTLE-FED PUPPIES

This process is the same as described for normal puppies, but begins at about two and a half weeks. First encourage the puppies to lap, and as soon as this is mastered, introduce meat. Hand-reared puppies usually learn to lap several days earlier than puppies on the bitch, which makes life easier for you. Take great care that the puppies don't suffer a setback at this stage due to being slow to get enough food from the saucer. Continue feeds with the bottle until you're sure that all the puppies are feeding well and gaining weight satisfactorily.

A hand-reared puppy feeding
This puppy has learned to eat solid food.

Hand-rearing puppies

In general, newborn puppies don't need hand-rearing. The mother performs the task automatically. But this is not always the case and you may need to undertake some, or all of the care of a single puppy or even a litter, from birth. This involves bottle-feeding, stimulating bowel function and sometimes, maintaining adequate warmth (see p.130). Puppies needing active care may be: ☐ orphaned ☐ weak ☐ ill ☐ premature ☐ rejected ☐ unable to be fed by mother. Occasionally, your vet may suggest a foster mother for orphan puppies. If not, you will have to hand-rear them. It is important to distinguish weak puppies from strong, healthy ones (see *Detecting a weak puppy*, p.131).

Feeding healthy puppies
Strong, healthy puppies can be started immediately on standard bitch milk substitute – ask the vet which one to use. Mix the feed using a kitchen mixer to avoid lumps. Make up fresh milk every day, store it in the refrigerator and feed it at about 38°C. (To wean bottle-fed puppies, see p.133.) Alternatively, make up your own feed.

RECIPE FOR PUPPY FEED

Ingredient	Amount
Whole milk	800 ml (28 fl oz)
Single cream	200 ml (7 fl oz)
Egg yolk	1
Sterilized bone flour	6 g (1½ teaspoons)
Citric acid powder	4 g (1 teaspoon)
Pediatric vitamin drops	2–3 drops

BOTTLE-FEEDING A PUPPY

Anyone with a whelping bitch should obtain a nursing bottle just in case, although many vets stock them for emergencies. Use a special pet nursing bottle or premature baby bottle. Avoid eye droppers; they force in too much air. Newborn puppies should be fed two-hourly at first, and then three-hourly; amounts will depend on their appetite.

1 First sterilize the bottle with sterilizing fluid. Mix the feed, add it to the bottle, and heat to about 38°C by placing the bottle in boiling water.

2 Hold the puppy, supporting its rib-cage, and guide the teat into its mouth. Let its legs move freely while feeding, to allow the "kneading" reflex.

Feeding weak puppies

Milk substitute can be too rich for weak puppies. For the first few feeds, give them cow's milk, diluted with one-third the volume of water and with 10 g glucose added per 500 ml. To compensate for vitamins in colostrum (first mother's milk) add two drops of a pediatric vitamin mixture per 500 ml.

Heat the mixture to about 38°C and feed at least two-hourly (very weak puppies may take tiny amounts as often as half hourly until they pick up).

A puppy which won't feed will rapidly fade and die. Try dripping a little milk into its mouth. If this fails, after two hours consult the vet who can feed it with a tube. Forcing milk into a puppy is dangerous – you could flood its lungs.

Bowel and bladder problems

Every time you feed the puppies you must simulate the normal cleaning activity of the bitch, who would be busily licking them and cleaning up their urine and faeces. Clean each puppy's face, and wipe away any milk on its fur. It is also important to stimulate the bowel and bladder actions of newborn and young puppies.

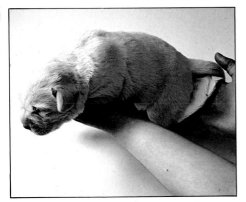

Stimulating bowel and bladder function
After feeding, gently massage the abdomen and anal area with damp tissue. Apply a little petroleum jelly around the anus afterwards.

Constipation
Puppies can become constipated when fed milk substitutes. You can help by using a stubby bulb thermometer to introduce some petroleum jelly around and into the anus. A drop of sunflower oil or liquid paraffin can be given in the feed or directly until the puppy is back to normal (stop the treatment so as not to cause diarrhoea). If there is no response after 24 hours, call the vet.

RETURNING PUPPIES TO THE BITCH

You may wonder whether or not to replace hand-reared puppies with their mother between bottle feeds. There is no simple answer to this – it depends on your relationship with the bitch and your knowledge of how she may react. With a highly-strung bitch, the slightest interference with her puppies can result in total rejection. The fact that you have handled a puppy can cause her to clean it frantically, licking and nibbling so much that she may even kill and eat it. If a discreetly supervised trial period suggests that she won't fully accept a weak puppy, it is best hand-reared away from her.

On the other hand, some nervous bitches seem to take pleasure in selected humans becoming involved with the litter. Never take advantage of this precious confidence and remember that young puppies should be handled minimally. When you do need to handle puppies kept with the mother, begin by washing your hands without soap (to avoid carry-over of scent), then stroke the bitch with both hands. This is to mask your human scent and avoid leaving it on the puppies. If you are feeding a premature litter, it is better to keep them with the bitch and take them out for feeds. The presence of puppies can encourage the production of milk and hopefully hand-rearing will only be temporary.

Veterinary puppy-care

Your vet will give your puppy the vaccinations it needs. He'll also tell you anything you need to know about worming, teething and any other aspects of the puppy's health.

Worming

Nearly all puppies have roundworm, passed on through their mother before birth and possibly also through her milk. It is important to worm puppies regularly. Worming involves giving each puppy a drug which kills the worms so that they are passed in faeces, and does no harm at all. Breeders normally start worming at about three weeks old, repeating the dose every two to three weeks.

If you're acquiring a new puppy, your vet will advise you when to worm it and what to use. It is best to continue the worming course until the puppy is 16 weeks old. After this, worm it at six months and again at 12 months. (For types of worm affecting adult dogs, see pp.250–1.)

Vaccination

Your puppy needs protection from a range of dangerous diseases that could kill or damage it. These are:
- CD – canine distemper
- CVH – canine viral hepatitis
- CL – canine leptospirosis (two forms – hepatitis and nephritis)
- CP – canine parvovirus
- Rabies (in certain countries)

The first injections against all these diseases (except rabies) are usually given to puppies at eight to ten weeks, although in some high-risk cases they may be given at six weeks. CP (parvovirus) vaccination is sometimes treated separately. For more about these diseases, see the *Health Care* chapter; for rabies, see p.152.

The reference chart opposite shows the best time to get your puppy injected for various diseases – although the timings may be modified by your vet, based on local experience.

Passive immunity injections
Some puppies are sold inoculated with a measles vaccine to give temporary protection against distemper. Injections of antiserum giving passive immunity are sometimes given by animal welfare organizations. Your vet may give such an injection to hand-reared puppies lacking the passive immunity which is given via the colostrum in bitch's milk. *Neither of these stop-gaps is an alternative to a full course of vaccination.*

Teething

Like human babies, puppies are born toothless. Between three and five weeks, the puppy's set of small, sharp temporary teeth appears. In the fourth month the growth of the permanent teeth makes the gums a little inflamed and swollen as the permanent teeth press on the roots of the temporary teeth. The signs of teething are varied. Puppies often become restless, off their food, salivating and even vomiting. Many show a desire to chew hard objects. This encourages the temporary teeth to fall out, stopping the pain caused by pressure on the roots.

Tooth retention
Sometimes, the eruption of permanent teeth doesn't push out the temporary teeth as it should. This is a common problem with toy breeds. Consult your vet if a temporary tooth is still firmly in position when the permanent tooth looks half-erupted – he may want to extract the temporary tooth.

TAIL DOCKING AND DEW CLAW REMOVAL

Tail docking causes controversy and is something you'll need to decide about if your puppy belongs to a breed whose Kennel Club standard requires a docked tail. Not all vets will carry out tail docking, and you may have to ring round to find one willing to do it.

The best time to dock puppies' tails is at three to five days old; younger puppies may be adversely affected and blood on the tail stumps can provoke the bitch to cannibalize them. Older puppies suffer more pain and there's more bleeding. The procedure involves cutting the tail at the appropriate point with surgical scissors, staunching the bleeding, then stitching the skin over the stump. This last step is crucial with some breeds to avoid unsightly scarring. Often no anaesthetic is used and the puppies may suffer some pain.

Dew claws Removal of the dew claw (equivalent of the thumb, on the side of each foot), is another common practice and should also be carried out at three to five days. There are various reasons for removal. Being off the ground, the dew claw doesn't wear down like the other claws. In some dogs, it grows round in a circle, penetrating the toe in a very painful way. Working dogs can catch these claws in the undergrowth. In some breeds, they are removed simply to give a smooth, sleek look to the legs. The breed standard may also require removal of all, or one pair of the dew claws.

YOUR PUPPY'S HEALTH CARE DIARY

Weeks	VACCINATION INJECTIONS CD, CVH, CL, CP	Rabies	TEETHING	WORMING
1				
2				First worming
3			Temporary canines.	First worming
4	First (high risk cases)	Two injections, two to four weeks apart, in countries where disease exists (not in U.K.)	Temporary incisors. First three temporary cheek teeth	Second worming
5	First (high risk cases)			Second worming
6	First (high risk cases)			
7				
8	First (normal cases)			and every two to three weeks until 16 weeks (3½ months)
9	First (normal cases)			and every two to three weeks until 16 weeks (3½ months)
10	First (normal cases)			and every two to three weeks until 16 weeks (3½ months)
11				and every two to three weeks until 16 weeks (3½ months)
12	Second			
Months				
4	Third (CP only)		**4 months** Permanent premolar (carnassial). Temporary fourth cheek tooth. Central and lateral permanent incisors. **5–6 months** Corner permanent incisors. Permanent canines. First three and fifth permanent cheek teeth. **6–8 months** Sixth cheek tooth lower jaw, (not always upper).	
5	Third (CP only)			
6				Worming
7				
8				
9				
10				
11				
12				Worming

Your puppy's new home

The question of when a puppy should move to its new home causes more problems than any other. There can be psychological conflicts between a caring breeder parting with a litter of puppies and a new owner eager to acquire one of them. A breeder may even delay selling a particular puppy because it has show potential and could command a higher price later, or even to be too good to sell.

For getting to know its new family, six to seven weeks is the best time to move a puppy. From this age, the more human contact it experiences, the better its temperament will be. Strangely enough, the eight to nine-week period is said to be the equivalent of a "fear period" seen in babies of eight months, and it is usually best to avoid changes of home during this time. Smaller, more

MAKING YOUR HOUSE AND GARDEN SAFE

Houses are designed for people and can contain hidden hazards for dogs, particularly young puppies. In the house, watch out for any exposed electric flex in places where it can be chewed, especially in out-of-sight corners. Make sure the puppy can't fall down stairs or stair-wells by putting up guards. Although you may feel a little silly, it is well worth going round every room in the house on all-

fours, to see exactly what is within reach of an inquisitive, playful puppy!

Examine the garden to make sure your puppy can't get out. A garden gate is often a weak spot – cover it with wire netting to make it secure. You must also feel quite sure that no dogs can get in from outside before your puppy has had all its vaccinations. If possible, fence off a section of the garden where you can safely

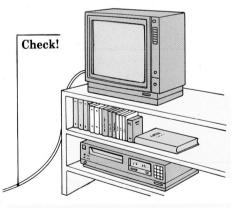

Check!

Check the house
- Exposed electric flex
- Stairs and stair-wells
- Any projections which could catch on the puppy's collar and strangle it
- Check rooms on all-fours

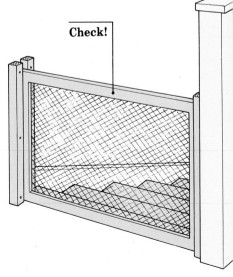

Check!

insecure breeds and puppies going to noisy homes with very young children are often best left until they are ten weeks old. There are no hard and fast rules, though, and if the breeder considers the new home suitable, the owners sensible and the puppy well-adjusted, six to seven weeks seems a good age to make the transfer.

If you're about to acquire a puppy, there are arrangements to make and equipment you need (listed below right) to ensure the puppy's happiness and safety in your home.

leave the puppy for short periods; it can also use this run as a toilet area.

Check your garage and garden sheds for items that could fall on the puppy and make sure that no dangerous poisons like weedkiller or slug and rat baits have been left around. Finally, put up guards to protect the puppy from any other garden hazards such as pools, ponds and steep drops at the edges of patios or lawns.

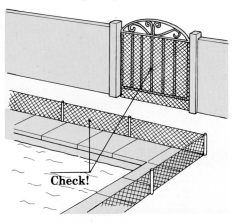

Check!

Check the garden
- Dog-proof boundaries, especially gates
- Garage and sheds
- Baits and poisons
- Ponds and steep drops

A place to sleep

A bed of its own makes a very important contribution to the puppy's sense of security in its new home. It will certainly miss its mother, brothers and sisters and previous home so will benefit from having its own "territory". The first bed doesn't have to be elaborate – a cardboard box with the front cut down provides a good start. The only bedding needed is newspaper with a folded blanket on top. Once the teething stage is over and the puppy chewing less, you can provide a sturdier bed (see p.146).

Food and water bowls

Your puppy needs separate bowls for food and water. When deciding where to put them, remember that the water should be available at all times, so choose an out-of-the-way place with an impervious surface. Place the bowls on newspaper to keep any stray food tidy; when the puppy is past the chewing stage, you can place them on a plastic wipe-down mat.

EQUIPMENT CHECKLIST

Use this list to make sure you're fully prepared for your puppy's arrival.
- Bed and bedding (see *Housing, Handling and Training,* p.146)
- Food and water bowls (see *Feeding,* p.171)
- Suitable diet (see p.133)
- Collar, lead and identity tag (see *Housing, Handling and Training,* p.145)
- Grooming equipment (see *Grooming,* p.178)
- Toys (see *Housing, Handling and Training,* p.148)
- Run or playpen
- Travelling box (see *Housing, Handling and Training,* p.149)
- First aid kit (see *First Aid,* p.278)

Collecting your new puppy

If possible, arrange to collect your puppy in the morning so that it has a whole day to get used to you and its new surroundings before being left alone for its first night. This is a big day, not only for you and your family, but for the puppy. It is a good time to find out everything the puppy's breeder can tell you about caring for it, and to have it checked by the vet.

Ideally, two people should fetch the puppy but if only one can go, you'll need a travelling box (see p.149). The upset will be minimized if someone can hold the puppy on their lap, protected by a blanket. Take newspaper and a roll of kitchen paper since most puppies are travel-sick, even on short journeys in the car.

QUERIES FOR THE BREEDER

If you've not already consulted the breeder, now is the time to find out about the following:

Pedigree If the puppy is pure-bred, the breeder will give you its pedigree.

Vaccination Find out which vaccinations the puppy has already had, and ask for the relevant veterinary certificates. The breeder should tell you when the puppy was last wormed and with what product.

Feeding Ask exactly what the puppy has been fed on. You may decide not to continue with the same diet, but any changes should be gradual and not sudden. In any case, keep the puppy on the same food for at least the first few days. Some breeders will provide a detailed diet sheet, listing all the foods your puppy has eaten to date, and with other suggestions. A good breeder will have used readily available foods or will sell you a week's rations of the foods he's been using.

Visiting the vet

It is well worth having your puppy checked over by the vet, particularly for the presence of any congenital diseases. The best time to do this is on your way home from collecting it. If the vet detects a serious problem, you may wish to return the puppy to the breeder. Far less upset will be caused to you, your family and the puppy than after you have had it for several days, or even weeks.

If your vet has an appointments system, let him know in advance that you'd like your new puppy examined. Take all the documents in with you so that the diet sheet can be checked and any further vaccinations arranged. If your puppy hasn't yet been fully vaccinated, stay in the car with it until just before the appointment. Never put the puppy on the floor inside or anywhere near the surgery; there may be sick dogs in the waiting room which could infect it.

Arriving home

On your arrival, don't let children fuss the puppy too much – it will already be nervous and bewildered.

Toilet training

Immediately the puppy arrives at its new home, give it the opportunity to relieve itself. Even in the first few minutes you should start toilet training the right way. Unless it is raining or snowing, take the puppy into the garden and keep it under supervision. Otherwise, lay some sheets of newspaper by the door to the garden. Most puppies should have the opportunity to relieve themselves at least every two hours and after every meal. This will pay dividends in later training. Some owners like to train their puppy to use a litter tray (although those dogs who do bury their faeces tend to do it rather vigorously and can kick litter over a considerable area). Later on this can help encourage the dog to use flower beds and not lawns. For more about toilet training, see p.153.

The first meal
It is likely that the puppy will still be at the four-meal-a day stage. Give it about one-third less than its normal feed for the first meal. It may be excited or nervous and has probably been sick in the car. Keep a discreet distance while your puppy eats the meal – your well-intentioned hovering could inhibit a nervous puppy.

Meeting other pets
Introductions to any other pets you may have should be made cautiously, under full supervision. Older, more aggressive animals (especially dogs rather than bitches) can resent the presence of new animals. Each case

needs judging on its own merits, but watch the animals carefully for at least the first week. Even a well-meaning adult dog could harm a puppy through rough play.

Social mixing is important – your training is reinforced when the puppy sees an adult dog behaving properly and copies it. Dominance and "pecking orders" become more important as dogs get older. This isn't a problem with two bitches, who usually live happily together, the older bitch taking seniority. With two dogs, however, as the puppy gets older and stronger, it will periodically challenge the older dog and they may fight.

Cats
Cats are usually very withdrawn with puppies and resent the intrusion. They may spend most of the time out of the house for the first few weeks until they begin to accept the idea of the new addition to the family. Eventually, there are usually no problems, but it can be a good idea to trim cats' front claws at first, to prevent them from damaging the eyes of a cheeky puppy.

The first night
Just before bedtime, give the puppy an opportunity to relieve itself again. Almost inevitably, your first few nights' sleep will be disturbed. The homesick puppy will be upset at night when you and your family disappear to bed and will probably cry. There are two approaches to this. You can ignore the crying until the puppy settles down. Never punish it for crying – this only increases its misery. After a quiet night, praise your puppy. The alternative is to place a pen in the bedroom of one of the family and let the puppy sleep there for a couple of weeks. This can cause problems in itself, since children especially tend to weaken your resolve to keep the puppy out of bedrooms and off beds.

Meeting the family's other pets
Most older dogs are kind to puppies once they're acquainted, but watch them carefully at first.

HOUSING, HANDLING AND TRAINING

Welcoming a dog into your home involves a new set of
responsibilities. It is important for you and your
family to start as you mean to go on; your reward for
careful handling and training will be a sociable,
obedient dog you'll be proud to be seen out and about
with. Responsible ownership means choosing the right
equipment for your dog – its own collar, lead and bed,
plus any extras like a kennel, travelling box or toys.
Exercise, in the form of walks, is an integral part of
every dog's life; playing games helps provide this too.
General care and equipment for young puppies is
covered in *Puppy-care* (see pp.128–41).

Handling a dog

When dealing with a friendly dog that already knows you, follow these general guidelines:
● Be gentle but firm at all times
● Speak in a reassuring voice
● Don't startle the dog
● Don't tease the dog or take advantage of its friendly nature

A responsible dog owner should have the trust of his dog and should be able to hold it still, pick it up or carry it without any panic or aggression. The degree of holding and cuddling that dogs will tolerate varies – it depends partly on temperament, partly on owner conditioning. Most dogs revel in it, given the opportunity.

However, it is also important to teach your dog to accept physical restraint from you. Train it by restraining it for very short periods from puppyhood so that it doesn't see your gesture as a threat. You'll need to restrain it at the vet's (see p.271).

HANDLING A STRANGE DOG

If you encounter a strange dog, perhaps in an enclosed space, it may show aggression (see p.219), growling or baring its teeth. There are a few things to remember in this situation:
● Speak in a calm, firm voice
● Don't make any sudden moves. If the dog shows any aggression, keep still
● Don't challenge the dog by staring
● If all is well, offer a clenched fist to be sniffed (fingers are vulnerable)
● Don't crouch by the dog unless you know it is safe. Stoop from the waist so you can straighten to avoid bites
● If you're uncertain, keep your distance. Don't threaten the dog or block its exit path
● Look around for an object for self-defence if this should prove necessary, but don't show it to the dog
● When you leave, invite the dog to come too; don't make it look like a retreat

PICKING UP A DOG

If you need to pick up or carry a dog, talk to it first so that it is not surprised to be handled. If you're alone and you're in any doubt about the dog's temperament, muzzle it first (see p.279).

To pick up a small dog, place one hand under its chest. Use the other to support its rear end, the way you'd lift a cat.

To lift a larger dog, place one hand or arm under its chest in front of its forelegs and one under its hind legs. Bend your knees before lifting the dog rather than bending from the waist. It often helps to have a second person gently holding the dog's head and talking to it. This stops it panicking and turning to bite your face.

The right way to pick up a dog
Whatever the size of dog, make sure that its front and rear ends are both supported.

Collars and leads

Pet shops stock a bewildering array of collars and leads. In general, choice depends on preference, but there are a few points to watch.

Choosing a lead

Leads are usually made of rope, leather, chain or nylon. For large breeds, choose a strong lead, either a stout leather one or the chain sort with a leather handle. Badly trained dogs that chew their leads also need chains. Nylon leads are easy to wash and lightweight, so they're handy to put in your pocket.

It is possible to buy a lead on a rewinding spool, extending to 4.5m or 6m. Although the lead is compact to hold, it lets the dog explore while you remain in control.

Choosing a collar

Most collars for dogs are leather, but chain and nylon ones are also available. A leather collar 12 mm wide is suitable for most dogs; larger breeds will need 2.5–4 cm width.

Several countries require a dog to wear an identity tag on its collar in case of loss or accident; several types are available.

A puppy's first collar

Even though a puppy isn't allowed out on the streets until after its course of vaccinations, it is a good idea to accustom it to collars and leads.

POINTS OF SAFETY

When giving a puppy its first collar:
- Don't fasten the collar too tightly; you should be able to slide several fingers underneath it
- Don't use a choke chain on a young puppy – you could damage its neck
- Don't leave anything projecting on which the puppy could catch the collar and accidentally hang itself

---

USING A CHOKE CHAIN COLLAR

A choke chain (or check chain) is a training aid and should *not* be worn all the time. It is meant to control a dog while out walking or during training. If worn continually, there's more risk of it catching things. Always have the dog on your left-hand side. It is important to put the collar on the right way round, so that the weight of the chain loosens the loop after the collar has checked the dog.

From the ring, the chain should pass in front of the dog's neck, round the neck and back through the ring to the lead.

Dog beds, kennels and pens

A bed or kennel is an important part of your dog's surroundings and provides it with its own territory, refuge and "reference point". Every dog needs its own place to sleep; some may also benefit from having a kennel and perhaps an outdoor pen.

A bed for your dog

A cardboard box is fine for a growing, teething puppy, and easily replaced if soiled or damaged. As the puppy grows up, you'll probably decide to buy it a proper bed or basket.

You can buy dog beds at most pet shops, although owners of giant breeds may need to spend time finding a suitable one. Choose one that will only leave a little space round your dog when it is fully grown, while allowing for bedding.

Bedding

Anything soft and warm – old towels, jumpers or blankets – is ideal. Wash them regularly. You can also place a bean bag in the bed or basket – line the bed with newspaper first.

Cleaning the bed

Dogs will happily sleep on beds which smell (to us) incredibly "doggy". This does little to enhance their personal freshness. You should wash bed and bedding regularly, every time you bath the dog and between-times as well. Scrub the bed or basket with a non-toxic disinfectant diluted with hot water.

Where to put the bed

Place your dog's bed in a secluded draught-free site. Dogs don't settle in

TYPES OF BED

Dog beds come in a wide range of sizes and shapes. **Wicker baskets** are traditional and popular; their friendly creaking may reassure a dog. However, they're hard to

clean and large pieces can be chewed off and swallowed – watch this. **Plastic beds** are resilient and suitable for dogs that seem to be reassured by chewing their bed. Some

small breeds like the "igloo" type sold for cats – these surround the animal snugly and securely. **Bean bags** make a self-contained bed on their own. They're ideal for dogs

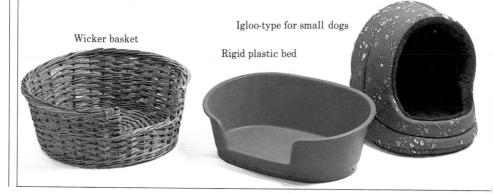

Wicker basket

Igloo-type for small dogs

Rigid plastic bed

very busy parts of the house.

Animals seek out warmth in cold weather, so place the bed near a radiator and turn it down if the dog seems too hot.

Kennels

Many owners, particularly those with working dogs, prefer to keep their dogs in outside kennels at night, and may restrict their range with a tethering chain or a pen.

It is quite acceptable to provide a dog with a snug outdoor kennel, for sleeping in at night or for spending a few hours in during the day when you're unable to give it your company and supervision.

You can either buy a kennel or make one yourself. The size of the kennel is dictated by the size of the dog. It should be large enough for the dog to have its bed at the back, well away from the entrance.

Most kennels are wooden, but they can also be built of brick or breeze block. The roof is usually of wood, covered with roofing felt. It should be removable for cleaning the bed.

A pen for your dog

A secure run in your yard or garden can contain your dog, giving you peace of mind while letting it move about freely in the open. Decide how large a pen or run you want, based on the size of your dog and the amount of time it will be spending there. The more space you can allow, the better.

A mesh-covered wooden framework is usually adequate, but very large dogs may need a solid wall about 60cm high below the mesh. If possible, arrange the kennel a few inches off the ground – the base may slope gently away from the kennel towards an outside drain. This arrangement is easy to clean with a hosepipe.

that enjoy vigorous "nest-making". Buy the type with a removable, washable cover. The outer fabric should be sturdy and the "beans" should be fire-retardant.

Bean bag

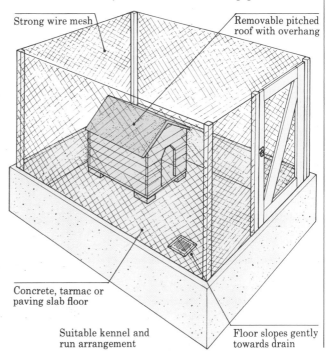

Strong wire mesh

Removable pitched roof with overhang

Concrete, tarmac or paving slab floor

Suitable kennel and run arrangement

Floor slopes gently towards drain

Play and exercise

Every dog needs regular exercise to keep it fit and healthy. Dogs which don't have enough exercise become obese. Generally, your dog will take as much exercise as you want to take yourself. However, if you're very athletic and enjoy hill-walking or long-distance jogs, your dog will need to build up to this gradually.

Avoiding over-exercise
Large dogs, particularly giant breeds, should never be over-exercised before they're 12 months old. Bones and muscles are still developing and too much exercise in puppyhood can cause long-term problems. It isn't easy to say exactly how much exercise to give individual dogs – just try to judge when your dog has had enough. Never walk puppies or young dogs to exhaustion; simply try to take the edge off their enthusiasm.

If your dog seems unable to tolerate moderate exercise without becoming tired out, or comes home lame for no obvious reason, consult the vet rather than simply assuming it is unfit. It may have a problem in its chest, muscles or bones (see also pp.266–7).

Toys
Play is a vital element in the development of a puppy. Since you won't always be on hand to amuse it, it needs to learn to play by itself. Providing proper toys prevents its desire to chew being directed towards you or your slippers. There are plenty of special pet toys on the market and older dogs enjoy them too. Puppies love the special rawhide chews which help give relief during teething.
Which toys are safe?
Toys that are safe for your pet vary according to the size of breed. All dogs love balls, but don't give them small ones. A tennis ball size is relatively safe; smaller balls could lodge at the back of a dog's throat and obstruct its airway. Football or softball types are the safest. Nylon bones are fine for most puppies and adult dogs of larger breeds, and squeaky toys give great pleasure – if you can bear the noise!

Toys are bound to suffer a certain amount of chewing and clawing, so use your common sense when buying them and keep these points in mind:
● Toys must be non-toxic.
● There must be no pieces which can be chewed off and swallowed.
● There should be no sharp edges.
● It should be impossible for the dog to swallow the whole toy.
● Beware of small balls or small, plastic childrens' toys.

The importance of games
Dogs love playing, especially with children.

Travelling with a dog

There will certainly be occasions when your dog needs to travel – to a dog show, a new home, or just to the local vet. Most dogs are only too pleased to be taken out; they'll be quite happy in the back of the car behind a guard, or held on a lead by a passenger. Some small dogs may feel more secure in a travelling box, though.

Travelling boxes

Special travelling boxes are available for all sizes of dog, but are really only used routinely for small dogs. Large boxes are used for big dogs travelling by air or rail.

Cardboard carriers don't withstand soiling and don't last very long, but may be useful for taking a puppy to the vet for vaccination. You can always use an ordinary cardboard box – don't buy an expensive fibreglass or wicker carrier if the puppy will be too big for it when fully grown.

The canine traveller
A wicker carrier is suitable for a small dog.

Transporting a litter of puppies
There may be occasions when it is a good plan to take the whole whelping box to the vet's. You might need to do this for a bitch having a Caesarian, or a litter of puppies having their tails docked. It is much less unsettling to take mother and puppies in their box in the car and leave whichever is not seeing the vet in the car during the appointment. Make sure any box you use for transporting puppies is completely draught-proof – puppies aren't efficient at regulating heat (see p.139). Pad the box well and add a hot-water bottle.

Travelling by car
Some dogs take to cars well but some are car-sick after half a mile and others start jumping up and down, barking and howling immediately they are put in the car.

Try to get your dog used to car travel from puppyhood. If it seems to dislike the car, build up to long trips gradually. Let the puppy investigate the stationary car and see that it is nothing to be afraid of. Take it on a short trip to the shops and leave it in the car with someone. Take some kitchen paper and make sure the puppy has an empty stomach. Once it is fully vaccinated, take it on short car journeys, followed by a walk, so that it associates the car with nice things rather than just visits to the vet.
Sedatives
Generally, these are not a good idea. Most interfere with dogs' heat regulation and if sedated in a hot car, they can suffer heatstroke. However, dogs that suffer from persistent car sickness may need travel-sickness tablets for long trips – ask your vet.

Guards and grilles

Under most circumstances, dogs travelling in the car are best confined behind a dog-grille or dog-guard. These provide a dog with its own area in which to settle down comfortably and prevent boisterous pets from being a nuisance.

Guards come in several types and sizes, ranging from lightweight adjustable versions (for small breeds and well-mannered larger dogs) to the more substantial models which can be fixed to the car body.

As an alternative to actually attaching the guard to the car, you can buy a cage which is assembled in the back. A "mobile cage" like this is particularly useful for show-dogs, which can be confined to stop them getting messy before a show. The car can be safely opened up for ventilation.

Window guards
Another useful car fitment is an adjustable screen which fits inside an open window so you can wind down the windows for better ventilation, yet prevent dogs jumping out. Although useful, don't rely on these guards making the car a safe place to leave a dog on a hot day.

Leaving a dog in a car

Never leave a dog alone in a car for long, especially in hot weather. On a still, warm day there is often no air current even if the window is open, and the interior of a car heats up like a greenhouse. Dogs suffer heatstroke easily (see p.281) and may even die.

TIPS FOR LONG JOURNEYS

- Before a long trip, give the dog a chance to urinate and defecate
- Give it a drink and something to eat before departure – about one third of its normal meal is enough. Some dogs can't eat anything before travelling but you'll discover this through trial and error
- Stop at reasonable intervals along the route – at least every 2–3 hours – to give the dog a chance to stretch, relieve itself and have a drink
- On very long trips, give the dog some more food after 4–5 hours. A little food in the stomach helps many dogs settle

---

A sturdy dog grille allows both you and your dog to travel comfortably, even over long distances.

Travelling by air

Air travel is fairly cheap for dogs. Its speed minimizes the period of distress; the dog is never more than a few hours away from a vet.

All dogs must travel in a container which complies with regulations laid down by airlines through the International Air Transport Association (I.A.T.A.). In addition to these rules, some airlines add their own. For example, British Airways will not carry any snub-nosed breeds of dog. Different government regulations apply in different countries, too. Find out about these before your dog travels.

Dogs should be given a light meal and a short drink about two hours before dispatch.

I.A.T.A. RECOMMENDATIONS

● Snub-nosed dogs (Boxers, Bulldogs, Pekingese and Pugs) must be free from respiratory troubles before travelling. The front of their container must have open bars from top to bottom
● Air travel is not recommended for bitches on heat
● Nursing bitches and unweaned puppies aren't acceptable for carriage
● Weaned puppies younger than eight weeks should not be shipped
● Puppies and kittens may travel well together, although some countries insist that each animal is crated individually
● A familiar article placed in the container helps to comfort a dog
● The dog's name must be marked on the outside of the container

CONTAINER REGULATIONS

Fibreglass, metal or rigid plastic
● Containers must have a strong framework, with stout joints
● The whole of one end must be open and covered with securely fixed bars, weldmesh or smooth expanded metal
● Access should be via a very secure sliding or hinged door
● The main ventilation must be supplemented by slots or holes distributed regularly over the opposite end of the container, as well as over the top third of the sides
● The container must be large enough for the dog to stand, turn and lie
● Noses and paws must not be able to protrude through ventilation holes
Wire mesh and wooden containers should conform to the above points. However, carriers made chiefly of wire mesh are unsuitable for international travel and wooden ones may be unsuitable for large dogs
Wicker containers These should only be used for puppies and small dogs

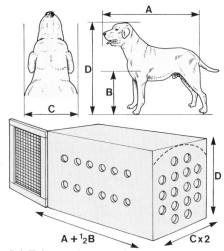

I.A.T.A container requirements
A = Length of dog from nose to root of tail
B = Height from ground to elbow joint
C = Shoulder width; $C \times 2$ = Container width
D = Height of container (top flat or arched)/height of dog in standing position.
Container to show mandatory "This way up" label and I.A.T.A. "Live Animals" label.

Travelling abroad

Transporting a dog to other countries calls for a great deal of organization. Your first priority will be to investigate the quarantine regulations both in the country you are travelling to, and the country you are travelling from.

The U.K. is one of the world's few rabies-free countries, and remains so by imposing strict quarantine laws.

When you bring a dog into the U.K. from abroad, it will be quarantined for a period of six months. During this time it will be given two anti-rabies inoculations. Even though the U.K. is rabies-free, a short quarantine period and/or an inoculation will often be required if you take a dog (or any other susceptible animal) from the U.K. to another controlled country. For more about rabies, see p.265.

RABIES

Rabies is a potentially fatal virus transmitted in the saliva of infected animals. The disease is endemic in many countries, and rabies-free countries impose strict quarantine regulations to stop its spread. Anyone who tries to evade these regulations when taking a dog (or any other controlled species) into a country with disease-control regulations breaks the law and endangers lives.

Rabies-free countries
These countries have very strict quarantine laws:
● Britain
● Australia
● New Zealand
● Hawaii

Precautions
In all countries without anti-rabies legislation, take the following precautions:
● Avoid close contact with free-roaming animals
● Don't allow your pets any contact with wild or feral animals

● Get your dog vaccinated regularly

Emergency action
If bitten by a suspect dog:
● Clean the wound with soap or disinfectant immediately. If this isn't possible, wash it with clean water or alcohol
● Seek medical attention immediately – prompt treatment with vaccine will save your life
● If possible, restrain the animal for investigation, but take care to avoid further injury
● If you can't safely catch the dog, inform the police

United Kingdom quarantine regulations
If you buy a dog abroad or take your dog overseas and then return to the U.K. with it even if it has been vaccinated abroad, it will still be subject to quarantine here. This six-month confinement is essential in order to keep the U.K. rabies-free. Registered quarantine kennels are comfortable, well-run establishments.

Of course, they have the same disadvantages as commercial kennels.
If you plan to bring a dog into the U.K., obtain the necessary documents before making your trip.

Incubation period
The rabies virus has a long incubation period (usually 10–120 days, but sometimes up to six months). The quarantine system is therefore an essential part of the safeguards designed to keep the human and animal populations of rabies-free countries safe from this fatal disease.

Anti-rabies vaccinations
British policy is *not* to use vaccines, for various sound scientific reasons applicable to an island that has been free of infection for many years. However, if you are going to live or work abroad and you intend to take a dog to a country where rabies vaccination is advisable or compulsory, vaccine can be given in the U.K. by your vet under licence.

Toilet training your puppy

Begin house-training as soon as you obtain your new puppy. As it will relieve itself frequently, there will probably be quite a few "accidents" before the puppy is trained. But never punish it if it relieves itself in the wrong place – you could cause problems such as submissive urination (see p.224).

Success depends on your ability to predict the call of nature. Common times are after activity, waking or eating. Some dogs circle round and sniff the floor first.

You must first decide whether to paper- or house-train your puppy.

House-training

If you are at home most of the time and access to the outside is easy, this is the simplest method.

Take the puppy out when it wakes, after every meal, when it has been active, if it hasn't urinated for some time or if it shows signs of wishing to do so. Let the puppy walk out with you rather than being carried, since it will then recognize the route and learn to go to the door when it needs to go out.

Until the puppy is able to go through the night without accidents, put newspaper by the door at night. You'll soon be able to discard it.

PAPER-TRAINING

If you live in a flat, or are out for much of the day, then paper-training is a good idea. It also makes a back-up to house-training.

The aim is to teach the puppy to relieve itself indoors on newspaper, which you can eventually place outside. When the frequency of urination and defecation is reduced to the level where you can be sure of being present when the puppy needs to go out, progress to full house-training. Some puppies dislike the feel of newspaper under their feet, particularly those that circle before relieving themselves. In this case it is probably best to go straight to house-training.

1 Confine the puppy to an easily cleaned room, and cover the floor with newspaper. When the puppy develops a preference for one area, remove the paper from the rest of the floor. You can then gradually move the paper, and eventually place it by the door.

2 On a fine day, place the paper outside. The next day, remove the paper altogether. Hopefully the puppy will then relieve itself outside. Praise it when it does this. Keep an eye out for the warning signs, including the puppy looking for its paper near the doorway.

The principles of dog training

The aim of training a dog varies from simple control in the park to strict obedience-style training for competition or police work. Most owners wish simply for a well behaved dog, which is under full control when out of doors.

A training system

What form should the training take and what should you be able to command your dog to do? Aim to teach it to come when called, walk to heel, stop and sit, stay, wait and come to you, and lie down. Once your dog has mastered these lessons, you'll have no worries when taking it out and about. You should be able to leave it outside a shop, for instance, and know it will be waiting for you when you come out.

Initially, use a collar and lead as a training aid. The lead gives you control over the dog's movements until you have full verbal control.

What signals are suitable?

The signals you give your dog when you want it to act in a certain way are important. Hand and arm signals can be used but are restricted by the dog needing to have a clear view of you. Sound is more often used because it has great range and dogs' ears are capable of appreciating a variety of audible signals. A well-known method of training uses spoken commands reinforced by hand/arm signals.

To start with, you can reinforce the sound signals by repetition and by suitable gestures. For instance, when training your dog to "COME", try turning away as you give the command. This plays on a dog's pack instinct. It sees its "pack leader" begin to leave and wants to stay with the group, so it follows.

Dog training classes

Training classes can be fun and may be of special benefit to older dogs going through the training process or needing a "refresher course". However, distractions may present a problem. Some people find that their dog behaves perfectly in the class with the trainer and the other dogs present, but won't obey at all outside; with others, the opposite applies. This is often related to how well the animal interacts with other dogs and people. If your dog is apprehensive of the trainer and the other dogs at the class, its attention will be concentrated more on staying with, and pleasing, you. If it gets on well with other dogs, its attention may wander during the class because it wants to play. Dogs like this are probably best trained at home.

The value of reinforcement

In training, you can give either positive or negative reinforcement – reward or punishment. Punishment has little value in training dogs and none in the basic training described here.

The best approach is positive reinforcement – giving praise when a command is obeyed; if your dog fails to obey, simply withhold your praise. You're playing on its instinctive desire to be accepted as part of the pack (the family) and to please you, the leader.

Force is not a good training tool. Hitting a dog simply trains it to stay out of range, but training needs close contact and a good relationship so this counteracts your objective.

The occasional punishment

There will be times, however, when you have to punish your dog – probably to stop it doing something and to gain its attention. Think carefully why you are using the punishment and be sure in your own mind that the dog will understand why it is being punished. There is no point in scolding it for something it has done some time earlier; any retribution must be speedy otherwise it is just counterproductive.

The right way to punish a dog
Never beat a dog repeatedly – you could injure it. A reasonable punishment is to grasp the skin at the back of the neck (in large dogs, use both hands, either side of the neck) and raise the dog off the ground (this is how a bitch would naturally punish an unruly puppy within the pack). Give it a good shake and a harsh verbal scolding at the same time. As a simpler measure, a light slap on the rump will often suffice.

TIPS FOR TRAINING SUCCESS

- Take the training steps one at a time, in the order given in this chapter
- Accompany punishment and reward with verbal signals like "BAD DOG" and "GOOD DOG". Later, these will be sufficient punishment and reward in themselves
- Try not to get too short-tempered with a young dog. Your mood may upset it
- Bribery with tit-bits does have a place in training – as an occasional extra
- Keep your voice pleasant; always use the same form of words for verbal commands
- Keep your dog on the lead near traffic or farm animals

The first commands

There is no fixed age to begin training, but the best time to learn walking to heel is probably at about 12–14 weeks (when vaccination is under way). It usually takes about three months to train a young dog with no ingrained bad habits; older dogs take longer. Lead training is the first step and very few puppies actually enjoy it. However, getting it right is vital for

TEACHING YOUR DOG TO WALK TO HEEL

1 Be very calm and help your dog to get over its initial reaction by speaking reassuringly and holding the lead firmly. Shorten the lead and insist that the dog comes in to the required position, its right shoulder beside your left leg. Don't let the dog chew the lead – a bad habit which should be discouraged.

2 Having established mastery of the lead and your dog's movements, begin walking in a straight line. As you start off, say "HEEL" firmly. Continue speaking in a pleasant way to reassure your dog that all is well even though it may feel that something strange is happening! Check your dog if it pulls forward or hangs back.

3 At this stage, make any turns carefully. Initially, restrict yourself to making right turns – away from your dog. Turning to the left can panic it at first since it may worry about becoming entangled with your legs. Once your dog is used to walking on the lead, introduce the left turn.

the future. You and your dog will both enjoy going for walks far more if it is able to walk to heel willingly. Training sessions should be no longer than ten minutes for puppies and twenty for adult dogs, or the animal will lose interest. In fact, the first sessions should only last five minutes and can be repeated several times daily for the first few days, before you progress to ten minutes. Speak reassuringly, take your time, and give commands firmly.

Make sure no-one interferes with your training session. Puppies get confused if the whole family are involved, so decide on one person to be responsible for training. The rest of the family can learn the commands later.

WALKING: OUT AND ABOUT

After a few quiet sessions training your puppy to walk to heel, take it out on the streets and let it see other people. Everyone will want to pet the puppy. This encourages boisterous behaviour because it then expects everyone you meet to make a fuss of it. If possible, don't stop.

When you see other dogs, just keep walking. Obviously avoiding them makes the puppy think they're a threat, which can lead to aggression.

How soon you expose a young dog to noisy traffic and crowds depends on its temperament, but it is an important part of training. Don't begin too soon, or the dog will see it as a punishment.

Walking don'ts
- Don't stop to talk to people
- Don't allow sniffing of lamp posts
- Don't avoid other dogs
- Don't go among traffic and crowds too soon

TEACHING YOUR DOG TO SIT

When your dog is able to walk to heel properly and enthusiastically, continue the training process with the "SIT". When walking to heel, choose a quiet place to stop. Place your left hand on the dog's back, just above the pelvis, and apply gentle but firm pressure to make the dog sit. As you do this, say "SIT". Soon you can dispense with the lead and the hand.

Remember that dogs don't speak English. Saying "SIT" over and over again won't make your dog automatically understand. You must *show* it what you mean as well.

Hold your lead hand up

Bend your knees slightly

The next steps

Once your dog has mastered "SIT" and will do it on command without your hand or the lead, it is time to introduce "STAY". This is an important landmark in your dog's training. By staying still while you go out of sight, the dog shows its total trust in you. Then, when you have taught it to stay, with the implication that you will return for it, it is useful to teach your dog the alternative command – "WAIT – COME".

TEACHING YOUR DOG TO STAY

1 Walk with your dog to heel, then make it sit. Holding the lead vertical and taut, command "STAY" and walk round the dog. Correct any attempt to move with a gentle but firm jerk of the lead. Repeat the command as you move round the dog. When it begins to understand, slacken the lead and widen your walking circle.

2 Now try the "SIT – STAY" command without the lead, again gradually extending your distance from your dog. To reinforce the command, stretch one arm away from your body, palm upwards, towards the dog. This psychologically lessens the gap between you. Gradually go further away until you are actually out of sight. When you return, praise the dog for its obedience, then continue walking.

TEACHING YOUR DOG TO WAIT AND COME

Don't be too anxious to try this without the lead as, initially, the command is easily broken. Your dog may push its luck and refuse to come, or sit just out of range. In this case, punishment is no use. Go back to lead training for a while. Remember never to scold your dog if it doesn't come on odd occasions – it should never be afraid to come to you. Always praise it when it does come – this is an important lesson.

For this exercise, you'll need a long lead – use the extending type if you have one, or extend your regular lead with 10–15 metres of nylon cord.

1 The procedure for learning "WAIT" is the same as for "STAY", so your dog will learn this quickly. Command the dog to sit and when it sits, command "WAIT", then turn and walk away.

2 Once you're a few metres away, turn and call the dog by name, stressing the additional command, "COME". You may need to give a little tug on the lead to show your dog what you mean.

TEACHING YOUR DOG TO LIE DOWN

This is usually comparatively simple to teach. The "DOWN" position is a natural extension of the "SIT" position. Use the lead in the same way as for "STAY". Start with the "SIT" command. Now show the dog the "DOWN" position by moving its front legs at the same time as giving the "DOWN" command repeatedly and gently reassuring the dog. Praise it if it maintains this position, but not if it gets up.

At first, it is important to show your dog the meaning of "DOWN".

7

FEEDING

Your dog needs the right foods for growth, work and body maintenance. And a correctly balanced diet is all part of owning a happy, healthy dog with bright eyes and a well-conditioned coat. You'll soon be able to tell if you're not doing it right!

The principles of feeding a dog are the same as for all animals. There are a few nutritional differences between dogs, cats and humans, for instance, but these are to do with detailed requirements of specific nutrients. All dogs need certain nutritional components in the right proportions. Whether you're using pre-packed dog foods or giving your dog a home-cooked diet, feeding do's and don'ts should be carefully observed. It's important to adopt the right approach to amounts of food, supplementation, feeding bowls, titbits and mealtimes. Weaning and feeding of young puppies is covered in *Puppy-care* (see pp.128–41).

The dietary needs of a dog

It may seem odd to consider exactly *why* you feed your dog, but the objective is important. It is to provide sufficient food for body maintenance plus enough for extras like growth, work, pregnancy and lactation. So what should a dog eat and how much?

Feeding for growth

When considering how much food to give your dog, you may feel tempted to promote its growth by giving it large quantities. Seeking maximum growth, particularly in large and giant breeds, can cause serious growth abnormalities. There is evidence that rapid growth and weight gain can aggravate diseases like hip dysplasia. Heavy feeding and supplementation carried out by owners of giant breeds seeking to boost their dog's growth may contribute towards the shorter lifespan of these breeds.

It isn't a good idea to give your dog as much food as it will eat. In practice, the quantity which seems to produce the best results in terms of growth is about 80 percent of what a dog would eat if unchecked. More than this can cause obesity; less may curb growth potential.

The "raw materials" of a dog

The statement "we are what we eat" applies to dogs as well as people. Just like the food it eats, a whole dog can be considered in terms of raw materials. This helps us to understand what's needed for the dog's growth and maintenance.

In the same way, a diet can be considered in terms of various nutritional components. These are:
□ Protein □ Fat □ Carbohydrate
□ Vitamins □ Minerals □ Fibre.

Raw materials of the average dog

Protein	16 percent
Fat	23 percent
Carbohydrate	1.7 percent
Minerals	3.5 percent
Water	56 percent

N.R.C. dog nutrition requirements

The N.R.C. (National Research Council) in the U.S.A. has assembled all the data on dog nutrition and produced a set of guidelines for manufacturers of dog foods which can be summarized in a table (see overleaf). The requirements for growing puppies are double those for adult dogs' maintenance.

The value of protein

All animal tissue contains a relatively high level of protein, so your dog needs a continual supply of protein in its diet to maintain itself and to grow. The "building blocks" of protein are the amino acids; about 25 are involved in protein. Ten of them are essential in the diet and cannot be made from others. It is to get enough of these that the needs of the body for dietary protein are so high.

Unexpectedly for a carnivore, the dog's ability to digest protein is variable. Although most offal and fresh meat is 90 to 95 percent digestible, dogs only digest 60 to 80 percent of vegetable protein. Too much indigestible vegetable protein can cause colic and even diarrhoea.

The value of fat

Fats are present in the diet as molecules called triglycerides which are basically three fatty acids linked together. Some of the fatty acids are essential to a dog. A deficiency of them causes a dog's skin to become itchy and it may develop a harsh, dry coat with dandruff, often leading to ear infection. Fatty acid deficiency can make a dog dull and nervous, too.

Apart from being necessary for very important metabolic processes, fat is an important energy source for dogs. If a dog can obtain most of its energy from fat, intake of protein can be reduced, lessening the demands on the liver and kidney. Fat increases the palatability of food for a dog and is an essential carrier of fat-soluble vitamins. Fats are virtually 100 percent digestible in a healthy adult dog – even puppies can digest them efficiently.

The value of carbohydrates

These incorporate sugars, starch and cellulose. The simplest sugars are the easiest to digest. Adult dogs can't digest lactose, the sugar naturally present in milk (excess milk causes diarrhoea), although they can cope quite well with ordinary sugar (sucrose).

It is interesting to compare the carbohydrate levels in terms of energy in foods comonly fed to dogs. Very high levels are contained in boiled potatoes, rice and carrots, with dry dog food mixer and wholemeal bread a little lower on the list. All-meat canned food, fresh meat and fish have no carbohydrate-derived energy but meat/cereal canned dog food and complete dry food contain 30 to 50 and 40 to 50 percent respectively.

The value of vitamins

Many vitamin disorders have been recognized in dogs, but these are now rare because the vitamin level in prepared dog foods is carefully balanced. For dogs needing extra, there are very good proprietary supplements on the market (see p.168).

The value of calcium and phosphorus

Dogs need some minerals in large amounts and others in trace amounts. Calcium and phosphorus are closely related and are two of the most important minerals in a dog's diet. An optimum balance minimizes the need for Vitamin D.

Calcium and phosphorus are needed for bone formation and development. (At birth, puppies have relatively low levels of these elements.) It is important to supply enough but not too much; over-supplementation in larger breeds can cause bone deformities and diseases like rickets (see p.247).

THE FUNCTIONS OF FIBRE

High-fibre diets have recently become popular for humans. How helpful is fibre to a dog? In general, a dog should be given about five percent of its total diet as fibre (dry weight). Fibre is valuable in several ways because it
● Increases the rate of food passage through the gut which can reduce problems of diarrhoea or flatus (breaking wind)
● Seems to aid digestion even though food is passing through the system more rapidly
● Eases metabolic stress in liver disease (adsorbs toxic by-products of digestion)
● Acts as a bulking agent for obese dogs (rather like slimming tablets for humans). Use as ten to 15 percent of the diet
● In diabetic dogs, fibre controls and eases absorption of glucose after a meal. Use as ten to 15 percent of the diet

DAILY NUTRITIONAL REQUIREMENTS OF A DOG

Component amount	Dietary sources	Main functions in body
Protein 4.8 g (see p.162) Fat 1.1 g (see p.163) Linoleic acid 0.22 g (see fats, p.163)		

Minerals

Component amount	Dietary sources	Main functions in body
Calcium 242 mg	Bones, milk, cheese, bread.	Bone/tooth formation, nerve and muscle function, blood clotting.
Phosphorus 198 mg	Bones, milk, cheese, meat.	Bone and tooth formation, plus many roles in metabolism.
Potassium 132 mg	Meat, milk.	Water balance, nerve function.
Sodium chloride 242 mg	Salt, cereals.	Water balance
Magnesium 8.8 mg	Cereals, green vegetables, bones,	Constituent of bones and teeth, helps in protein synthesis.
Iron 1.32 mg	Eggs, meat, bread, cereals, green vegetables.	Part of haemoglobin, needed in respiration, energy metabolism.
Copper 0.16 mg	Meat, bones.	Constituent of haemoglobin – needed for incorporation of iron.
Manganese 0.11 mg	Many foods.	Involved in several enzymes and metabolism of fat.
Zinc 1.1 mg	Many foods including meat and cereals.	Part of digestive enzymes and probably helps tissue repair.
Iodine 0.034 mg	Fish, dairy products, salt, vegetables.	Part of thyroid hormone.
Selenium 2.42 μg	Cereals, fish, meat.	Associated with Vitamin E.

Vitamins

Component amount	Dietary sources	Main functions in body
A 110 I.U.	Cod liver oil, milk, butter, cheese.	Associated with bone growth.
D 11 I.U.	Cod liver oil, eggs, dairy produce, margarine, meat.	Promotes bone growth and increases calcium absorption
E 1.11 I.U.	Green vegetables, cereals.	Assists cell membrane function.
Thiamine 22 μg	Pig meat, organ meats, whole grains, peas, beans.	Co-enzyme in various functions with carbohydrate metabolism.
Riboflavin 48 μg	Most foods.	Part of enzymes involved in energy metabolism.
Pantothenic acid 220 μg	Most foods.	Central to energy utilization.
Niacin 250 μg	Liver, meat, cereal grains, legumes.	Part of enzymes involved in many aspects of metabolism.
Pyridoxine 22 μg	Meats, vegetables, cereal grains.	Amino acid metabolism.
Folic acid 4 μg	Legumes, green vegetables, wheat.	Amino acid metabolism, blood.
Biotin 2.2 μg	Meat, legumes, vegetables.	Amino acid metabolism.
B12 0.5 μg	Muscle meat, eggs, dairy produce.	Transfer of carbon.
Choline 26 μg	Egg yolk, liver, grains, legumes.	Involved in fat metabolism.

I.U. = International unit, μg = microgrammes, mg = milligrams.
Amounts shown represent a dog's daily requirements for every kg of its body weight.

Pre-packed dog foods

Supermarket shelves are packed with an endless variety of proprietary dog foods, sold in cans or packets. Commercially prepared foods are well balanced and are generally of very high quality. Large dog food companies have their own testing laboratories to check palatability and suitability in all sizes of dog and at all phases in the dog's life.

There are three main types of prepared dog food: dry, semi-moist and canned.

Dry foods

Despite their name, these in fact contain about ten percent water. Although all brands have a similar nutritional analysis, different raw materials are used, so some may be more palatable or digestible than others.

Among the advantages of dry foods are their low cost – a bonus if you own a large dog. Dry food can be bought and stored in quantities to last several weeks; kept for too long, however, it may go off and lose its vitamin content. Dry foods are high in bulk and can help dogs which suffer from dietary upsets. Note that the more voluminous faeces can be a problem to clear from the lawn (although there's less odour). One word of warning – they're initially easy to overfeed, causing obesity.

Semi-moist foods

Sometimes called "soft-moist", these foods contain about 25 percent water. They are usually presented as simulated mince or chunks of meat. They're often more acceptable to owners than dry diets because they do look more like meat. Semi-moist foods come packed in average servings and store well without refrigeration.

Semi-moist diets can be rather expensive but they provide a good alternative for dogs used to fresh meat if this becomes difficult to obtain. Some rather fussy small dogs love them. They have a high sugar level which, although not usually a problem, makes them unsuitable for diabetic dogs.

Pork crackling treat/training aid

Crunchy treat/training aid

Meat flavour snack bars

Semi-moist diet

All-meat
canned food

Complete canned food

Dog biscuits

Canned foods

This is probably the most familiar form of dog food to most people, but many don't realize that there are two types which should be fed in different ways. Some have a cereal component which makes them a complete diet; others are meat only and you need to add biscuit at home to provide a balanced food. Always check the method of feeding a particular food. Feeding an all-meat diet without added biscuit is expensive since you need more food to satisfy the dog. And despite the extra cost, it isn't a nutritionally balanced diet. Each brand has a different formula and may require different amounts of biscuit per can. If your dog won't eat biscuit, try one of the complete meal types. Note that although convenient, these are heavy to carry and need extra storage space (you're carrying and storing more water than with other foods).

Canned foods are available in a wide range of flavours to suit most tastes. You'll probably find that the ingredients in some don't agree with your dog and cause diarrhoea.

Special canned foods are also available – these include finely textured puppy food, high palatability foods for fussy small breeds, and a variety of special prescription diets for dogs with specific medical problems (available from vets).

Biscuits

Dogs which won't eat biscuit with their meal will often eat separate dog biscuits. It is quite in order to feed your dog an all-meat food and supplement this during the day with dog biscuits given as tit-bits.

ANALYSIS OF PRE-PACKED DOG FOODS

Type of food	Percentage in food of:				Total energy (kcals per gram)
	Protein	Carbohydrate	Fat	Water	
Dry (complete)	22	51	7	15	3.4
Semi-moist	19	38	10	26	3.0
Canned (complete)	8.2	12	4.8	72.5	1.0
Canned (all-meat)	9.3	1.5	4.7	81.9	1.3
Biscuit	10	69.9	6.1	8.4	average 3.5

Individual products may vary from these values but manufacturers will normally supply analyses on request.

The energy needs of a dog

Dogs need energy for growth, work, lactation and so on, and obtain it by "burning up" (digesting) protein, carbohydrate and fat. The table below left shows the breakdown of each pre-packed food type in terms of protein, carbohydrate, fat and water. It also gives the energy content of each food in kilocalories per gram.

How much of the dog's energy need is supplied by which components? Most of the energy in dry dog foods comes from carbohydrates (50 percent) with the remaining 50 percent split between protein and fat. In semi-moist products, most of the energy comes from protein (43 percent). Available energy in a complete canned food is well balanced between the three main elements, but in all-meat canned food, it is fat which provides 52 percent of the total available energy, protein 41 percent, and carbohydrate only seven percent.

The increased contribution of fat as an energy source in the all-meat foods makes them useful supplements for working dogs fed on a dry diet. Relatively small quantities of all-meat canned food supply useful amounts of energy for a dog.

How much food does my dog need?

The amount of food a dog eats is based on its energy needs. All dogs have different metabolic rates (rate of turning food into energy), even within the same breed. Like people, dogs become fat if they take in more calories than they can "burn up" by exercise, so keep an eye open for obesity problems. However, it's possible to get a rough idea of the ideal daily food amounts for individual dogs based on their weight.

Take the amount of kcals (kilocalories) of energy needed for your dog according to its weight from the table below and refer to the table (left) for the energy content of the various types of pre-packed food. For example, a beagle weighing 15 kg requires approximately 1010 kcals energy daily. If fed on a semi-moist diet providing three kcals per gram, the beagle needs about 337 g daily, less if you wish to replace some with biscuit (again, see chart for energy value).

These values should be increased for the following circumstances:
● Growing puppies × 2–2.5
● Pregnancy (6–9 weeks) × 1.5
● Lactation × 3–4

THE DOG'S ENERGY REQUIREMENTS

Dog weight (kg)		Energy needed (kcals per day)	Examples of breeds
small	2	230	Papillon, Chihuahua
	5	450	King Charles Spaniel, Toy Poodle
	10	750	Dachshunds (standard), Corgis, small terriers
medium	15	1010	Beagle, Staffordshire Bull Terrier
	20	1250	Airedale Terrier, Basset Hound
	25	1470	Bulldog, Collies, Samoyed
large	30	1675	Boxer, Labrador, Irish Setter
	35	1875	German Shepherd, Old English Sheepdog
	40	2070	Borzoi, Greyhound

Vitamin and mineral supplements

Most pre-packed dog foods need no extra supplementation except under particular circumstances such as convalescence, pregnancy, lactation and growth. However, fresh diets do need extra vitamins and minerals. (For the importance of these in the diet, see p. 163.) The basic home-made diet shown opposite has its own built-in supplements, but if you wish to feed your dog other freshly-cooked foods, such as combinations of lights, melts, heart, liver, egg, table scraps, bread and vegetables, you should add this simple supplement. (Take care not to over-supplement.)

To every kg of fresh food, add
● 2–3 teaspoons bonemeal
● 2000–3000 I.U. Vitamin A
● 200–300 I.U. Vitamin D

USEFUL SUPPLEMENTS FOR DOGS' DIETS

Proprietary vitamin/mineral supplements
There are so many of these that it is probably safest to choose a well-known brand. Never exceed the manufacturer's dose; an occasional month's course combined with one weekly dose is usually sufficient for most dogs.

Bonemeal
This provides valuable calcium (30 percent) and phosphorus (15 percent). Use it to correct the calcium deficiency of fresh meat. Feed it as described above.

Eggs
These are a good source of easily digestible protein. Note that raw egg white contains avidin which is antagonistic to the B vitamin, Biotin, plus another substance which interferes with digestion. If you want to feed eggs regularly, you should cook them lightly.

Milk
A good protein and calcium source, although many adult dogs lack the enzyme to digest lactose (sugar in milk), so may suffer from diarrhoea.

Vegetable oils
Some vegetable oils are rich in linoleic acid (an essential fatty acid). When dogs are deficient in this, their coats become dull and poor-looking. Most pre-packed dog foods provide more than the required one percent, but a little extra does no harm, especially at the start of a moult.

There are special oil supplements for dogs; you can also use corn and safflower oils. Remember that oil is a type of fat and too much can cause obesity. The daily corn oil dose for a 10 kg dog is $\frac{1}{2}$ teaspoon, increasing to two teaspoons for a 50 kg dog (give one-third the amount of safflower oil).

Cod liver oil
This is a good vitamin source, but should be used in tiny amounts to be safe. One 5 g teaspoon supplies the daily requirement for a 50 kg Great Dane – on a diet which does *not* already contain the necessary vitamins.

Yeast
Yeast preparations are rich in the B vitamins and some minerals. They're useful for older dogs or those with weak livers and are also safe used in excess.

Herbal preparations
Many of these are available, among them seaweed tablets, given for their iodine. Sulphur blocks in the water bowl (for "cooling the blood") are said to relieve some coat problems such as itching.

Home cooking for dogs

If you wish for any reason to avoid pre-packed dog foods, it is possible to prepare a nutritionally balanced diet for your dog at home. Using the basic meat and rice recipe below, suitable diets can be planned for a variety of circumstances. The liver, bonemeal, corn oil and salt provide the essential vitamins and minerals.

Don't buy mince for adult dogs – it can contain too much fat. Medium fat cuts or chunks of meat are best – you can mince it yourself.

Using other foods

When making up fresh meals for your dog, remember that nutritional balance is essential while variety isn't – don't chop and change too much.

Vegetables

Dogs are basically carnivores which benefit from a certain amount of vegetable matter in their diet. Even if you are vegetarian, it is cruel and unnatural to impose a possibly deficient vegetarian diet on a dog.

Table scraps

Non-fatty scraps from your own meals provide some acceptable variety, particularly, leftover meat, stews and vegetables with some gravy. Avoid carcasses and small bones.

Bones

Although dogs in the wild would naturally eat bones, they can cause severe constipation. However, the odd bone provides hours of pleasure; to some extent it also cleans the teeth and exercises the jaw. Small bones (poultry, chop, rabbit or lamb) aren't suitable. The only safe bones are large "knuckle" bones which won't splinter. Keep an eye on a dog with a bone, though.

BASIC RECIPE FOR HOME-COOKED DIET

Below is a basic diet plus three variations:
● **Basic** For normal adult maintenance

● **Meaty** For normal maintenance of small dogs and large dogs needing extra for growth and work

● **Reducing** For overweight dogs
● **Geriatric** For older dogs

Ingredient	Basic diet	Meaty diet	Reducing diet	Geriatric diet
Rice, uncooked	$\frac{2}{3}$ teacup	$\frac{1}{3}$ teacup	$\frac{1}{3}$ teacup	$\frac{1}{3}$ teacup
Meat, medium fat	$\frac{1}{3}$ teacup	$\frac{2}{3}$ teacup	$\frac{1}{3}$ teacup (lean)	$\frac{1}{2}$ teacup
Wheat bran			$\frac{2}{3}$ teacup	$\frac{1}{2}$ teacup

All quantities are per 10 kg dog weight.

All diets	Grams	Teaspoons	Contribution
Raw liver	30	6	Vitamins and minerals
Bonemeal (steamed)	5	1	Calcium
Corn oil	5	1	Linoleic acid, Vitamin E
Iodised salt	3	$\frac{1}{2}$	Iodine

Method Mince the meat and cook in a little water. Boil the rice in water and mix it with the cooked meat. When this mixture is cool, add remaining ingredients and feed to your dog either warm or cold.

Feedtime techniques

Most adult dogs over 12 months have one feed per day, usually given in the evening. Some small breeds will only eat a small amount at one "sitting" and need two meals daily. Overfeeding a dog may result in vomiting or diarrhoea. Dogs will obligingly fit in with the household routine and are often happy to be fed at around the same time as the rest of the family. This helps to prevent them from scrounging for food while you're eating your own meal.

Unfortunately, after an evening feed, some dogs can't get through the night without needing to relieve themselves – an apparent breakdown in your careful house-training. The answer to this problem is usually to change the feeding regime – moving feedtime to earlier in the day, or giving half the food early and half in the evening. For guidelines on feeding puppies and young dogs, see p.132.

Where to feed your dog

A dog likes to have a regular feeding place. This enforces its routine and encourages it not to take too long over its meal.

Where to feed your dog is a matter of personal preference. Most dogs are tidy eaters, but it is sensible to choose a place which is easy to clean – such as a kitchen or conservatory floor or an outside covered area. You can place food and water bowls on a wipe-down plastic mat. Some dogs like to pull pieces of meat from their bowl and sit on the floor chewing them like a lion with its kill. Put down newspaper for these dogs otherwise you'll have to clean the floor after every meal. As with puppies, don't leave uneaten meals on the floor for too long.

FEEDING TWO OR MORE DOGS

If you have more than one dog, each should have its own bowl and be fed a little way away from the others. Discourage dogs from sharing each other's bowls; the practice can lead to the following problems:
- One dog may become overweight through eating the "lion's share"
- Diffident dogs get pushed out
- Individual dogs may need diet supplements
- Fights can occur, even if dogs are used to communal feeding
- It is difficult to detect a dog off its food through illness, since the other dog often eats what's left

Need for water

Water is crucial to all animals. On a weight for weight basis, most dogs' bodies consist of about two thirds water. Fatter dogs may drop to 50 percent water, leaner ones can be as much as 75 percent water. All dogs lose water from their body through: sweating, panting, via the gut, via the lungs and via the kidneys. This must be replaced, and so you should make sure that fresh water is always available for your dog.

How much water is needed?
To maintain the correct balance, a healthy dog should take in about 40 ml per kg of body weight per day. This can come from all sources including the moisture contained in food.

Weight of dog	Water needed per day
10 kg	400 ml
20 kg	800 ml
30 kg	1200 ml
40 kg	1600 ml

Your dog will want to drink more water in hot weather when water loss through panting and the lungs is increased. More is also needed in dogs with diarrhoea or kidney disease. The tabled quantities are merely guidelines and you should know the amount of water your dog normally drinks.

There are several diseases of which thirst is a common symptom. If you notice excessive thirst, contact your vet as soon as convenient.

Eating between meals
Don't accustom your dog to tit-bits between meals; this only encourages begging and makes the dog a nuisance with visitors. Once the principle of "no scrounging" is established, you should have no problems. It's often more difficult training the family to accept this than your dog! Non-fatty scraps from the family meal can be placed in your dog's bowl for its next meal.

Tit-bits are best used as a reward for good behaviour or as a training aid. When combined with your praise, this is much more effective than punishment for bad behaviour. Remember that tit-bits are still food and if used in excess can cause obesity. Make the gift a token only – it is the pleasure of being given something by its owner which means the most. *Suitable tit-bits are:*
● Semi-moist dog food – only suitable given in very small amounts
● Special crunchy treats for dogs
● Chocolate drops – special dog chocolates can be used, again in moderation
● Raisins – use in moderation
● Broken biscuit – very suitable
Warning Vitamin/mineral supplements are most unsuitable – an overdose can easily occur.

TYPES OF FEEDING BOWL

Choosing a feeding bowl is a matter of personal preference and price. Plastic bowls are the cheapest, but are often scratched and chewed, making them difficult to clean properly. Stainless steel bowls are excellent for cleaning but can be knocked over as they're generally light. The familiar glazed earthenware bowl is both stable and easy to clean, although in time it can become chipped and will obviously break if dropped.

Breeds with long, floppy ears like spaniels, Bassets and setters sometimes trail their ears in their food bowls – a practice that can cause dermatitis on the ear flaps. Special deep, narrow feeding bowls are available to exclude the ears from the feed and avoid this problem.

Dogs which are inclined to choke while feeding because of soft-palate problems combined with their eagerness to eat fast may be more comfortable with their food bowl raised a few inches off the ground. This keeps the head up and encourages the food to go in the right direction.

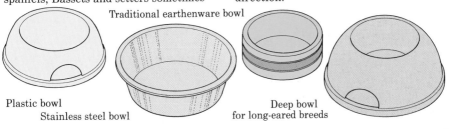

Traditional earthenware bowl

Plastic bowl

Stainless steel bowl

Deep bowl for long-eared breeds

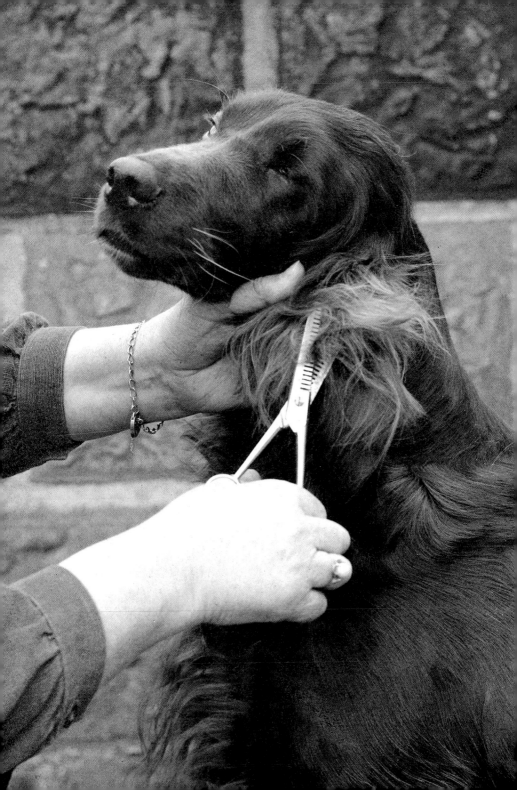

GROOMING

When you acquire a dog, you take on the
responsibility for keeping it clean, tidy and well-
groomed. People often base their choice of breed on a
glossy picture in a dog book or a luxuriant-looking
specimen seen on television. If you aren't aware of the
range of coat types found in dogs, this can lead to
disaster. The dog in the book or on television was
probably the product of hours of grooming
immediately prior to its appearance. Grooming isn't
just for show-dogs. Whatever your dog's coat type,
regular, correct grooming keeps it looking and feeling
good. Most dogs enjoy grooming sessions, so they
deepen your mutual trust and sense of
companionship. Use the sessions to check your dog
for any other problems – it may need its claws
clipping, it may even need a bath! You may spot
early signs of impending health problems given in
Health Care (see pp.226–75).

Basic grooming

If you're the prospective owner of a long-haired breed such as Lhasa Apso, an Old English Sheepdog or an Afghan Hound, don't delude yourself over the amount of grooming time required. Up to an hour's work may be involved daily, and you should be prepared for this, or choose a breed which needs less grooming. If you intend to show your dog and it has one of the more "tricky" coats, the chances are it will need a certain amount of professional grooming as well as your routine care. Some breeds are better clipped professionally, but it certainly isn't essential for a pet dog.

It is a popular misconception that breeds which are kept clipped or stripped need only the odd visit to a grooming parlour to remain in perfect condition – this just isn't the case. It is no good opting out of grooming – it is all part of responsible dog ownership.

The dog's coat

There are five basic types of dog coat – long, silky, non-shedding curly, smooth and wiry. To these we can add a sixth group of "extremes". Each type of coat has its own special grooming needs (see the chart on pp.176–7) but the principles of hair growth and the factors which produce a healthy coat are the same for all of them. The coat types requiring the most routine grooming are the curly coat, the wiry coat and any long-length coat.

The main aims of grooming are to remove dead hair and to clean the skin and the living hair. Every dog has several different types of hair on its body. Hairs grow in follicle complexes of several hairs per hole. In each follicle, there is a primary, or guard hair which belongs to the dog's outer

coat, and several secondary hairs which constitute the undercoat. Other more specialized and sensitive hairs – the "tactile hairs" – are the eyelashes, the hair on the external ear, and the whiskers on the muzzle. For more about the function and growth of the dog's coat, see p.32.

Hair streams
The direction of hair growth follows lines called "hair streams", which run from the head, down the back, spreading down the body and legs to the feet. You can feel these if you stroke the dog.

Moulting

Moulting – loss of hair and a change of coat – usually happens in Spring and Autumn, lasting four to six weeks. The new coat grows in three or four months. The poodle group (non-shedding curly coat) doesn't shed any hair at all.

While your dog is moulting, groom it daily. A little dandruff is no problem, but if there is an excess, bath your dog.

In the wild, a moult is provoked by changes in temperature and hours of daylight as winter comes and goes. However, smooth-coated domestic dogs are susceptible to slipping into a permanent light moult. The reason isn't certain but it may be connected with central heating, artificial lighting or diet (see *Hair loss*, p.269).

BASIC GROOMING PROCEDURE

Here's a useful step-by-step reference plan for a "top-to-toe" grooming session for all types of dog.

Although you don't need to carry out all the steps at every session, it helps to know the right sequence in which to perform the various tasks for the best results. The needs of different coat types are described overleaf. For how to use the various tools, see pp.178–181.

1 Use a wide-toothed comb to break up the coat and remove mats.

2 Use a fine comb under the chin and tail and behind the ears.

3 Brush as required for the breed, following hair streams.

4 Strip or pluck the coat with a dresser or stripping knife.

5 Use scissors to tidy hair round eyes, genitals and anus.

6 Thin the coat with scissors or shears if required.

7 Bath or dry shampoo the dog (see p.182 for correct techniques).

8 Give the entire coat a final brush and possibly a polish (see p.209).

GROOMING NEEDS OF DIFFERENT COAT TYPES

BREED GROUP	BASIC GROOMING

Long coat with undercoat

German Shepherd, Collie, Newfoundland, Old English Sheepdog, the Spitz breeds.

Bath twice-yearly in Spring and Autumn. Brush and comb the coat forwards over the head and shoulders before combing it back; brush the flanks in the direction of the "lay" of the coat. Comb the dense undercoat, especially during moulting.

Silky coat

Afghan Hound, Yorkshire Terrier, Maltese, Lhasa Apso, setters, spaniels and Pekingese.

If neglected, these coats quickly become a mess. They all need frequent brushing to avoid mats, and relatively frequent baths.

Non-shedding curly coat

Bedlington Terrier, poodles, Kerry Blue Terrier.

These dogs don't moult, but hair growth is continuous, so they need a clip and a bath every six to eight weeks. Give short parts of the coat a thorough brush every couple of days. Longer, fluffier parts of the coat need combing first.

Smooth coat

Short, fine coat types: Whippet, Boxer and Smooth-haired Dachshund. Longer, denser coat types: Labrador and Corgi.

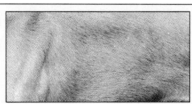

The easiest group to groom. The longer coats require a comb and a bristle brush, while a hound glove is sufficient for the short coats.

Wiry coat

Most of the terriers – West Highland White, Sealyham, Cairn, Norwich, Lakeland, Airedale. Also the Wire-haired Dachshund and the Schnauzers.

These dogs need regular combing to avoid mats. The top coat should be stripped and plucked every three to four months, followed by a bath. Alternatively, machine clip every six to eight weeks. Use scissors carefully round eyes and ears.

Extremes

"Out of the ordinary" breeds with distinctive coats.

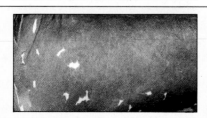

Every breed needs grooming, whatever its coat type. There are some breeds with very little hair, like the Mexican Hairless and the Chinese Crested Dog. Although minimal, this hair still needs combing and brushing.

PARTICULAR GROOMING NEEDS

Use a fine comb under the chin and tail and behind the ears.

If the dog needs an additional bath between its two "major" seasonal ones, use a dry shampoo.

Afghans, setters and spaniels need to be stripped of dead hair every three months, followed by a bath. Spaniels' coats need a trim at the same time. Trim "Yorkies" and Maltese about four times a year. Some show specimens (particularly Afghans and Yorkshire Terriers) need their hair oiled and wrapped in curling papers before a show.

Most of the dead hairs shed by this type are secondary hairs, so neglect usually results in a "felt matting". The same type of hair occurs in the dogs' ear canals and shed hair may be retained. So check the ears frequently to make sure they don't become plugged with wax and hair (see p.252).

How often you bath these dogs depends on how dirty they get, but most dirt and mud can be brushed out once dry. Don't bath these breeds too frequently or you'll wash out the natural waterproofing oils produced by the skin for protection.

Puppies
Give the puppy its first trim – around the head and tail – at about four months.

Breeds like the Hungarian Puli and the Komondor have dense, corded coats which should be oiled and twisted as they grow to maintain the cording.

SPECIAL CARE

Old English Sheepdog
Many Old English Sheepdog owners keep their coats clipped to about 2.5 cm. Like this, the dog is more comfortable than it would be poorly groomed. Even well groomed, it can be very uncomfortable on a hot day or in a centrally heated house. Grooming the dense coat takes up to an hour per day.

Spaniels
Pay special attention to feet and ears. Hair growing between the toes can become matted. Excessive hair on ear flaps and in the ear canal can lead to disease. Keep country spaniels well trimmed in these areas as their coats have an uncanny attraction for grass seeds which work their way to the ear canals and can penetrate the skin between the toes.

Puppies
The first clip should take place at 14–15 weeks old. The noise of clippers can frighten a young puppy, especially if it has to go away from home to be clipped. Accustom the puppy to the noise by gradually bringing an electric razor close to it and holding it against the puppy's skin. Trim the area under the tail with scissors at first.

Breeders and your vet can give you specialized information on dealing with any particular unusual coat.

Grooming equipment

At the very least, every dog needs its own brush and comb for grooming. Brushes fall into the category of bristle types, hound gloves and carders. Brushes and combs are the main tools you need, but several others are available for different coat types – mostly stripping and thinning tools.

Keep all your equipment together in a dry box to prevent scissors and knives rusting. Each time you finish a grooming session, clean hair and excess grease off your tools before putting them away. Dogs seem to have an uncanny desire to ferret out their grooming equipment and try to destroy it, another good reason for keeping the tools safe.

Fine comb

Bristle brush

Wide-toothed comb

Carder

Hound glove

USING A COMB

Combs are available in metal or plastic, although the plastic type often ends up broken and can be chewed by dogs. Whatever the comb is made of, the teeth should be rounded, both at the tips and in cross section, to avoid tearing the skin or hair. All dogs need a wide-toothed comb with teeth about 2 mm apart; finer-coated dogs and breeds prone to mats and tangles should have a finer comb too.

1 Insert the wide-toothed comb to its full depth into the coat and use it to break up any coarse mats or snags, particularly in the outer coat.

2 Use the finer comb to separate the undercoat and bring out any dead hair which is no longer firmly attached. Don't pull too hard, or you'll hurt the dog.

3 If you encounter any resistance in the coat, take the comb out, and work on the knot a little at a time, teasing it apart with the wide comb or your fingers.

USING A BRISTLE BRUSH

This is the tool used for the bulk of routine grooming. It is useful for "finishing off" after combing, particularly on the longer-coated breeds, and for giving a well-groomed dog a quick "once-over" after a run. The bristles should always be long enough to reach through the dog's coat to its skin. An inadequate brush may cause mats.

Short, dense-bristled brushes are fine for short-haired breeds. To brush a smooth-coated dog, follow the normal "lay" of the hair and the direction of the hair streams, beginning at the dog's head and working back towards the tail. If your dog has a long coat, you'll need a brush with longer, wider-spaced bristles set in a rubber base.

Professional groomers are wary of synthetic bristles, believing that they generate too much static electricity and cause hair breakage, so it is worth buying a genuine bristle brush if possible.

Brushing a long coat
On long-haired dogs and breeds whose hair is meant to stand out from their body, brush gently against the "lay" of the coat. Push the brush into the coat and twist it *slightly* against the natural growth, working in very short strokes. Never brush the whole coat in the wrong direction – you'll weaken or break hairs.

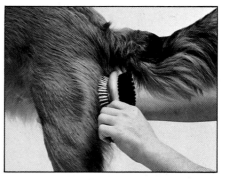

Brushing a medium coat
With medium-length coats (such as a Labrador's), pay particular attention to the hindquarters. The guard hairs in these coats are long enough to retain dead hair, and the dog's movements and its licking can make this move within the coat towards the dog's hindquarters where it accumulates in dense pads.

Using a carder
This is a kind of wire-bristled brush, consisting of a rectangular board with short, bent wire teeth mounted on it, and a handle. The function of the carder is to bring out dead undercoat on shorter-haired breeds. Use it in a similar way to the brush on long-haired dogs, working the teeth gently through to the skin and then twisting the carder out towards the surface.

Using a hound glove
Hound gloves are useful for short-haired dogs, particularly the hound types, to give a polish to the outer coat and to remove any dead undercoat. The glove has short bristles, wires or rubber bumps set into it, and you can slide your hand inside it, giving you a "bristled palm". A hound glove isn't really effective on coats longer than that of a Labrador.

Cutting tools

There are various cutting tools for use on dogs' coats. Stripping combs, knives, scissors and shears can all be useful, whether your dog needs a trim, a thinning out, or just a routine tidy-up. There are also special nail clippers available for pets. Electric clippers are probably best restricted to professional use unless you're an expert. Handling them badly can harm a dog's skin.

Thinning shears

An effective tool with one regular and one serrated blade. The aim is to thin the coat without affecting its appearance too much, so the shears are usually used on the undercoat, the top coat being combed up out of the way. This preserves the colour of the outer coat in dogs which have a different coloured undercoat.

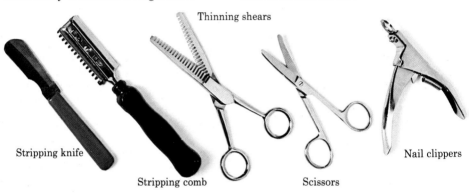

Thinning shears

Stripping knife

Stripping comb

Scissors

Nail clippers

USING A STRIPPING KNIFE

Stripping combs ("dressers") and knives provide a serrated metal cutting edge for removing dull, dead hair. The stripping comb has a removable guard-plate on one side and comprises a razor blade mounted against a comb. A stripping knife is just a metal blade with a handle, like a butter knife.

Stripping is often combined with "plucking" – using the thumb and forefinger to pluck out dead hair.

1 Brush the coat well to fully separate all the hairs. For silky-coated dogs, chalk powder dusted into the coat gives you a better grip.

2 Grasp a section of hair between knife and thumb and pull the knife away with a twisting motion. Dead hair comes out, live hair is trimmed.

Scissors

Barber's scissors can be used on dogs, but for safety's sake they must be the type with round-ended blades. The most useful size is 12.5 cm. Use scissors for trimming "wispy hair" in delicate areas, especially around the eyes, ears, lips, feet, anal and genital areas. Never cut the sensitive whiskers on a dog's muzzle. Scissors can also be used in conjunction with a comb to remove mats and snags (see box, right).

Special care for show-dogs
Scissors and thinning shears are used on show dogs in the same way, although the extra grooming that show animals need actually cuts down on the need for scissors. Both tools can be used to make minor adjustments to the coat or to shape it in order to "balance" the look of the dog. A dog may need last-minute touches such as a thinning over the shoulders or a slight trim on the legs before being presented in the show-ring. Take care not to trim off too much hair.

USING SCISSORS

Careful use of scissors round the eyes can prevent the problems suffered by some spaniels and terriers, particularly where hair irritating the eye causes a sticky discharge. Use scissors to improve the vision of non-show Maltese and Old English Sheepdogs; trim the fringe, then thin it.

The tactile hairs on the ears and muzzle are too sensitive to be stripped or plucked, but you can trim these areas with scissors if you take care to leave any "whiskers" intact. Hair between the pads of the paws can be trimmed on long-haired breeds, to avoid matting or dirt in the house.

Hair around the penis of male dogs may need an occasional trim for hygiene; this can be necessary in the vulval area of bitches too. Similarly, it is sensible to keep hair in the anal region short to avoid matting. Use a comb to lift the mat away from the skin, then cut above the comb. Once a mat is reduced, it can be combed out.

CLIPPING A DOG'S NAILS

Trimming a dog's nails is often done at the same time as routine grooming. With care, you can do it yourself. Use the guillotine type of clippers that cut rather than the pliers type that crush. Crushing a nail can cause pain to the sensitive nail bed inside.

Ideally, get an expert to give you a demonstration first. The length of the nail bed varies in dogs, and if cut, it will hurt and bleed copiously. With clear or white nails, you can see most of the nail bed, but it narrows right down at the tip, so make allowances for this. Dogs with black nails tend to have longer nail beds. Err on the side of caution and learn by the first one you cause to bleed.

Place the dog on an easily-cleaned surface. Have a styptic pencil or other caustic to hand to stop any bleeding. You may also need to apply a light dressing (see *First Aid*, p.282).

Check the dew claws on the inside of the leg if your dog hasn't had these removed. They don't wear down and, if covered with hair, may be forgotten.

Clipping a dog's nails
Take care not to hurt the dog.

Bathing your dog

There's no simple answer to the question "How often should I bath my dog?" A dirty or smelly dog needs a bath, although a little dirt can often be brushed out when dry. Many dogs need more baths in summer, others need a regular monthly bath, but few need a bath more often than this. Some dogs, particularly Scottish Terriers, tend to get dirty skins through a build-up of dandruff. They may need a bath every two to four weeks. If this becomes a problem, consult your vet.

Always groom your dog before bathing it, or you could make matting much worse. Never use household detergent or carbolic soap; many dogs' skins react badly to these. You can use a mild "human" soap, but a special dog shampoo or baby shampoo is best. The water should be comfortably warm.

You can use your own bath for your dog as long as you wash it down well afterwards. A baby bath is ideal for a small dog – you can place it at an easy working height indoors or out. For large dogs, you could use a child's paddling pool but watch that the dog's nails don't puncture it. A rubber car mat can prevent this; used in the bath it also helps stop the dog slipping. If your dog does slip, it may panic and soak the room!

Dry shampoo
This is excellent for a quick clean but doesn't deal with a really dirty dog properly. Dry shampoo is a powder, used to remove excess oil in the coat (which may be a little dirty and smelly). This brightens the coat colour and the talc in the shampoo enhances any white parts. Dust the powder well into the dog's fur and brush it out. The coat may "stand on end" because of static electricity, so don't aggravate the problem by using a brush with synthetic bristles.

HOW TO BATH A DOG

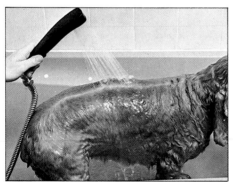

1 Try and enlist the help of someone else to hold the dog steady while you shampoo it. Take off the collar and place the dog in the bath. Using a jug, shower attachment or slow-running hosepipe, wet the dog's back and work the water into the coat on back and sides.

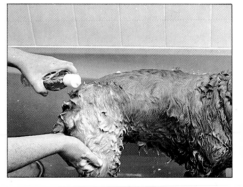

2 Apply some shampoo to the back and work it in, extending all the way to the rear of the dog and down the legs. Wash the head last, being careful not to get any shampoo in the dog's eyes. It is when its head gets wet that it is most likely to want to shake!

DEALING WITH MATS AND TANGLES

Small tangles can usually be teased apart with a wide-toothed comb. Once broken up, they should be thoroughly combed, first with the wide-toothed comb, then with a finer one.

Large mats which don't respond to this treatment can simply be removed by sliding a comb under the mat and cutting with scissors just above it. The result can be messy, and you may prefer to try dividing the mat with a knife or scissors, teasing it out in sections, then combing it. You can have this done professionally.

Removing a tangle from the coat
Lift the knot gently before you cut.

Special care for long-haired dogs

If you're using carders, hound gloves and short bristle brushes on your long-haired dog, you may not be grooming it properly at all. Although the outer coat may look smooth the hidden undercoat can build up into dense mats if tools don't reach it.

A dog that has been "surface-groomed" like this looks fine for a time but feels uncomfortable; eventually its outer coat becomes involved in the underlying mat. At this stage, the only answer is to shave the coat – a time-consuming job which upsets the dog. It may have to be done at the vet's surgery under anaesthetic and can be costly.

Shaving an Afghan is particularly tragic and is impossible to do neatly – the dog may take as long as 18 months to come back into coat. It may need steroid treatment for bruising caused by parting its matted coat from its skin. The moral of this is: never neglect the grooming of your long-haired dog. Make sure you're using the right tools and techniques.

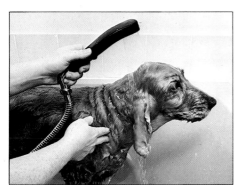

3 Now rinse the dog thoroughly, starting with the head and working back. Squeeze out any excess water. In summer, a good run in the open air followed by a brush is enough to dry off most dogs, although long-haired dogs will need some towelling.

4 In winter, towel your dog and let it dry somewhere warm, otherwise it could catch a chill. You can use a hair-dryer, but be very careful introducing the dog to it – the noise and sensation may frighten it. Don't hold the dryer too close to the dog.

BREEDING

Breeding dogs is a rewarding experience. From simple genetics to successful whelping, this chapter tells you all you need to know to give yourself the best chance of ending up with a happy, healthy litter of puppies. Even if you're not planning for puppies, it helps to be aware of all the stages in your bitch's reproductive cycle, so that you can understand her behaviour, and the changes taking place in her body. Mating, pregnancy and whelping need careful management. Avoiding unwanted pregnancies can be a full-time job too. Dogs in the wild mate naturally at their first "heat", and, if unchecked, domestic dogs will readily do likewise. Care of newborn puppies is covered in *Puppy-Care* (see pp.130–31). For ailments and problems relating to the reproductive system, see *Health Care* (pp.226–75). If your bitch is expecting a litter, keep your vet informed of her progress. He'll give you all the help and support he can.

Introduction to genetics

The basic unit of all life is the cell. This is true of everything from the smallest single-celled bacteria to man himself. A dog is made up of the same "building blocks". The cells in each dog are unique to that individual.

Apart from the sex cells, all cells in an animal contain the same set of instructions since they are all produced from the same fertilized egg. These instructions enable the cells to develop in different but co-ordinated ways into a whole animal.

Inside each cell is the "cytoplasm" – a complex mixture of chemical structures. At its heart is the "nerve centre" or nucleus, which contains the "blueprint" for the design of the dog.

Genes and chromosomes

The information needed to carry out this incredibly complex organization is carried by structures in the nucleus called "chromosomes". Chromosomes can be thought of as strings of different coloured beads.

Broadly speaking, the various beads are represented by genes. Genes work singly or in concert to control all aspects of structure and function of the body, whether it be hair and eye colour, bone growth or the efficiency of blood clotting. Unfortunately, genes are responsible for many canine diseases and disorders, too. There are genes controlling everything that makes a dog a dog.

THE PRINCIPLE OF DOMINANCE

The inheritance of black coat colour in cocker spaniels is a good example of dominant and recessive genes. The gene for coat colour in this case has two alleles: B (black, dominant) and b (brown, recessive). Individual dogs may be BB (black), Bb (black, because B is dominant) or bb (brown). Here there are three genotypes (BB, Bb and bb) but only two phenotypes – black and brown.

Different mating possibilities may produce different offspring:

BB with BB produces all black (BB) puppies.

BB with Bb produces all black (two BB and two Bb) puppies.

BB with bb produces all black (Bb) puppies.

Bb with Bb produces three black (one BB, two Bb) one brown (bb).

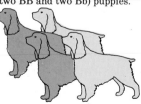

Bb with bb produces two black (Bb) and two brown (bb) puppies.

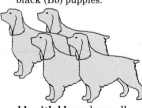

bb with bb produces all brown (bb) puppies.

A dog has 78 chromosomes which fall into 39 pairs, representing the "blueprint" for the dog. These can divide to produce identical copies of themselves.

Sex chromosomes

Although chromosomes are paired, one pair in each dog is not necessarily an identical pair. These are the chromosomes which determine the sex of the animal. The female has a pair of identical X chromosomes (XX); the male has one X and one Y chromosome (XY). When the egg and sperm cells (the sex cells) meet at conception they combine to form a full set of 78 chromosomes. It is the male's contribution (the sperm) which governs the sex of the offspring, depending on whether an X or Y sperm reaches the egg first.

Complementary genes There are many modifying factors in the genetics system; one of these is complementary genes.

The incidence of black in cocker spaniels' coats (see left) is dependant on another gene – E when dominant, e when recessive. This is inherited in the same way as B and b. When a dog inherits two recessive e alleles, its black pigment distribution is restricted to the eyes and nose. The complementary effects of E and e on the two inherited B alleles permit a whole range of colour expression:

● **BB + EE, BB + Ee, Bb + EE or Bb + Ee:** all black.

● **BB + ee or Bb + ee:** red, with black nose and eyes.

● **bb + EE or bb + Ee:** brown, liver or chocolate with a brown nose.

● **bb + ee:** pale red, yellow or cream with a pink nose.

SEX CHROMOSOMES

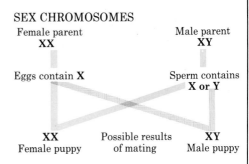

Female parent
XX

Male parent
XY

Eggs contain **X**

Sperm contains **X or Y**

XX
Female puppy

Possible results of mating

XY
Male puppy

Inheritance of parental characters

At the moment of conception, the new cell formed receives a copy of one chromosome from each of its parents' pairs. Therefore there are two genes present for each character. These are usually called "alleles". One comes from each parent, and they're not necessarily the same. There may be a series of different alleles relating to a character such as coat colour. An allele which can act on the appearance of a dog when present singly is "dominant". If both alleles need to be the same before they can express themselves, the allele is "recessive" (see examples on p. 186).

The unique gene pattern that represents an animal is called its "genotype"; its final appearance – the result of the genotype's effects – is called the "phenotype".

MUTATION

Due to radiation, rearrangements of the gene "beads" may occur, allowing new genes or new combinations to be created. These changes are called "mutations". It is spontaneous gene mutation which is the basis of evolution, creating new types of animal, new breeds or simple breed variations. For millions of years, natural selection has been retaining the successful mutations, allowing all forms of life to evolve and change.

The reproductive system

Unlike a male cat, the male dog is easily distinguished from the female by the penis, hanging within the prepuce along the underside of the abdomen. The two testes are also obvious, located in the scrotum which hangs between and behind the hind legs. The sexual organs of the bitch are located inside the body.

The male dog
The testes consist of a mass of coiled tubes which produce sperm (male reproductive cells). This is stored in a sac called the *epididymis*. The production of sperm begins at puberty and continues throughout the dog's life, although output is reduced through age or disease.

The common outlet for both urine from the bladder and semen from the testes and associated glands is the *urethra*. This leads out of the bladder and through the penis.

Sexual development of the dog
The testes develop inside the unborn puppy, and are attached to the scrotum by a ligament. As the newborn puppy grows, the ligament contracts, causing the testes to descend through the

inguinal canal into the scrotum. They should be fully descended by about two weeks of age. At this stage, they can often be felt. As the puppy grows, fat in the scrotum may make them difficult to feel again until about four months of age. It is important that a dog has two descended testes. If not, it is cryptorchid (see *Health Care*, p.260).

The female dog
Externally, the vulva is visible below the anus. Inside the abdomen are the two ovaries, each about 1.5 cm long. These hang from the roof of the abdomen, close to the kidneys. They are surrounded by a fatty sac, the *bursa*, which catches eggs produced in the ovary and channels them into the fallopian tube, which in turn leads into the uterus (womb). This consists of two separate large "horns" which meet at a part called the "body".

Between the uterus and the vagina is a thick section called the cervix. This stays shut except during oestrus and whelping. The vagina leads into the vestibule, the walls of which form the vulva. The outlet from the bladder (the urethra) enters the system here.

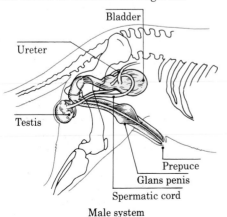

Male system

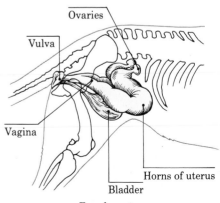

Female system

THE BITCH'S REPRODUCTIVE CYCLE

A bitch usually has her first "season" or "heat" between six and twelve months of age. Smaller toy breeds and terriers usually begin between six and nine months, but some giant breeds may not begin until two years old.

There are four phases in the cycle, which usually lasts six or seven months, although the anoestrus stage is very varied.

1 Pro-oestrus This is the first noticeable phase. There's usually some swelling of the vulva plus a clear discharge which then becomes bloody. You may miss the discharge, but you'll normally see the blood. It may simply be "spotting". Most bitches are fastidiously clean and lick the discharge from the vulva very quickly, so you may notice the licking first.

Some bitches have a heavy discharge and no swelling; others may have no discharge but heavy swelling. Some bitches, particularly giant breeds, show almost no external signs. During this time, a bitch is attractive to dogs. Most bitches are flirtatious, although usually all but the most experienced will refuse mating.

2 Oestrus Normally, the bleeding has stopped. The vulva is less turgid but still swollen. There may be a clear or straw-coloured discharge. Now the bitch may seek out dogs and will usually accept them.

Ovulation is said to occur on the second day of oestrus, making it the best day for mating. Several matings around this time increase the likelihood of conception.

3 Metoestrus Although there are often no external signs, this stage still represents an active time in the bitch's uterus as it prepares for a period of quiescence (anoestrus).

False pregnancy
The hormones in the body at this time can cause the distressing problem of false pregnancy (see p.261). A non-pregnant bitch may think that she is pregnant, make a nest and actually come into milk. If this occurs, consult your vet.

4 Anoestrus This is the quiet period of variable duration when there is no activity in the bitch's reproductive tract.

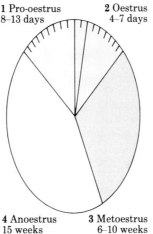

1 Pro-oestrus
8–13 days

2 Oestrus
4–7 days

4 Anoestrus
15 weeks

3 Metoestrus
6–10 weeks

SPAYING AND CASTRATION

Spaying of a bitch may be necessary for one reason or another. It is one way of guarding against unwanted pregnancy, and basically involves removing the ovaries and uterus. Although this is a routine piece of surgery, it requires considerable surgical skill. Vets dislike performing it on fat bitches – the surgery takes longer and there is an increased risk of problems. So be guided by your vet if he suggests a diet prior to spaying.

Castrating a dog involves removing both testes, thus eliminating the source of sperm. Dog owners may have this done to stop a dog wandering, but the operation may change its character. Although it can sometimes solve problems of excessive aggression, make sure it's really necessary before making the decision to have your dog castrated.

Deciding to breed from your bitch

Letting your bitch have a litter of puppies is rewarding and fun, but should never be undertaken without serious thought. You probably won't profit financially, particularly when you take into account the work and inconvenience involved plus the expense of feeding and vet's fees.

Far too many unwanted puppies are produced by irresponsible owners. Make sure you'll be able to sell yours at the "going rate" before taking your bitch to stud. It is morally wrong to bank on selling puppies cheap to get rid of them easily. You'll just be increasing the amount of unwanted dogs that jam the doors of animal shelters daily.

Breeding from poor stock does no-one any good. The progeny may be so poor that they require euthanasia due to congenital disease. People argue that using poorer stock maintains variation in a breed and a wide "gene pool", but it only produces more unwanted pets.

When to breed from your bitch

Pregnancy and birth causes a major metabolic change in a bitch and she should be physically fully mature first. A young bitch's bones stop growing at between ten and 12 months of age and in larger breeds, a general filling out and "muscling up" of the body occurs after this.

It is best to let a bitch have one normal "heat" before breeding from her – there's a better chance of a good-sized, healthy litter. Female dogs in the wild mate naturally at their first "heat". They usually become pregnant, often resulting in small litters which die because the bitch wasn't in the top physical condition to rear them.

Dealing with "accidents"

Dogs mate readily by instinct and accidental mating (misalliance) is fairly common, especially if a bitch's owners don't supervise her properly during her heat. Bitches can be given a canine version of "the pill" or injections to stop them cycling. If you don't plan to breed from your bitch, most vets advise spaying rather than long-term medication.

If you know your bitch has mated and you don't want puppies, she can be injected within the first 24–48 hours after mating (95 percent certain to prevent conception). However, there is a risk of side effects and your vet will warn you about these. If you want to breed from her again, it may be best to let her have this litter, even if the puppies are cross-bred.

WHAT STEPS TO TAKE

Before breeding from your bitch:
● Discuss it with the breeder of your own dog, at least one other breeder, and your vet. During these discussions, you'll probably hear of a suitable dog with which to mate your bitch
● Read all you can about your breed and its particular problems. Decide whether your bitch is close enough to the breed standard. There are testing procedures for a number of the more serious congenital diseases which you should discuss with your vet
● If you're breeding pedigree dogs, make sure both prospective parents are Kennel Club registered. If not, you won't be able to register the puppies as pedigree
● Arrange booster vaccinations for your bitch before the heat at which you wish to breed and be prepared to worm her in the week prior to mating

Mating

Some breeders say that ten days after the beginning of the discharge (pro-oestrus) is the best time for mating; others prefer 12 days. A good compromise is a double mating – either on the tenth and 12th days, or on the 11th and 13th days.

If your bitch shows few external signs of her "heat", the vet can take a series of vaginal smears to assess the stage of her cycle and help you judge the correct time for mating. This is expensive and dog owners normally resort to it after a few failed matings which they may have considered due to bad timing.

The stud dog

Most stud dogs are "initiated" at around ten months old, preferably using an experienced bitch. Using an untried dog (even a show-dog) on a maiden bitch can be tricky and upset both dogs, so if this is your bitch's first litter, make sure the stud dog is sufficiently experienced.

MATING PROCEDURE

On the day fixed for mating, take your bitch to the dog rather than the other way about. Most bitches are aggressive on home territory, and it is the dog which needs to be assertive in this situation.

If possible, let the dogs socialize and romp around a little before actually mating. A bitch may refuse to mate if she isn't used to other dogs. Breeds with a more aggressive nature can be difficult.

It is usual to hold your bitch firmly throughout to avoid her causing any aggressive damage to a valuable dog.

Stage 1 When the bitch is ready, she holds her tail to one side. The dog mounts the bitch and the first part of ejaculation takes place. Part of the dog's penis (the *glans penis*) swells up, holding it in place so the two animals are joined.
Stage 2: "The tie" After about a minute, the dog dismounts and turns to stand back to back with the bitch, the two still joined. This usually lasts about 20 minutes and comes to an end naturally. Don't be alarmed – it is quite normal, although it isn't essential for fertility and often doesn't occur.

Although supervision at this stage is usually unnecessary and it is a bizarre background for small talk with the dog's owner, you must stay with the dogs. A bitch can get vicious or wrench away too soon, damaging the dog (see p.260). For the same reason, never force the dogs apart yourself.

Pregnancy

You won't see much change in your bitch for at least four weeks after mating. In fact, a few bitches show no signs of pregnancy at all until their puppies are born!

Pregnancy lasts an average of 63 days, although puppies may be born alive up to seven days either side of this. (The greater the divergence from the due date, the lower the survival rate.) So from the date of mating, you can work out when the litter is due.

It is usually possible for a vet to diagnose pregnancy at around 24–32 days. The growing, fluid-filled amniotic sacs which surround the puppies can be felt as small, tense spheres in the uterus. This may be a waste of time with large, fat or nervous bitches. If there are few foetuses, the result will probably be an educated guess. After 49 days, bitches can be X-rayed to see how many puppies are present.

Care of a pregnant bitch
If it is the first whelping for both you and the bitch, consult the vet three or four weeks after mating. At this stage, he can check the bitch, confirm pregnancy if possible, and give you advice on care and feeding.
Feeding
When the bitch is five to six weeks pregnant she needs more food – from one-third to a half extra. Meals should be small and frequent because the growing foetuses occupy a good deal of abdominal space and larger meals will fill her up too quickly.

The theory that "milk makes milk" is misguided. To promote lactation the bitch needs good quality protein. Some milk is valuable, but she requires cheese, eggs and meat too, as well as prescribed doses of a vitamin mineral supplement. You can use other natural supplements, too (see p.168).

THE WHELPING BOX

A proper whelping box is useful, particularly if you're planning to breed from a bitch again. You can construct one yourself or use a cardboard box with the front cut down enough for the bitch (not the puppies) to get in and out.

Introduce the bitch to the box about three weeks before whelping. Try to guide her into choosing it as a place to whelp. If you suddenly put her in a strange place at the last minute, she'll already have decided for herself where she wants to have her puppies, and it won't be your box if she's not familiar with it. Line it with plenty of newspaper.

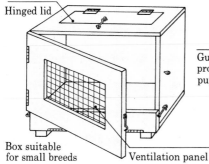

Hinged lid

Box suitable for small breeds
Ventilation panel

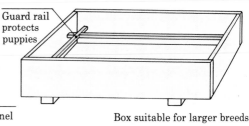

Guard rail protects puppies

Box suitable for larger breeds

SIGNS OF IMMINENT WHELPING

As the whelping date approaches, be on the lookout for these signs:
- The bitch's temperature will be slightly lower than normal (38°C) during the last weeks of pregnancy. In the last 24 hours before whelping it drops further to about 36°C
- The development of the breasts is very variable. In some bitches, they may fill up with milk a month before whelping; in others they may not fill until a day or so afterwards, when you'll need to temporarily hand-rear the puppies
- Most bitches refuse meals in the last 24 hours, but may pick at some of their favourite foods. Some vomit a little shortly before whelping
- There is often a sudden discharge of green mucus a couple of hours before whelping as the placenta begins to separate

Green discharge
Some bitches have a persistent light green mucus discharge throughout pregnancy – a substance called *uteroverdin* produced in the placenta. This is no problem and often decreases in the last two weeks. You'll see more of it during whelping.

Exercise
Pregnant bitches need exercise but don't encourage too much rough-and-tumble, particularly after the four-week stage. In the later stages, continue with regular short walks, but let her do things at her own pace without becoming overtired.

Preparing for whelping
It is easier for newborn puppies to find their way to a nipple if you trim the hair round the mammary glands of long-haired bitches. Similarly, to avoid a long-haired bitch becoming too messy during whelping, trim the hair round the vulva carefully with scissors.

Once the bitch is a day overdue, consult the vet. If your bitch had multiple matings, tell him if nothing has happened by the last due date.

Anticipating a difficult birth
It is important to involve the vet early with a potentially difficult birth. Try to anticipate the problem before it actually happens.

If a Caesarean is necessary, it is much better for your bitch to have it during the day than in the night. In the daytime there'll usually be plenty of the vet's staff around to revive the puppies. Very few practices have separate staff for night duties. The vet you see at night will often have worked the previous day and be working the following day too. It makes sense to see him when he is at his most alert and when maximum assistance is available. A difficult birth is a veterinary emergency, requiring at least two, and often several people to assist. In a multi-vet practice, only one vet will be on duty each night, so you may not see the one you prefer. If your bitch is in distress, though, don't hesitate to ring the veterinary surgery, whatever the time.

THINGS TO HAVE READY
- Your vet's emergency telephone number
- Paper towels and plenty of newspaper
- Clean towels
- A safe skin disinfectant for your hands
- Fine cotton thread and scissors
- Fresh bedding for the bitch
- A notebook and pen to record the timings of the various events

The birth

The bitch will probably manage the whole process of whelping with the minimum of assistance from you, but watch for the various stages. Keep a detailed record of the times of:
□ the first stage □ green discharge
□ straining □ the arrival of each puppy and its placenta.

Stage 1: dilation of the cervix

In some bitches, this stage isn't noticeable, but in others it may last between three and 24 hours.

Short contractions "sort out" the foetuses and present the first one into the pelvis. This brings the foetal membranes into the cervix and stimulates it to open. The bitch is uncomfortable and restless, unable to settle and often frantically rearranges her bedding. She will probably pant, and her pulse quickens.

Stage 2: expulsion of the foetus

The total length of the second stage depends on the number of puppies. It rarely exceeds six hours and even with a large litter should not exceed 12.

When the first puppy enters the pelvis, contractions become stronger, longer and more frequent. The bitch's hind legs often straighten out during the strongest waves of contraction. She may empty her bladder at this stage.

Eventually the water bag (*amniotic sac*) is pushed out. Sometimes the first puppy will be pushed through the sac membrane before it shows externally, and you'll see a little gush of liquid. The bitch will rupture the sac if it has appeared and may pull with her teeth on any visible membranes. These membranes give the birth canal a slippery lining to ease the passage of the puppies.

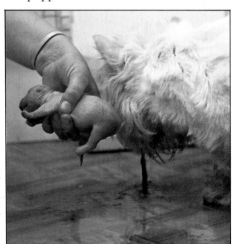

The stages of whelping
A West Highland White bitch (left) in her box prior to whelping. The floor of the box is covered with plenty of newspaper. When the first puppy arrives, the bitch should clean it and will probably chew off the umbilical cord (above). The latest arrival (right) is cleaned by its mother as the other newborn puppies sleep or feed.

By this time, the bitch is normally lying down. She turns frequently to clean herself; each turn is accompanied by a powerful contraction.

Don't rush to help, but observe the bitch from a distance. Some neurotic bitches need their owner at their side giving reassurance but not interfering. These are in the minority, though; other bitches are definitely put off by the presence of their owner.

Don't panic if the puppy arrives rear end first – up to 40 percent of puppy births are breach. Once the head or rear of the puppy is visible, the bitch may give a short pause before expelling it.

The first puppy

A maiden bitch usually produces her first puppy within three or four hours of beginning to strain. When the puppy arrives, she'll clean it vigorously, licking it all over. This removes all the membranes which the bitch usually eats; she also chews off the umbilical cord. The puppy, stimulated by these cleaning activities and the air in its nostrils soon seeks out a nipple and immediately begins to suck, helping to promote the supply of milk.

The puppy's placenta may come out with it, or follow up to 15 minutes later. (Where there are several puppies, one may bring with it the placental membranes of previous puppies.)

The rest of the litter

The second puppy follows at any time up to two hours later. Occasionally it may be longer, but you should seek veterinary advice after a delay of two hours. Rest periods between the puppies usually get shorter. If the litter is very large – 12–14 puppies – the bitch may "take a couple of hours off" in the middle. A bitch with experience of whelping usually gets it over more quickly. The process of expulsion is often quicker and easier, with shorter rests between puppies.

Stage 3: expulsion of membranes

This is a complex phase where there is more than one puppy. Placental membranes are usually passed within 15 minutes of each puppy. They may arrive along with the next puppy.

The bitch will probably attempt to eat these placentas. This won't do her any harm – she may vomit them up later or have green diarrhoea. If you can collect some of them without causing her too much distress, do so, although this isn't essential. It's more important to make sure the same number of placentas are passed as puppies produced.

Information for the vet

If you need to contact the vet at any stage, he'll need certain information.
- Breed and age of the bitch.
- Date of mating (or matings).
- Number of days since mating.
- Has the bitch been eating normally? When did she eat last?
- Is there a vaginal discharge?
- Has she been ill recently? Has she vomited? Is she distressed?
- What is her breeding history – any previous problems?
- Did her dam (mother) have any problems whelping? (You may not know, but it can be useful if you do.)

HOW YOU CAN HELP

If the bitch shows no signs of dealing with a puppy, clear the membranes away from its nose and rub it with a towel to stimulate it. Don't do this unless absolutely necessary, and take care not to rub all the fluid off the puppy – let the bitch clean it. She could reject a puppy on which you've lavished too much attention. Never take a puppy away – just do what's necessary and replace it with the bitch. Let the bitch lick the puppy, then gently rub its face on her mammary glands to encourage it to suckle.

If a puppy is visible for more than a few minutes before completing its arrival and the bitch is straining persistently, help by pulling it out and downwards, very gently. If this achieves nothing, ring the vet.

Dealing with the cord
When cleaning membranes off a puppy, you may also have to sever the umbilical cord. Make sure your hands are clean and sterile. Tie a ligature of fine cotton thread tightly round the cord, about 1.5–2.5 cm away from the puppy. Snip off the thread ends, then cut the cord 5 mm–1 cm further along. Take care not to pull on the cord at all.

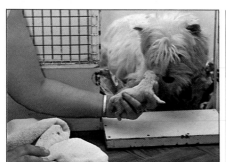
Stimulating a newborn puppy
Towel the puppy, then return it to the bitch.

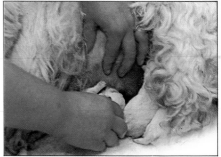
Helping a puppy to suckle
Some puppies need encouraging to feed.

The Caesarean

Your vet will decide if and when a Caesarean section is necessary. Although all general anaesthetics carry a small degree of risk, this operation is nothing to worry about. No vet would advise it unless it was the safest available option.

You will have to transport the bitch to the veterinary surgery. Often, you'll be able to wait at the surgery and take the bitch and any puppies home $1\frac{1}{2}$ to $2\frac{1}{2}$ hours after the start of the operation. At night, you might even be asked to help veterinary staff revive the puppies.

A Caesarean involves making an incision in the midline of the belly, or in the flank, removing the puppies from the uterus and stitching up the incision. Once the bitch is home, check this incision several times daily and report any problems to the vet.

Care of the new mother

Most bitches have a slight bloody/green discharge for at least 24 hours after whelping. After the birth of a large litter, this can last up to a week. Bathe it off with an antiseptic wash. If it persists, consult your vet.

The bitch may also vomit or have diarrhoea due to eating placentas. If you take care not to give her too fatty a diet, this should settle down.

Feeding

A heavily lactating bitch needs up to three times as much food as normal. For her to eat this amount, it must be presented almost continually, and should include good quality protein, plus supplementary vitamins and minerals.

Mammary glands

Check the mammary glands regularly for mastitis (painful, red swollen areas). You'll have an opportunity to do this when the bitch leaves the puppies to go and relieve herself. Report any symptoms to your vet. Abnormal swelling sometimes occurs 24 to 48 hours after whelping. Bathe the glands in warm water and draw off excess milk by alternately squeezing and releasing (to allow refilling) around the nipple. The problem usually sorts itself out as soon as the puppies start taking more milk.

ECLAMPSIA

For the first month after whelping, make sure there's always someone around to check that the nursing bitch is happy and comfortable. This is particularly important with toy breeds, especially Yorkshire Terriers. These dogs are prone to a condition called eclampsia (lactation tetany), caused by calcium deficiency.

Symptoms The problem usually occurs just before whelping, or within the first month of lactation. It tends to strike bitches with large litters which have been in heavy milk. The bitch becomes unsettled, wandering round, panting, whining and getting up and down. As the problem worsens, she becomes stiff, with twitching muscles and obvious lack of co-ordination. Eventually, she will collapse with convulsions, and if not treated, will die.

Treatment Eclampsia is a veterinary emergency. Once you suspect it, contact your vet immediately – he'll need to give the bitch a calcium injection. Feed the puppies by hand for at least 24 hours.

Prevention It isn't always possible to prevent the condition, which occurs due to the large amounts of calcium transferred to puppies in the womb, and later via the milk, but give pregnant and nursing bitches proper vitamin and mineral supplements, including calcium.

DOG SHOWS

There is much more to showing a dog than just putting a collar and lead on it and trotting it round the show-ring a couple of times. Far from being an initiation, your dog's first appearance at a show should be the end result of months of training and preparation. Showing isn't all hard grind, though. If you and your dog enjoy it, you'll both get a lot of pleasure out of it. Apart from the thrill of success if your pet is a good performer, there's real comradeship between owners of show dogs, and an atmosphere of excitement and friendly competition.

To find out exactly how your dog should look for a show, consult *Dog Breeds* (see pp.42–119). Grooming is covered in *Grooming* (see pp.172–83). The right techniques for obedience training are given in *Housing, Handling and Training* (see pp.142–59). Buying a puppy for show is covered in the chapter on *Choosing a Dog* (see p.126).

The world of the dog show

The first dog shows took place in the 1830s and 1840s. They were low-key affairs, held in public houses, and probably invented as a result of the ban on dog-fighting and bull-baiting which left dog fanciers with little outlet for their competitive instincts. The idea of shows soon caught on, though, and the first organized dog show was held at Newcastle-upon-Tyne, England in 1859.

Dog shows grew in popularity with the building of the railways, since breeders could travel from show to show. However, problems arose when people in different areas had conflicting ideas about how a breed should look. No single body or group was responsible for dog shows and standards varied tremendously. There was much controversy over standards and a great deal of faking. Clubs were therefore established to reach a consensus over what were and were not desirable characteristics of the various breeds.

THE KENNEL CLUB

The Kennel Club in Britain was founded in 1873 to oversee the showing of dogs. The Club registers the standards which describe exactly what the ideals of each breed should be. These standards are set by the individual breed societies but held by the Kennel Club. (For concise versions of the official standards for those breeds shown in this book, see pp.50–119.) All pedigree dogs must be registered with the Kennel Club before they can be shown as such in shows held under Club rules. The main functions of the Kennel Club are to:
- Promote the improvement of dogs, dog shows, field, working and obedience trials
- Classify breeds
- Register pedigree dogs
- Oversee transfers of ownership
- Grant licences to dog shows
- Establish and enforce the Kennel Club rules
- Give awards

An "International Dog Show", held at the Agricultural Hall, Islington, in 1865.

Advice for newcomers to showing

Anyone contemplating breeding dogs for show should appreciate that it is hard work, with little or no financial reward, except for the lucky few. Entering dog shows is something most people do for love rather than money.

Launching yourself into serious dog showing will only be fun if you remember not to get down-hearted. For serious showing, you do of course need a pedigree dog; some of the more light-hearted country dog shows run competitions for mongrels, but only registered pedigree animals may be entered at official shows. The competition is intense, and at times, it will seem as if the same handful of dogs wins at every show.

Much depends on your chosen breed of dog. Of course it is much harder to gain awards in those breeds where many dogs are in competition; a dog has to be that much better to do well.

Crufts Dog Show
Some of the entrants waiting on their benches at this large show, held annually in February.

Grooming for shows

A smart appearance plays a large part in a dog's success in the show-ring. At any show held under Kennel Club rules, the dogs which do well are sure to be as well groomed as they can possibly be. With long-haired breeds such as Afghan Hounds, Old English Sheepdogs and Yorkshire Terriers, appearance on show day is dependent on their owners' efforts over the previous six to 12 months.

The *Grooming* chapter in this book tells you about basic grooming skills and special care for different coat types. The Breed Society for your dog can supply detailed information on correct show grooming for the breed. In addition to a coat in top condition, make sure your dog has clean feet (the claws clipped if necessary, see p.181), plus clean eyes, nose and teeth.

There are rules governing the extent to which you are allowed to "alter" your show-dog's appearance in terms of grooming, cosmetic and surgical procedures. It's worth checking up on these, as failure to comply will mean disqualification and disappointment (see p.208).

The importance of vaccination

Vaccination is a very important factor which is neglected by many people showing dogs. You should keep a dog's vaccinations up to date under any circumstances, but dogs visiting shows and mixing with other dogs from all over the country are particularly at risk. Canine carriers of disease do come to dog shows – when parvovirus disease first appeared, its initial spread was closely linked to the show circuit.

The general public are allowed into dog shows and are an enthusiastic audience. However, their desire to pat and stroke the dogs can cause them to transmit disease with the most innocent of motives, so watch for this.

How is dog showing organized?

There are several different types of dog show. Besides the various local, regional and national "beauty shows", there are also special Obedience shows, plus Working Trials and Field Trials for working dogs.

Championship shows

Chief among the Championship shows in Britain is Crufts, established in 1886 by Charles Cruft, a supplier of dog biscuits. The most prestigious dog show in the U.S.A. is New York's Westminster Dog Show, inaugurated in 1877. Because of the charismatic appeal of these shows, entry has to be restricted to dogs which have won the required certificates at other Championship shows.

At a Championship show, classes are organized with the dogs separated into breeds, then further divided into several age and handicap groups such as Puppy, Junior, Novice, Open and Veteran. Dogs and bitches are judged separately in each class. There's a "Best-of-Breed" class, with a certificate awarded to the winner of the best dog and the best bitch. The best dog and best bitch each receive a Challenge Certificate. In the next round, the Best-of-Breed winners in each group are judged to select the best in each group (Gundogs, Hounds, Working Dogs, Terriers, Toys and Utility). Ultimately, the best of the various groups are judged to award the "Best-in-Show".

Other types of dog show

"Open shows" are organized in a very similar way to Championship shows, but aren't such long affairs – the Best-in-Show is judged from the Best-of-Breeds.

Your local Dog Show is likely to be an "Exemption Show". These shows have permission to waive Kennel Club rules, and make a very good introduction for dogs new to the show-ring. As well as giving amateurs a chance to try their hand at showing a dog, they allow enthusiasts to show new dogs in conditions similar to those at a Championship show.

"Club shows" are those organized by

A parade of Basset Hounds being presented by their handlers at a Championship show.

the individual Breed Societies. They usually offer a combination of serious classes for enthusiasts, plus exemption-type classes and "fun and games" for the owners.

Obedience shows and classes

Some classes aren't judged on breed or appearance, but simply on ability. Different breeds and mongrels may all compete together. The kind of thing that the dogs are required to do begins with the commands given in *Housing, Handling and Training*, pp.156–9. Dogs are asked to move left and right, walk, run, stop, lie down, sit, stand and negotiate obstacles – all on verbal commands. The classic breeds for this type of contest are Labrador Retrievers, German Shepherd Dogs and Border Collies, although many breeds take part. In addition, there are various types of Utility classes which involve tracking or searching and retrieving. For all these types of competition, there are special training classes and clubs for dog owners which teach both dogs and owners what is required of them. Many long hours of work are needed for success and not all dogs are capable of it.

Field trials

These competitions are held to put gundogs through their paces – they involve complex retrieving operations both on land and in water. Once again, there are specialist clubs which owners can join to learn with their dog the techniques of Field-Trial work.

Sheepdog trials

These specialized shows involve working sheepdogs competing against each other, usually on a faults and time basis. The aim is to complete a specific herding operation at long range, the dogs being controlled by whistle signals.

A country dog show
A lighthearted dog race at an Exemption show.

A working Welsh sheepdog, directed by whistle signals, rounds up a group of sheep at a trial.

Dog show procedure

If you're planning to enter your pet at a dog show held under Kennel Club rules, you must enter for the appropriate classes well in advance. You'll be sent an entry ticket and a benching number. You'll also be asked to attend by a specific time.

What to do when you arrive

When you arrive at the show, buy the catalogue which gives full details of all the classes. Next, make your way to your numbered bench.

Make your dog comfortable. Dogs are benched according to breed and sex. If yours is a small dog, the bench may be a cage; for larger breeds it will be a stall – which is why you need a benching chain (see *Equipment Checklist*). Settle your dog with its own bed and a drink of water, but don't feed it until after it has finished its classes of it may feel (and look) sleepy.

Organizing your dog

The classes for which you've entered will have been confirmed to you by the show organizers. Check your entries in the catalogue and note the times of the various classes. Only the first class in each section has a definite time, but all the classes are numbered and follow each other in order. As a particular

Show-dogs in action
One of the entrants in the Irish Setter class at a Championship show being examined by an official judge (top left). The judge is assessing head carriage and the dog's neck. All show-dogs should be happy to be handled in this way.

Dogs of every breed are welcome at this local country dog show (below left). It isn't an official show, but each owner is practising the proper method of presenting his dog.

An Afghan Hound being gaited is a fine sight (right). The handler adopts a brisk pace to help the dog look its brightest and most alert.

class is being judged in the show-ring, its number is displayed on the judges' table. This is how you can judge the progress of the order of classes.

Don't have your dog waiting by the ring for class after class or it will become stale and bored. Like a film star, you should bring the dog from its dressing-room to the ring where it will hopefully give a flawless, Oscar-winning performance, retiring immediately afterwards to the dressing room for a rest.

There are normally small exercise areas where you can have a "dry run" or rehearsal before the real thing. You'll find out by experience how much of a warm-up your dog needs on the day of a show.

SHOW EQUIPMENT CHECKLIST

- Grooming equipment – combs, brushes, scissors and dry shampoo
- Dog's bed and blanket
- Drinking bowl and water bottle. Every show should provide water, but it isn't always conveniently placed, and you may need some on the way
- Food and feeding bowl for long days
- Titbits. Many handlers use titbits in the ring to focus a dog's attention These are usually kept in the pocket in a plastic bag which makes an obvious rustling noise
- Benching chain. You'll need one at some shows to attach your dog's collar to the staging
- Show lead – usually made of nylon or fine leather

Handling a show-dog

For success in the ring, a dog should appear confident and familiar with the handling, stance and movements required of it. Your dog's "presence" is a crucial feature in show judging – almost as important as anatomical excellence. This "presence" has a lot to do with good handling. If you're not sufficiently confident yourself, it is in fact possible to employ an experienced handler to take your dog through its paces in the ring.

A show-dog is accompanied in the ring at all times by its handler, and proper presentation begins with the handler. Dogs pick up human moods and fears rapidly; a gloomy owner will soon transmit his feelings to his dog and their combined performance will be drab and lack-lustre.

One of the elements of successful dog handling is dressing neatly and practically. If you own a large dog, remember when choosing footwear that you'll have to run in the ring.

Gaiting

One of the most important aspects of your dog's performance is the way it moves. The judges will expect to see each dog moving at a brisk trot. It is the responsibility of the handler to give the dog enough space and freedom to move correctly, and to move freely himself without impeding the animal. It is also up to the handler to select the route for the run. Although the judge will indicate the general direction, you should survey the field first. Dogs aren't usually keen to move freely over a patch soiled by another dog, even if it has been cleared. Outside, make sure the route is level, with no dips or mounds which may alter the dog's gait.

Techniques for the "trot"

Gauging the speed of trot for the best presentation of the dog's gait needs practice at home, with someone experienced watching. Finding the correct pace and length of lead for your dog is very important, so

An Old English Sheepdog being gaited in the ring. The handler keeps a careful eye on the pace.

experiment. Expert handlers in the ring make it look as if there's nothing to it. This is in fact the aim of all handlers – the dog should look as if it is moving completely freely. A very short lead might help some dogs to tighten their shoulder action, but in other dogs it may cut short the stride.

Although you and your dog should move harmoniously as a pair, be very wary of imitating the dog's stride as you run beside it. It may unwittingly begin to imitate *you* and adopt a stilted action. Depending on the size of the dog, you may need to move at a fast walk or a run. Large breeds like German Shepherds or Borzois need a fit owner to allow them to move correctly. You may be moving in a line with other dogs and handlers, so make sure you leave enough room ahead of you so that you and your dog aren't forced to shorten your steps.

Techniques for the "collected trot"
As well as seeing your dog gaiting from the side, the judge will want to see its action when it is coming towards him and moving away from him. For this, a slower, more "collected" trot is often preferred. It is very important that the dog moves in a straight line. "Fighting" with the lead can result in paddling of the feet and a crab-like gait, the rear end swinging out at an angle. Practise gaiting clockwise and anti-clockwise, on both sides of the dog. Careless footwork on the part of the handler is a common cause of the problem so watch this carefully, especially in the ring.

THE STAND

Practise arranging your dog's stance in front of a mirror so you can see the effect. Don't pick up the dog under its belly; this causes many dogs to "roach" their back for a moment. And don't overspread the back legs since this can cause the front legs to bend and the back to dip.

When you're asked to present the stand, choose a level piece of ground, free of leaves or debris. A dog will stand off-balance in order to avoid objects on the ground.

Good handlers accomplish the stance with the minimum of fuss. The best technique is to place one hand under the chest to raise the front end, then run the hand up the neck to present the head correctly. With the other hand, adjust the hind legs and tail with as little interference as possible, more as if petting the dog than arranging it. A dog with a slight dip in its back ("soft topline") can be induced to tighten its abdominal muscles for a moment by a gentle touch under the last rib.

Presenting the stand: this Whippet's handler holds her lead hand up to lift the dog's head.

Show judging

Dog show judges have a very difficult job and try in all good faith to do it the best they can. Of course, different judges do place dogs differently due to their own preferences within the standard. Nevertheless, a judge should be familiar with the official standard of the breed that he is judging.

A show judge is faced with making a decision based on all the factors shown in the diagram below. He may have to choose from 30 dogs, of one breed or of many breeds, depending on the class. It is interesting to go round the benches trying to assess these factors yourself.

RULES AND REGULATIONS

At an official show, there are certain rules governing appearance and grooming. If a judge detects an infringement of any of these, he'll be forced to disqualify the dog. A dog may not enter the show-ring with:
- Excess chalk or talc in the coat
- Lacquer or hair spray in the coat
- The setting of its teeth artificially altered
- Any dyes, tints or bleach having been used to alter the colour of its coat

THE JUDGE'S ASSESSMENT

The diagram shows the routine points a judge will check when assessing a dog. He will also assess:

- General demeanour, stance and "presence"
- Movement and temperament

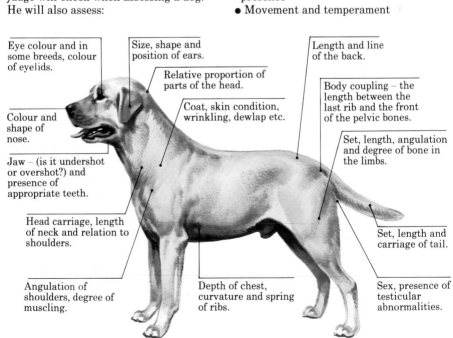

Eye colour and in some breeds, colour of eyelids.

Size, shape and position of ears.

Relative proportion of parts of the head.

Length and line of the back.

Colour and shape of nose.

Coat, skin condition, wrinkling, dewlap etc.

Body coupling – the length between the last rib and the front of the pelvic bones.

Jaw – (is it undershot or overshot?) and presence of appropriate teeth.

Set, length, angulation and degree of bone in the limbs.

Head carriage, length of neck and relation to shoulders.

Set, length and carriage of tail.

Angulation of shoulders, degree of muscling.

Depth of chest, curvature and spring of ribs.

Sex, presence of testicular abnormalities.

Show techniques

A show-dog's appearance is all-important for success. Obviously, every competitor does all he can to make sure his dog looks its best. There are many "tricks of the trade" which you'll only pick up over a period of time. To make the stand appear better, for instance, an experienced handler might take advantage of a slight hump in the ground, placing the dog's forelegs on it to lift its front end.

Legal and illegal practices

Over the years there has been considerable faking involved in showing dogs. In the U.K., the surgical aspects of faking are now banned by the R.C.V.S. (Royal College of Veterinary Surgeons). Vets aren't permitted to perform "cosmetic surgery" for show purposes. Common techniques now forbidden include modifying ear carriage by severing cartilage, straightening tail carriage by severing tendons and implanting plastic testicles in cryptorchids.

Some breeders try to manipulate ear carriage, particularly in puppies. To make the ears stand up, they wax the insides of the ear flaps, use leather supports, or apply straps round the base of the ear. The only one of these techniques which a breeder might actually use in the ring is ear waxing; this is illegal and grounds for a ban.

Even coat colour can be tampered with. A breeder may pluck out stray hairs of the wrong colour, or dye a whole patch of the coat. Chalk and inert powders such as talcum may be used on white dogs as long as none remains in the coat during showing (see *Rules and Regulations*, left).
Therapeutic surgical procedures
These are permitted, and include treatment of problems like the eye disorders, entropion and ectropion (see p.256). But since many of these conditions are inherited, it is best not to show or breed from sufferers.

POLISHING A DOG

Long coats require the most attention before a show, but here's a good tip for pre-show preparation on a short coat to give it an extra-healthy shine. This works especially well on dark and uniform colour coats.

Rubbing down the coat brings out any loose hair. You can then polish it with a piece of soft fabric and use a special spray to add a final finish (don't use a spray household polish).

1 Rub down the coat with a damp chamois leather then with a piece of silk or velvet.

2 Use a specially formulated spray to give the coat a final sparkle before a show.

UNDERSTANDING
YOUR DOG

A relationship with a much-loved pet dog can be one
of the most special in your life. Mentally, dogs aren't
so complex as human beings; nevertheless, every dog
is an individual with thoughts and a personality of its
own. Learning more about what "makes your dog
tick" can only enhance your relationship with it.
Do you know, for example, which aspects of a dog's
behaviour are based on instinct, which on feelings
like fear, loneliness and aggression? Why do dogs wag
their tails, bark, bite, chase cats? Fathoming
out reasons for behaviour – whether problematic or
not – can be tricky, but by taking steps towards
understanding it, you'll improve the quality of life
for you and your dog. Temperaments of different
breeds are described in *Dog Breeds* (see pp.42–119).

The intelligence of the dog

The empathy between humans and dogs has developed over the thousands of years of domestication of the dog. To a large extent, selective breeding has changed a wild pack animal into one which seems content to live with a pack of two-legged animals controlling everything from its food and water supply to its access to the outside world. Occasionally a dog will seem more like its wild, wolf-like ancestors – seeking the company of other dogs and challenging human authority unless it is enforced by strength. But in general, the favourable light in which dogs view their owners is based on a deep mutual trust.

The responsible dog owner should be able to read the signs given by his own or other dogs and react accordingly. Understanding what a dog is trying to say through its posture or its behaviour is crucial and many sensitive people are very gifted when it comes to intuitive understanding of their pet. Unfortunately, some people overdo this anthropomorphism, ascribing very complex human behaviour and emotions to dogs. Most of this is in the eye of the beholder. Dogs are motivated on a far more basic level and are much more easily contented than many people think.

How clever is a dog?

The intelligence of a dog is a difficult concept; the extent of it is still disputed by scientists. It is difficult enough to compare humans conditioned by different cultures. With dogs, the question is even more tricky – different breeds have developed different physical abilities and natural instincts. Just think of the immediately apparent differences between toy breeds and giant breeds, guard breeds and sight hounds, fighting dogs and herding dogs.

The dog's brain is much smaller than man's (see p.23). Its ability to truly think isn't absent, but much reduced, although dogs occasionally give the impression of thinking things out and behaving in a surprisingly "human" way. The most famous canine example is "Greyfriars Bobby", a Skye Terrier who, after his master's death, followed the coffin to the churchyard and denied all efforts to send him away. The dog spent the next 14 years until his own death living around the churchyard, appearing to grieve for his lost friend and master.

Expert dog trainers measure intelligence by the speed with which a dog learns new tasks. Dog owners, on the other hand, often measure intelligence by the sensitivity a dog shows in detecting their moods and wishes. Whether these concepts actually represent the same kind of intelligence shown by man is debatable. Dogs certainly show the ability to learn, to understand signals and to associate a signal with a particular movement or task. They don't obey blindly, though, and are quite capable of deciding that they *don't* want to do something. They have a high degree of "animal intelligence" but seem to lack man's ability to reason and associate complicated abstract ideas.

A dog's power of association

Dogs are capable of linking two ideas in their mind (Pavlov's dogs' association of feeding time and the sound of a bell ringing is a famous example). However, dogs don't associate events which are separated in time. For instance, if your dog runs off while you're on a walk, punishing it on its eventual return, two hours later, won't have the desired effect. The dog associates the punishment with its return to you; it doesn't understand that the punishment is for failing to return two hours ago. The secret is to make the dog *want* to come back *to please you.* If returning to you is a pleasurable experience and it receives kind words, a friendly pat or a tit-bit, the dog will return because it knows you want it to.

Do dogs understand people?

Dogs are very good at detecting subtle signals from humans, whether these are unconscious signals of pleasure, distress or anger, or simply the intention to do something. This is, after all, the way individuals in a pack of wild dogs interact, using body language and sounds to express emotions. Obviously a dog doesn't understand our actual language – what means more to it is the pattern and tone of the sound. Sound signals are just as eloquent given by whistle, provided the dog has been taught to recognize the whistle as a signal as is the case with sheepdogs.

Dogs' ability to appreciate visual and audible signals is used by trainers at a sophisticated level in putting together dog acts for films, television and circuses. It isn't fear which trains a dog, but the wish to please. This can motivate them to learn complex manoeuvres to be carried out in response to signals, even at long range.

The scope of dog training
Posting a letter for its master (left) is within the reach of a large dog like a German Shepherd. The circus dog (above) has been taught a complicated trick involving doves.

The instincts of a dog

The innate behavioural traits of many breeds are well known. Without any special training, retrievers love to pick up objects in their mouth and carry them round, often showing them to their owners with great pride. Pointers unconsciously "point" at things which interest them before investigating. Sheepdogs love herding all animals, including people. And Spitz-type breeds, the Dobermann and terriers are all instinctive guards.

Territorial instincts

Protecting the home and its occupants from human or canine interlopers is a basic instinct of dogs. Although birds and other animals are often ignored, a dog regards humans and other dogs as its own kind, so unknown members of these species are viewed with suspicion.

The pack instinct

A dog's owner is usually seen as the leader of its pack, responsible for the pack's defence. If a stranger (human or dog) is accepted without aggression by the pack leader, he or she will generally by accepted by the dog. In the absence of the pack leader, the dog takes over the role and behaves quite differently. Even a small, quiet bitch may show territorial aggression.

"Chasing the postman"

Transient visitors to the "territory" (a classic example being the postman) serve to reinforce this protective behaviour. Because the dog warns them off, they depart rapidly. This is seen by the dog as cowardice, and eventually it recognizes their uniforms as the mark of a person it can chase and who will retreat. Tackle this behaviour by arranging supervised introductions between the dog and the visitors. And let your dog see regularly that you, as "pack leader", obviously accept the visitors' presence.

Characteristic behaviour of dogs
The postman (left) is apprehensive of the Great Dane. His tentative approach only reinforces the dog's territorial behaviour as it guards the gate. Many dogs love digging (right), sending up showers of earth with their front paws. This Jack Russell may be searching for a buried bone. The instinct to bury food stretches back to the early ancestors of the domestic dog which stored food in the ground to help them survive the leaner hunting days.

Predatory instincts

Although dogs have been domesticated for many thousands of years, some still instinctively go through the motions of hunting and catching prey. They may stalk, catch and even kill small animals, but frequently, they take an impressive-looking run at the prey which is aborted at the last minute.

Chasing cats

Dogs regard cats more as good sport than dinner. Cats appeal to the natural predatory instinct of dogs in being small, furry, quick to move and inclined to run away. Usually the chase is harmless and the only result is hissing and spitting from the cat.

A dog can distinguish between cats and will coexist happily with its own family's cat, tolerating its cheeky behaviour. Indeed, it may rush outside and chase the cat next door, then come indoors and curl up in the same basket as the household cat.

Sheep worrying

Sheep are natural prey – they run when chased. And dogs unaccustomed to sheep will often chase them. Some settle for a herding manoeuvre and give up the activity when the sheep are huddled together in a corner of the field. Other dogs may continue

harassing the sheep, biting and even killing some. This behaviour is very serious and a farmer may well shoot a dog seen worrying sheep. When walking near sheep, don't take any risks, keep your dog to heel on the lead.

The importance of smell

Sniffing anything unfamiliar – including other dogs – is one of a dog's strongest instincts. Where humans interact on the basis of sight and sound, dogs rely heavily on smell. The dog's sense of smell is remarkably well developed (see p.27).

Socialization sniffing

Smell is part of any greeting between dogs. Initially they may virtually touch noses, while displaying heads and tails held high. Any show of aggression will push this into conflict, but part of the intial "sizing up" is circling each other and sniffing.

Scent marking

The importance of smell is also shown by the male dog's desire to urinate frequently. (Bitches do it too, but not so noticeably.) By doing this, the dog leaves its own scent and marks what it considers to be, or is trying to claim as, its own territory. (Similarly, a dog uses the strong-smelling secretion from the sebacious glands in its anal sacs to put its own smell on its faeces). The reason a dog urinates so often is that it is competing with all the other local dogs, trying to mask *their* scent.

Another form of scent-marking is scratching the ground with the hind paws, kicking up earth. This leaves the scent produced by the sweat glands in the hind paws.

Dogs sometimes apply their own type of "after-shave", rolling in strong-smelling substances to enhance their own smell. These smell terrible to us, but delightful to a dog – top favourites are pig manure and bird droppings.

Body signals

Dogs are unable to use speech to express feelings like uncertainty, fear, aggression, pleasure or playfulness. But every dog has a range of "body signals" that it can use to express these emotions. Visible signs of how your dog is feeling can be shown by its whole body and also by its face. Barks, growls and whimpers give other clues. As a dog owner, it is important that you should be able to read these signals. Be alert and "tuned in" to recognize signs based on: □ body posture □ vocalization □ ears □ eyes □ lips □ tongue □ tail □ hair standing on end.

The invitation to play
A playful dog, tongue hanging out, keen to initiate a game with a ball. The dog looks up with bright eyes at a human, or a larger dog.

The dog's voice

Most dogs are fairly vocal. They can produce a range of sounds ranging from whimpers, through rolling growls to proper barks. Dogs use their voices to express themselves, raising the pitch or volume of their bark to indicate frustration or emotion. Barking isn't necessarily aggressive. It is more likely to mean "hurry up, come and play!" or "nice to see you!" than "one false move and I'll tear your throat out!"

Growling is more often aggressive in adult dogs than puppies. Some dogs "play growl", but their mood is always obvious. Many can make a rolling sound like a growl, fluctuating in pitch. The pitch of an aggressive growl may be constant or increase with the aggressive body posture.

The "normal" dog

A happy, alert dog carries its tail well, with no tension in its body. It moves freely and holds its head high. The tongue may loll out and the jaws are relaxed.

Asking to play

When it wants a game, a dog often dips down at the front into a crouch. It gives little yips and barks or rolling growls with high notes. It may raise one foot and lean to one side, its head almost on the ground. It may jump backwards and forwards, the head looking up at you with relaxed jaws.

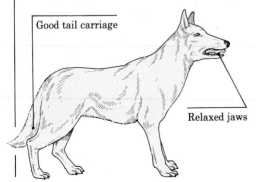

Good tail carriage

Relaxed jaws

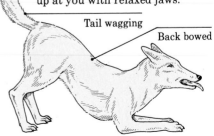

Tail wagging

Back bowed

FACIAL EXPRESSIONS

Like ourselves, dogs are blessed with facial muscles capable of giving different expressions to the face, although these muscles and their control system are not as efficient as man's.

The lips can be curled back to expose the teeth. Baring the teeth is not always aggressive – some dogs seem almost to laugh, and when very pleased, their lips are drawn back to expose the incisors. In aggression, the lips are drawn back further, often exposing the pointed canine teeth as well.

The ears are extremely mobile and can turn to follow sounds – even drop-eared dogs such as spaniels can move their ears into an alert position, although they don't have the range of expression of those breeds with erect ears.

The eyes are expressive too. When a dog is happy, there is a distinct brightening of the eyes. Some dogs raise their eyelids when surprised or quizzical – this is often exaggerated by a tilting of the head.

Staring Fearful aggression (see p.219) may give the dog a wild, wide-eyed look; the skin is drawn back, exposing the whites of the eyes and often the pupils are dilated. But in dominant aggression (see p.220), the pupils will probably be constricted, daring eye contact and fixed on your every move. To a dog, a fixed stare is a challenge. Usually, a person staring at a dog will cause the dog to look away and become submissive. A dog sure of itself and of its relationship with the owner may simply react with a questioning look. However, don't try to "stare out" a dog unless you're confident that you can handle the potential attack that may follow your losing this eye-to-eye contest.

Questioning and aggressive expressions
A quizzical look from a Weimaraner, its head held on one side, and unmistakable aggression on the face of a Husky, showing fearsome teeth.

Submission

The invitation to play may quickly change into a submissive posture with the dog in a lower crouch. It still raises its front feet in a mild play invitation, teeth are hidden. There is no tension in this posture and the dog is probably silent. As it crouches lower it may lick a little. A submissive dog often turns side-on to present its flank.

Complete submission

Now the dog's ears are folded down. It drops its tail and folds it round one leg; very nervous animals will tuck it right under. The head is down to avoid eye contact; with reassurance it comes up.

The final stage in submission is rolling over, one hind leg raised. Unless afraid, the dog usually raises its ears a little to show the submission stems from trust.

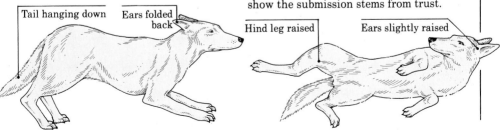

Tail hanging down   Ears folded back

Hind leg raised   Ears slightly raised

HOW THE DOG USES ITS TAIL

A dog's tail is an integral part of its communications system. The dog wags its tail to show pleasure or as an invitation to come for a walk or to play. It can be lowered as part of an aggression display, or tucked under in fear and submission.

Apart from its use as a tool of communications, the tail has physical uses. For example, water-dogs use their tail as a rudder when swimming.

Many breeds suffer the indignity of tail docking (see pp.49 and 137). But the importance of the tail for self-expression is obvious from the attempts docked dogs make to wag their stumps. Some of them wag their entire rear end in joy, but the more subtle signals aren't available to them. This can cause problems – they may find it impossible to signal submission adequately and end up in a fight. In fact, the initial aim of docking in breeds like Dobermanns, and Rottweilers, was probably to force aggression by preventing adequate expression of submission.

It is difficult to justify the idea of tail docking, although many breeds' official standards require it. Removing a dog's tail does make it easier to judge in shows, but there's no argument for removing the tails of working dogs. Responsible grooming will ensure that feathered tails of working dogs such as spaniels are kept tidy.

The tail used as a counter-balance
A German Shepherd negotiates an obstacle.

Fearful aggression
The dog shows its teeth, emits a constant low growl or snarl, or even barks. The ears are laid back. The whole body is tense, with the back legs held ready for rapid movement. The hair down the centre of the dog's back stands on end. The tail is held down and rigid.

Dominant aggression
Rather than simply warning you off, the dog advances confidently with its tail and ears held high. It will look straight at you, teeth bared, snapping and ready to bite.

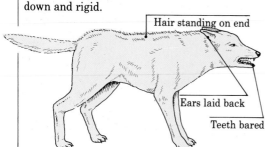

Hair standing on end

Ears laid back

Teeth bared

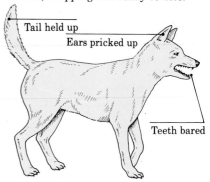

Tail held up

Ears pricked up

Teeth bared

Aggression and how to deal with it

There are several different forms of aggression in dogs. Learning to recognize their signs and causes gives you a far greater chance of solving any problems. The main types are:
- Fearful aggression
- Dominant aggression
- Protective aggression
- Aggression towards other dogs

The posture of an aggressive dog is not unlike one showing submission (see p.217), but the aggressive dog looks more "hunted" – its face has a drawn look. As the aggression deepens, the dog sinks lower and tucks its tail between its legs.

Treatment techniques

Modifying problem behaviour in a dog is a very specialized task. Real problem cases which require complex analysis of the problem are normally referred by vets in general practice to other vets or animal psychologists, for detailed study and therapy.

In general, punishment is a poor tool and may be dangerous when used on large, aggressive dogs. You should never push a dog into showing aggression or you'll take several steps backwards in training. Most types of aggression can be countered with reward-based techniques. Calling in a third-party professional trainer is usually no help. Sometimes it succeeds, but it can make the situation worse.

Never resort to striking a dog or to devices which cause local pain like pinch collars or electric shock collars. These often escalate the aggressive outburst. Anti-mugging alarms (which emit a very loud noise) are used in some cases, usually under specialist direction. They may solve aggression problems, but are probably best kept as the last resort – people find the noise nearly as unpleasant as dogs.

Ignoring a dog is one of the most effective punishments – dogs hate being deprived of your attention. Don't offer a dog any tit-bits or ball games in an attempt to change its mood; they will only be interpreted as a reward and reinforce the bad behaviour.

Fearful aggression

A dog showing this type of aggression is on the defensive. It feels frightened, threatened or in pain. Warning signals to watch for include a flattening of the ears and the dog alternately approaching and backing off from the source of aggression.

What to do

The technique for dealing with fear-based aggression is known as "desensitization". It involves facing the dog with the person or thing it fears, at a safe distance, and rewarding non-aggression with food or praise. Reduce the distance between the trigger and the dog over successive training sessions. Reward good behaviour and punish shows of aggression by ignoring the dog.

Fearful aggression
This dog is afraid of whoever is approaching.

Dominant aggression

Dominant aggression happens more often between two dogs than between dogs and people; when it does occur with people, it can be serious. In the eyes of the family dog, there's usually a particular "pecking order" in the household, and the dog tries to establish its place in the hierarchy as it did in prehistoric times in the pack. If the dog sees itself at the top, it may show aggression to the whole family. More often, it will simply consider some individuals, perhaps children, as subordinate to it. Strangely enough, people outside the family may present no threat to the dog and it may be perfectly friendly to them.

The dog may also begin urine marking in the house to stake its claim positively. In a confrontation situation, the dominantly aggressive dog will anticipate your movements and try to block them with its body.

What to do

Try to pick up the warning signs of dominant aggression in puppies or young dogs and establish your own dominance by grabbing the scruff of the dog's neck and holding it down on the floor in a submissive position. You could give it a little shake first.

Controlling the problem in an adult dog is more difficult, and the approach used with puppies can be dangerous or impossible. However, even adult dogs are dependent on you for their food. The family members who have been the targets of the aggression should take control over feeding and other things the dog likes which can then be used as a reward for good behaviour.

Conditioning submission

A technique which may succeed against dominant aggression is conditioning submissive behaviour in the dog, at times when it would normally show aggression – forcing a role reversal.

The dog which demands to be petted is showing dominant aggression. Reject the dog for a few minutes, then call it over for petting, making *you* the dominant party.

A dominantly aggressive dog
This dog is exhibiting all the usual body signs of dominant aggression (see p.218), and its whole body is taut. Not all dogs show these warning signals. Some will interpret an action of their owners as an attempt to dominate them, and react without warning by attempting to counter this with aggression. Triggers for this sort of behaviour could include grooming, unexpected petting or picking the dog up.

Protective aggression
A dog's protective instinct may be directed towards its home or owner. Noises of someone approaching the house may trigger it; sudden close contact between the owner and other people may be seen as a threat. Warning signs are barking and growling.
What to do
In this case, it is important to arrange a supervised introduction between the dog and the person it feels is threatening it. The "pack leader" (probably the head of the household) should indicate to the dog that the person is quite acceptable.

Aggression towards other dogs
Trouble between two dogs (dominant or fearful aggression) usually happens with dogs of the same sex. The generally submissive dog will follow its normal pattern with other dogs, showing the "body signals" described on p. 217. The dominant dog, even if well controlled in its owner's presence, may quickly seek to dominate other dogs and a fight may ensue if the other dog doesn't immediately look submissive and cowed.
What to do
Follow the advice given for treating dominant and fearful aggression, but if the problem persists, consult the vet.

Eradicating other bad habits
The desensitization technique is useful for treating a number of other problems, such as destructive behaviour when the dog is left alone.

Leave the offending dog on its own initially for very short periods under circumstances which would normally trigger the behaviour. Again, reward good behaviour, but simply ignore the dog if it behaves badly. Gradually increase the periods of time during which you leave the dog until it is happy at being left.

SEEKING YOUR VET'S ADVICE
Before trying to sort out problem behaviour, discuss the question with your vet. In many cases, there are medical reasons for behavioural disorders. What appears as aggression of one kind or another may in fact be associated with local pain. For example, passing urine indoors may be due to a problem like diabetes (see p.245). In such cases, there may be a medical solution to your dog's particular problem; several types of drug can be used effectively in this way:
- Hypnotics and sedatives
- Anti-anxiety sedatives
- Anti-psychotic tranquilizers
- Mood-stabilizing antidepressants
- Progesterones

PROBLEM DOGS
Given time, many behavioural problems of dogs can be solved satisfactorily. But absolute uncontrolled aggression in a dog is really too dangerous to deal with under most circumstances; sadly, such dogs are probably best destroyed. One potential cause which must be considered in certain cases is rabies (see p.152). Fortunately this is absent from Britain, but it should not be ruled out as an outside possibility.

There are a very few psychotic dogs whose behaviour defies explanation. With people they may display all the signs of a big welcome, wagging their tail and looking pleased, but their sole aim is to lure the unwary (particularly vets) close enough to take a large lump out of them. There's no defence against such dogs as they give no warning. Fortunately, however, they are rare.

Antisocial behaviour in adult dogs

In most owner-pet relationships, the owners see their dog as far more than a simple possession. Any antisocial behaviour that develops is often tolerated, partly because the owners couldn't contemplate the loss of the dog and partly because they feel the problem is due to some failure on their part. Understanding these problems is a big step towards solving them. The main kinds of problem are:

● Aggression (different kinds, see pp.219–21)
● Separation behaviour
● Phobia due to loud noises
● Barking
● Mounting
● Urine marking

The dog which bites

One of the worst aspects of aggression in dogs is the danger of their biting people. Although dogs can be trained to attack on command, this is thankfully a rare occurrence. Usually, such dogs are trained to grab and hold the arm of their victim rather than to truly bite and savage.

Luckily, most dog bites are minor ones. Statistics show they are most often inflicted on children, away from home. This implies that at least part of the reason may be a child's inexperience in interpreting the warning signs, or even provocation.

Most accidental dog bites are probably due to territorial, protective or defensive aggression. Any of these may be caused by a stranger.
What to do
It is very important to warn children not to run up to strange dogs and not to extend their fingers towards them, but to offer a clenched fist if the dog is friendly. See pp.219–21 for how to deal with different types of aggression in terms of corrective training.

Training is ineffectual when a dog is frightened and in pain. If the dog is threatening to bite because it has been in a road accident or a fight and is hurt, handle it carefully with slow, calm movements and use a soothing voice (see p.278).

Separation-induced behaviour

This is most often seen in puppies when they move to their new home (see p.224). It can also occur in adult dogs whose behaviour was not properly controlled during puppyhood and in adult dogs who have a change of owner. This may cause a feeling of distress and insecurity in a dog and the effect is over-dependency on humans.
What to do
You should try to reduce your dog's dependency on yourself and your family. Pet the dog on your return from absence, but don't make any farewells when you leave. Try also to reduce the amount of contact between you and your dog when you're at home.

Noise phobias

Phobic problems in dogs develop from an early age. Most are linked in some way to loud noises, ranging from gunshots to car sounds, fireworks and thunder. Sometimes, a noise becomes linked in the dog's mind to another feature associated with it, so that a fear response to thunder may lead to a fear of all the other aspects of a storm such as lightning, rain and wind. Sometimes telephone bells, vacuum cleaners and hair-dryers can trigger these fearful responses. Generally, these problems are associated either

*Curbing excessive
barking*
*Dogs that frequently
howl or bark can make
their owners unpopular
with the neighbours.
The solution is a sharp
"No", supported if
necessary with a light
smack on the behind to
get the dog's attention.
To a dog, the worst
punishment is being
ignored and banished
to a room on its own. If
your dog barks outside,
put it on the lead and
keep it to heel.*

with a traumatic event or with fear of the unknown. As the dog gets older, they become generalized.

What to do
It is important to notice any fear reactions in your young dog and try to allay the fear before phobias develop.

Use the desensitization technique if possible. If your dog panics on firework night, put it in a quiet, dark room and ask your vet to prescribe a sedative the next time there are fireworks.

Mounting
This is an annoying problem and can be embarassing. It is most often seen in small, young dogs such as poodles and terriers. The behaviour is usually directed at people, often children, although some dogs often choose objects such as cushions. The development of this behaviour is abnormal, since most dogs have a low sex drive. If the problem does occur, it is usually at puberty.

What to do
The solution is firm physical rejection and a sharp "NO". If the dog persists, reject and ignore it for a while. Keep your dog away from bitches on heat.

Don't rush into having your dog castrated. Mounting behaviour will often stop once the dog is mature and your vet may help with temporary hormone medication.

Urination problems
A dog may get carried away with the business of scent-marking and masking other smells (see p.215) and begin urinating in the house to cover scents like perfume or tobacco.

The urine of a bitch on heat contains strong odours, particularly pheromones, which excite the male and indicate her availability. Unfortunately, certain perfumes and aftershaves designed for humans also contain pheromones and these may lead to further problems in the dog, causing inappropriate urination in the house.

What to do
Removal of the cause (the scent which triggers the problem) is the first step. Ignore the dog if it continues urinating in the house; reward it if it behaves well. If necessary, use a reprimand. Failure to solve the problem may necessitate going back to the early stages of house-training (see p.153).

The problem puppy

Most puppies are playful and mischievous – they love exploring, chewing things and generally being a "handful". A certain amount of this behaviour is normal, but in some puppies behavioural disorders can be discerned. If you're experiencing these problems, try to decide exactly what's causing them – generally, the answer is *not* a rebuke or a punishment.

Problem behaviour in the first six months of a puppy's life is usually related to four major areas:
- Urination and defecation
- Separation-induced behaviour
- Teething behaviour and destructive chewing
- Aggression

Problems of submissive urination

The sign of this problem is your puppy squatting and urinating each time you approach it. Don't confuse this with a house-training problem (see pp.150–1). Initial development of the behaviour is related to insecurity, so punishing the puppy is likely to aggravate the problem. Understandably, a tiny puppy is likely to be intimidated by the approach of a large human with outstretched arms, making strange noises.

What to do
Make initial approaches to the puppy carefully and keep your body outline small by stooping slightly as you get close to it. If the puppy is still apprehensive and urinates, make your approach more pleasurable, offering tit-bits and crouching down further.

The essence of controlling submissive urination is to ignore the problem. Don't point it out to the puppy, but try to get it used to whatever is triggering the reaction.

Problems of excitement urination

This problem – a puppy seeming to have no control over urination when excited – is caused by immature control mechanisms. Again, punishment isn't a good idea since it may lead to submissive urination or attempts to escape.

What to do
Once urinary control mechanisms in the puppy's body are mature, the problem will disappear, so the best approach is to ignore it. Try to encourage play in places where urination *is* acceptable and discourage it where it is not.

Problems of separation

Problem behaviour may be caused by separation from the bitch or from the original owner. It first occurs when the puppy is collected from the breeder and taken to its new home (see pp.140–1). The major problem is likely to occur at bedtime and usually manifests itself in:
- Howling and yapping
- Destructive activities
- Urination and defecation

Don't interpret these signs as simply due to teething or a breakdown in your house-training. Great care is needed in dealing with this problem. Often, returning to see a crying puppy in its bed triggers hyperactive, excessive excitement. Many owners find this show of affection gratifying – they reward and pet the puppy. This can lead to reinforcement of the behaviour or excitement urination (see above).

What to do
The answer is *not* confinement in a smaller bed area; this is more likely to cause psychosomatic diarrhoea or hyperactivity when the puppy is released. Even punishment is not

effective – it can trigger attempts to escape or increase the degree of attachment.

The best approach seems to be patient management of the puppy and careful attention to the timing of its feeding, play and rest. Aim to organize the puppy's routine so that you confine it to its pen/bed area at its natural time to sleep – after feeding/defecation and a period of activity. When you leave the puppy alone, it should be ready to fall asleep and will soon come to link being "put to bed" with separation from the family.

Try to limit the puppy's range so that you keep it interested in one area (such as the kitchen), in which its bed is contained. If the kitchen is seen as the "home territory" where it feels comfortable, going to bed will be reassuring and pleasurable.

Problems of chewing and biting
Puppies often chew to alleviate the discomfort of teething, but it can be very annoying.
What to do
Try to re-direct the play activity to toys, particularly the chewy type which squeak (see p.148). Tug-of-war toys are great fun for a puppy. Some people misguidedly think that they cause aggression, but the growling that accompanies them is just play-growling (see p.217).

Problems of aggression
The most common type of aggression shown in puppies is possessive aggression while they are feeding. Don't tolerate this – it is linked to the potentially dangerous dominant aggression in adult dogs.
What to do
This is one of the few circumstances where punishment works. Carry out a training exercise, repeatedly offering the puppy food. Interrupt it and take the food away if it misbehaves, but reward good behaviour. This scheme usually produces a fairly rapid response and once your dominance is established, it probably won't be challenged.

However, when punished, some bold puppies escalate the degree of aggression to unacceptable levels. If your puppy does this, consult the vet and seriously consider the advisability of keeping the puppy – it may grow into an uncontrolled dog.

Preventing puppies chewing
Many puppies enjoy mouthing and biting people's feet or hands, and like babies, will chew during teething. If you respond by pushing the puppy away, it will probably misinterpret your behaviour as part of a playful game. However, punishing the puppy may provoke attempts to escape or defensive aggression. For a solution to the problem, see above.

12

HEALTH CARE

Every dog owner wants a healthy pet, but problems –
major or minor – are bound to arise from time to time.
It is important to understand the types of disorder
that can afflict your dog and how to observe the signs
of illness so that you can give an accurate description
to your vet. Basic signs of illness are dealt with in the
Diagnosis charts on pp.231–6. Use these to gain an
idea of what is wrong, how serious it is and what
action to take. Your dog relies on you for its health
and well-being. Make sure it has the appropriate
vaccinations to protect it against infectious diseases.
If you're in any doubt about its condition, contact the
vet. Once the vet has diagnosed the ailment and
treated your dog, it may need nursing at home.
Elderly dogs are prone to particular problems and
careful attention to these can make their remaining
years more comfortable. The techniques of first aid for
dogs are given in *First Aid* (see pp. 276–83).

How to use this chapter

The chapter begins with information that helps you to decide whether your dog is ill, including instructions on taking the temperature and pulse, and signs of ill-health. This is followed by the *Ailments* section, which is divided into areas of the body and systems within it. Finally, a section on care and nursing provides information on taking a sick dog to the vet, caring for an ill or elderly dog, and keeping your dog healthy.

Is my dog ill?

Dogs can't describe how they're feeling or what their symptoms are. As a dog owner, you're restricted to the clues that you can actually see – the *signs* of illness. So in this chapter, emphasis is placed on the "signs" of various problems and diseases, rather than their "symptoms".

Is my dog healthy?

There are a number of points on your dog that you should check regularly. A healthy dog has an upright stance and posture – it is alert, looking around and interested in its environment and in what is happening around it. The dog holds its head high and its ears follow sounds – you can sometimes see the ear flaps twitching. A healthy dog's nose is usually moist and there should be no discharges from its eyes or nose. The skin should look pink and healthy; the shine and depth of colour in the coat should be such that it just asks to be stroked. A healthy dog moves easily with no effort or lameness, and isn't overweight – there should be a little fat over the ribs so they don't "glare", but they should still be felt without difficulty.

AILMENTS SECTION

"See also" boxes
These reference boxes lead you to relevant information in other sections of the book.

Quick-reference boxes These help you to make decisions when you spot signs of illness.

Urgency advice
Crosses indicate how quickly you should contact a vet.

Special breed problems boxes If particular breeds are susceptible to certain problems, these are listed so you can watch out for them.

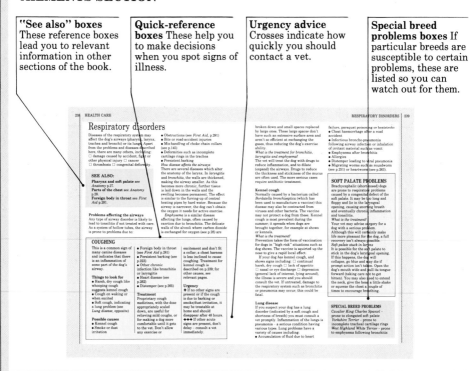

SIGNS OF ILLNESS

The first signs of ill-health you'll notice in your dog usually involve behaviour: it becomes duller, more introverted and less active. Also, its appetite is often affected and may decrease or increase.

Warning – acute signs: If your dog displays any of the following signs, consult a vet immediately: □ collapse □ vomiting repeatedly for more than 24 hours □ diarrhoea for longer than 24 hours □ troubled breathing □ bleeding from an orifice □ obvious pain.

The major signs of illness
□ Looking off-colour □ Vomiting □ Diarrhoea □ Troubled breathing □ Bleeding □ Scratching (see pp.231–6).

Other common signs of illness
On close examination, you may be able to detect other signs. If in doubt, watch out for the following:
Respiratory signs □ Coughing (see p.238)
Ear signs □ Painful ears (see p.253) □ Swollen ear flap (see p.252) □ Discharge (see p.252) □ Poor hearing (see p.253)
Eye signs □ Discharge (see p.255) □ Swollen eye (see p. 255)
Body signs □ Limping (see p.266)
Skin signs □ Scratching (see p. 269) □ Reddened skin (see p.269) □ Hair loss (see p.269)
Bowel/urinary signs □ Constipation (see p.248) □ Incontinence (see p.259).

DIAGNOSIS CHARTS

Back-up information
Following the quick-reference boxes, you'll find more detailed information on specific problems.

Prevention boxes
Where relevant, preventative measures are given.

Answer the questions and follow the arrows to an endpoint that suggests a likely veterinary diagnosis.

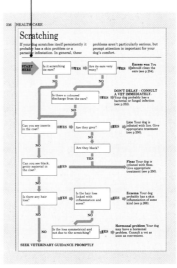

TAKING YOUR DOG'S TEMPERATURE

Don't rely on a dog's nose as a guide to its temperature or state of health. If you're unsure whether your dog is ill, taking its temperature is a useful guide as to whether or not you should contact the vet. The normal temperature is 38–9°C. Unless the dog is in a state of nervous excitement, which may push the temperature up very slightly, anything above this is abnormal and grounds for contacting your vet. Use a stubby-bulb thermometer (which doesn't break so easily as the more slender type).

1 Shake down the mercury in the thermometer to around 36°C.
2 Ask a helper to restrain the dog.
3 Lubricate the thermometer with a little petroleum jelly, or olive oil.
4 With one hand, raise the dog's tail slightly and move it to one side. Insert the thermometer about 2.5 cm into the rectum and hold it still, angled so that the bulb is against the rectal wall.
5 Wait 30 seconds, remove the thermometer and read it.
6 Shake it down, clean and disinfect it before replacing it in its case.

Inserting the thermometer
It is important to angle the thermometer correctly or you may damage the dog's rectum.

TAKING YOUR DOG'S PULSE

Measuring a dog's pulse gives you a direct count of the heart rate. The technique involves placing the ball of one or two fingers over an artery. The best place is the femoral artery on the inside of the thigh. In the centre of the upper thigh is a depression where the pulse can be felt as the femoral artery traverses the femur. However, with some dogs it is easier to feel the pulse over the heart area – low on the left-hand side of the chest (just behind the point of the elbow of a standing dog).

Use a watch with a second hand and count the number of beats in 30 seconds or one minute. Don't count for less time – multiplying to get the rate per minute may produce errors.

The pulse rate of small dogs is 90–120 beats per minute; large dogs have a slower rate of 65–90 beats.

Respiratory rate
When relaxed, your dog's normal rate of breathing should be around 10–30 breaths per minute (higher in small dogs than large dogs). Always be aware of your dog's breathing – it should be easy and smooth.

Finding a pulse
Try practising this when your dog is healthy, so that you know where to locate its pulse.

Looking off-colour

Your dog may show all the physical signs of health (see p.228) and yet not be itself. It may be off its food or show one or more of the signs below. If you're in any doubt about its health, telephone your vet or visit the surgery.

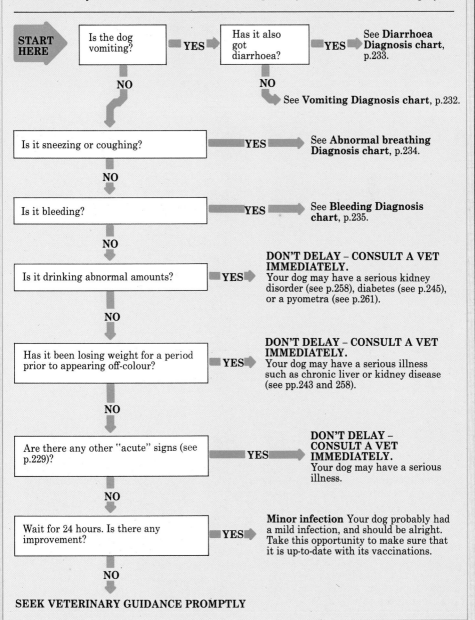

START HERE → Is the dog vomiting? — **YES** → Has it also got diarrhoea? — **YES** → See **Diarrhoea Diagnosis chart**, p.233.

NO (vomiting) ↓ / NO (diarrhoea) → See **Vomiting Diagnosis chart**, p.232.

Is it sneezing or coughing? — **YES** → See **Abnormal breathing Diagnosis chart**, p.234.

NO ↓

Is it bleeding? — **YES** → See **Bleeding Diagnosis chart**, p.235.

NO ↓

Is it drinking abnormal amounts? — **YES** → **DON'T DELAY – CONSULT A VET IMMEDIATELY.** Your dog may have a serious kidney disorder (see p.258), diabetes (see p.245), or a pyometra (see p.261).

NO ↓

Has it been losing weight for a period prior to appearing off-colour? — **YES** → **DON'T DELAY – CONSULT A VET IMMEDIATELY.** Your dog may have a serious illness such as chronic liver or kidney disease (see pp.243 and 258).

NO ↓

Are there any other "acute" signs (see p.229)? — **YES** → **DON'T DELAY – CONSULT A VET IMMEDIATELY.** Your dog may have a serious illness.

NO ↓

Wait for 24 hours. Is there any improvement? — **YES** → **Minor infection** Your dog probably had a mild infection, and should be alright. Take this opportunity to make sure that it is up-to-date with its vaccinations.

NO ↓

SEEK VETERINARY GUIDANCE PROMPTLY

Vomiting

There are many causes of vomiting in dogs, ranging from the mild to the very serious. If you're in *any* doubt about your dog's health you should telephone your vet or visit the veterinary surgery immediately.

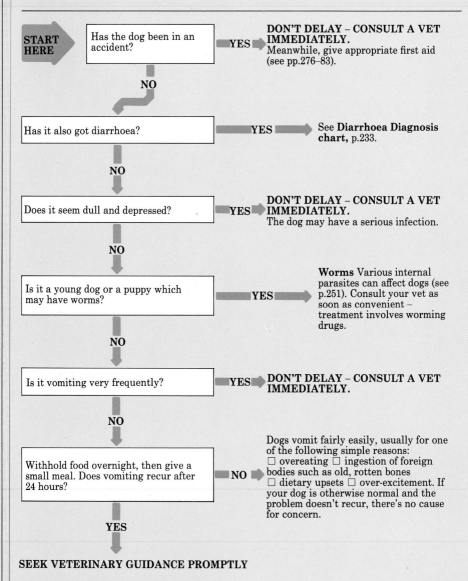

START HERE

Has the dog been in an accident?

YES → **DON'T DELAY – CONSULT A VET IMMEDIATELY.**
Meanwhile, give appropriate first aid (see pp.276–83).

NO

Has it also got diarrhoea?

YES → See **Diarrhoea Diagnosis chart, p.233.**

NO

Does it seem dull and depressed?

YES → **DON'T DELAY – CONSULT A VET IMMEDIATELY.**
The dog may have a serious infection.

NO

Is it a young dog or a puppy which may have worms?

YES → **Worms** Various internal parasites can affect dogs (see p.251). Consult your vet as soon as convenient – treatment involves worming drugs.

NO

Is it vomiting very frequently?

YES → **DON'T DELAY – CONSULT A VET IMMEDIATELY.**

NO

Withhold food overnight, then give a small meal. Does vomiting recur after 24 hours?

NO → Dogs vomit fairly easily, usually for one of the following simple reasons:
☐ overeating ☐ ingestion of foreign bodies such as old, rotten bones ☐ dietary upsets ☐ over-excitement. If your dog is otherwise normal and the problem doesn't recur, there's no cause for concern.

YES

SEEK VETERINARY GUIDANCE PROMPTLY

Diarrhoea

If your dog passes frequent liquid or semi-liquid motions it may be unwell. The cause is probably a minor infection but there's a possibility that it has something more serious. If you're in any doubt about your dog's health, you should telephone the vet or visit your veterinary surgery immediately.

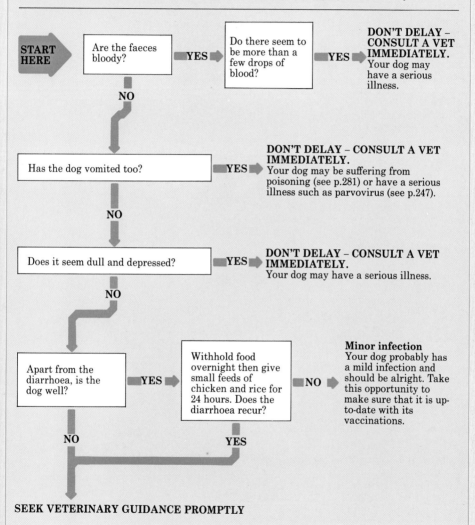

Abnormal breathing

A healthy dog's breathing is quiet and even, and consists of 10–30 breaths per minute. If your dog's breathing doesn't seem normal it may have a health problem or merely be resting or affected by hot weather or exertion.

START HERE

Is the dog's breathing slow and heavy, and fails to improve if disturbed? → **YES** → **DON'T DELAY – CONSULT A VET IMMEDIATELY.** Your dog may be suffering from poisoning (see p.281) or have a serious illness such as pneumonia.

NO

Is its breathing slow but improves when it is disturbed? → **YES** → **Resting** When resting, dogs slow down their bodily functions to a basic maintenance level. If your dog breathes normally when not resting, there is no cause for concern.

NO

Is it breathing heavily after recent exertion, or is the weather hot? → **YES** → **Over-heating** Dogs pant in order to cool down. If your dog seems otherwise normal, there's no cause for concern.

NO

Is it an older dog which tires easily and coughs when it wakes up? → **YES** → **Heart murmur** Consult a vet as soon as convenient. Your dog may have a heart murmur (see p.262) or other chronic chest problem.

NO

Is its breathing heavy, and are there other "acute" signs (see p.229)? → **YES** → **DON'T DELAY – CONSULT A VET IMMEDIATELY.** Your dog may have a serious illness.

NO

Is it breathing rapidly and has it a nasal and/or eye discharge? → **YES** → **DON'T DELAY – CONSULT A VET IMMEDIATELY.** Your dog may have distemper (see p.265).

NO

Is it breathing rapidly, but otherwise normal? → **YES** → Does it breathe normally if left alone? → **YES** → **Over-excitement** Your dog may have seen a member of the opposite sex! If it is otherwise normal, there's no cause for concern.

NO

SEEK VETERINARY GUIDANCE PROMPTLY

Bleeding

If your dog is bleeding you must investigate the source and take immediate action as it may need urgent veterinary attention. Advice on applying bandages is given in the *First Aid* chapter (see pp.282–3).

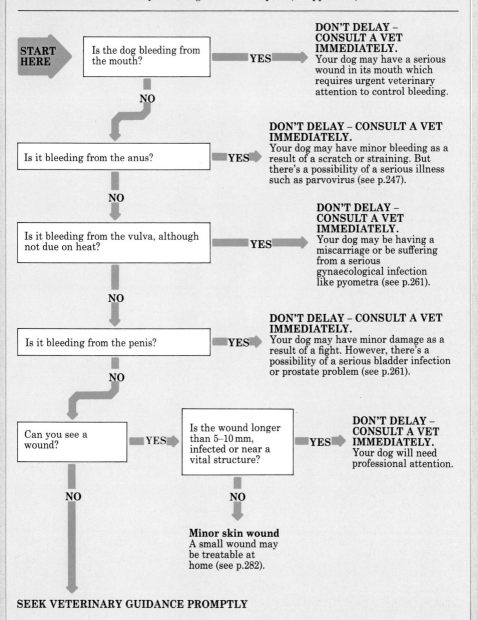

START HERE

Is the dog bleeding from the mouth? **YES**

DON'T DELAY – CONSULT A VET IMMEDIATELY. Your dog may have a serious wound in its mouth which requires urgent veterinary attention to control bleeding.

NO

Is it bleeding from the anus? **YES**

DON'T DELAY – CONSULT A VET IMMEDIATELY. Your dog may have minor bleeding as a result of a scratch or straining. But there's a possibility of a serious illness such as parvovirus (see p.247).

NO

Is it bleeding from the vulva, although not due on heat? **YES**

DON'T DELAY – CONSULT A VET IMMEDIATELY. Your dog may be having a miscarriage or be suffering from a serious gynaecological infection like pyometra (see p.261).

NO

Is it bleeding from the penis? **YES**

DON'T DELAY – CONSULT A VET IMMEDIATELY. Your dog may have minor damage as a result of a fight. However, there's a possibility of a serious bladder infection or prostate problem (see p.261).

NO

Can you see a wound? **YES**

Is the wound longer than 5–10 mm, infected or near a vital structure? **YES**

DON'T DELAY – CONSULT A VET IMMEDIATELY. Your dog will need professional attention.

NO

NO

Minor skin wound A small wound may be treatable at home (see p.282).

SEEK VETERINARY GUIDANCE PROMPTLY

Scratching

If your dog scratches itself persistently it probably has a skin problem or a parasitic infestation. In general, these problems aren't particularly serious, but prompt attention is important for your dog's comfort.

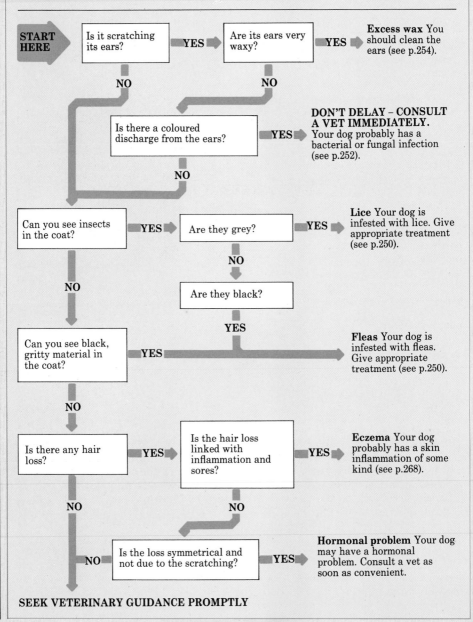

START HERE

Is it scratching its ears? — **YES** → Are its ears very waxy? — **YES** → **Excess wax** You should clean the ears (see p.254).

NO ↓ **NO** ↓

Is there a coloured discharge from the ears? — **YES** → **DON'T DELAY – CONSULT A VET IMMEDIATELY.** Your dog probably has a bacterial or fungal infection (see p.252).

NO ↓

Can you see insects in the coat? — **YES** → Are they grey? — **YES** → **Lice** Your dog is infested with lice. Give appropriate treatment (see p.250).

NO ↓ **NO** ↓

Are they black?

YES ↓

Can you see black, gritty material in the coat? — **YES** → **Fleas** Your dog is infested with fleas. Give appropriate treatment (see p.250).

NO ↓

Is there any hair loss? — **YES** → Is the hair loss linked with inflammation and sores? — **YES** → **Eczema** Your dog probably has a skin inflammation of some kind (see p.268).

NO ↓ **NO** ↓

Is the loss symmetrical and not due to the scratching? — **YES** → **Hormonal problem** Your dog may have a hormonal problem. Consult a vet as soon as convenient.

NO ←

SEEK VETERINARY GUIDANCE PROMPTLY

AILMENTS

This section is divided into different areas and systems of the body. Where practical, quick-reference boxes give basic guidance to help you make decisions when you spot signs of illness in your dog. Crosses are used to denote the likely degree of urgency with which you should seek expert attention (this ranges from one cross for "may be treatable at home" to three crosses for "don't delay – consult a vet immediately"). Following the quick-reference boxes, detailed descriptions of common problems, diseases and treatments are given. Where applicable, preventative measures such as vaccinations and special diets are also included.

This guide isn't meant to be a substitute for professional veterinary care. Diagnosis depends on the particular circumstances of the individual dog and can only be made by a qualified veterinary surgeon. The aim of this chapter is to inform you of the degree of urgency and help you understand what is wrong with your dog once a diagnosis has been made. The information included represents an understanding of veterinary knowledge at the date of publication.

The vet's examination
Whenever you take your dog to the surgery, the vet will give it a thorough examination to check for signs of ill health or injury.

MAJOR INFECTIOUS DISEASES

There are four major infectious diseases of dogs, each discussed in this chapter under the system they primarily affect. They are:

Canine distemper, sometimes called "hardpad" which may ultimately affect the nervous system (see p.265)

Infectious canine hepatitis, sometimes called "Rubarth's disease" which affects the liver (see p.244)

Parvovirus which affects the intestines and bowel (see p.247)

Leptospirosis which affects the liver or kidney (see pp.244 and 259).

Apart from leptospirosis, these serious diseases are caused by viruses and so have no specific treatment as there might be for a bacterial disease. If your dog should contract any of these diseases, its body must fight the illness itself while you and your vet help with symptomatic treatment. The aim of vaccination is to *prevent* the dog catching the disease at all. In the rare cases where a dog can't resist the disease completely, prior vaccination usually reduces its severity.

All puppies should be vaccinated against the four major infectious diseases (see *Puppy-care*, p.136). In addition, your dog should be protected by annual vaccination boosters. Keep in touch with your vet, and be guided by him or her.

Respiratory disorders

Diseases of the respiratory system may affect the dog's airways (pharynx, larynx, trachea and bronchi) or its lungs. Apart from the problems and diseases described here, there are many others, including: □ damage caused by accident, fight or other physical injury □ cancer □ thrombosis □ congenital deformity.

SEE ALSO:

Pharynx and soft palate see *Anatomy* p.27.
Parts of the chest see *Anatomy* p.28.
Foreign body in throat see *First Aid* p.281.

Problems affecting the airways

Any type of airway disorder is likely to lead to tonsilitis if not treated with care. As a system of hollow tubes, the airway is prone to problems due to:

● Obstructions (see *First Aid*, p.281)
● Bite or road-accident injuries
● Mis-handling of choke chain collars (see p.145)
● Deformities such as incomplete cartilage rings in the trachea
● Persistent barking

How disease affects the airways

There are several diseases which alter the anatomy of the larynx. In *laryngitis* and *bronchitis*, the walls are thickened, making the airway smaller. As this becomes more chronic, further tissue is laid down in the walls and the swelling becomes permanent. The effect is similar to the furring-up of central heating pipes by hard water. Because the airway is narrower, the dog can't obtain the oxygen it needs for active exercise.

Emphysema is a similar disease affecting the lungs, often caused by exertion due to bronchitis. The delicate walls of the alveoli where carbon dioxide is exchanged for oxygen (see p.28) are

---

COUGHING

This is a common sign of many canine diseases and indicates that there is an inflammation of some part of the dog's airway.

Things to look for
● Harsh, dry cough like whooping cough suggests kennel cough
● Cough on waking or when excited
● Soft cough, indicating a lung problem (see *Lung disease*, opposite)

Possible causes
● Kennel cough
● Smoke or dust irritation

● Foreign body in throat (see *First Aid* p.281)
● Persistent barking (see p.223)
● Other chronic infection like bronchitis or laryngitis
● Heart disease (see p.262)
● Distemper (see p.265)

Treatment
Proprietary cough medicines, with the dose appropriately scaled down, are useful for relieving mild coughs, or for making a dog more comfortable until it gets to the vet. Don't allow any exercise or

excitement and don't fit a collar; a chest harness is less inclined to cause coughing. Treatment for kennel cough is described on p.239; for other causes, see relevant pages.

Urgency
✚ If no other signs are present or if the cough is due to barking or smoke/dust irritation, it may be treatable at home and should disappear after 48 hours.
✚✚✚ If other acute signs are present, don't delay – consult a vet immediately.

broken down and small spaces replaced by large ones. These large spaces don't have such an extensive surface area and aren't so efficient at exchanging the gases, thus reducing the dog's exercise ability.
What is the treatment for bronchitis, laryngitis and emphysema?
The vet will treat the dog with drugs to reduce inflammation, and to dilate (expand) the airways. Drugs to reduce the thickness and stickiness of the mucus are often used. The more serious cases require antibiotic treatment.

Kennel cough
Normally caused by a bacterium called *Bordatella bronchiseptica* (which has been used to manufacture a vaccine) this disease may also be contracted from viruses and other bacteria. The vaccine may not protect a dog from these. Kennel cough is most prevalent during the summer; it spreads when dogs are brought together, for example at shows or kennels.
What is the treatment?
Prevention takes the form of vaccination for dogs in "high risk" situations such as dog shows. The vaccine is squirted up the nose to give a rapid local effect.

If your dog *has* kennel cough, and shows signs including: □ continual harsh, dry cough □ lack of appetite □ nasal or eye discharge □ depression (general lack of interest, lying around), the illness is severe and you should consult the vet. If untreated, damage to the respiratory system such as bronchitis or pneumonia may occur; this could be fatal.

Lung disease
If you suspect your dog has a lung disorder (indicated by a soft cough and shortness of breath) you must consult a vet promptly. Inflammation of the lungs is pneumonia – a serious condition having various types. Lung problems have a variety of causes including:
● Accumulation of fluid due to heart

failure, paraquat poisoning or heatstroke
● Chest haemorrhage after a road accident
● Infectious broncho-pneumonia following airway infection or inhalation of irritant material such as vomit
● Emphysema after bronchitis
● Allergies
● Distemper leading to viral pneumonia
● Migrating worms such as roundworm (see p.251) or heartworm (see p.263).

SOFT PALATE PROBLEMS
Brachycephalic (short-nosed) dogs are prone to respiratory problems caused by a congenital defect of the soft palate. It may be too long and floppy and lie in the laryngeal opening, causing snorting breath and eventually chronic inflammation and tonsilitis.
What is the treatment?
Your vet may advise surgery for a dog with a serious problem. Although this will certainly make life more pleasant for the dog, a full recovery isn't always possible.
Soft palate stuck in larynx
It is possible for the soft palate to stick in the dog's laryngeal opening. If this happens, the dog will collapse, go blue and may die if prompt action isn't taken. Open the dog's mouth wide and pull its tongue forward (taking care not to get bitten). You may also need to extend the neck, give the head a little shake or squeeze the chest a couple of times to encourage breathing.

SPECIAL BREED PROBLEMS
Cavalier King Charles Spaniel – prone to elongated soft palate
Yorkshire Terrier – prone to incomplete tracheal cartilage rings
West Highland White Terrier – prone to emphysema following bronchitis

Disorders of the upper digestive tract

The digestive system has a number of clearly defined sections. The mouth, oesophagus, stomach, liver, spleen and pancreas consitute the upper digestive tract, while the small and large intestines (gut), rectum and anus belong to the lower digestive tract. These all have their own special problems and are best considered separately.

> **SEE ALSO:**
>
> **Structure of the digestive system** see *Anatomy* p.30.
> **Lower digestive tract disorders** see *Health Care* p.246.
> **Treatment of vomiting and diarrhoea** see *Health Care* p.247.

Vomiting

One of the surest indications of digestive disorders is vomiting. All vomiting dogs should be assumed to have some form of inflammation in the system. (For treatment of vomiting, see p.247.)

Frequent vomiting is often a sign of *toxaemia* (poisoning by bacteria living in an affected part of the body) and may also be due to:
● Pyometra (see p.261)
● Liver or kidney failure (see pp.243 and 258)
● Foreign body blocking any part of the digestive tract.

Any problems involving frequent regurgitation of food should be investigated by a vet, since nasal damage can occur and food inhalation may cause lung damage. A vet will usually X-ray a dog with this type of problem for diagnosis prior to dealing with it surgically.

Problems of the stomach

Stomach or gastric disorders may be either acute (sudden, serious illness) or chronic (long-term, milder problem). Signs of colic (stomach pain) include:

□ whimpering □ hunched position □ tender abdomen when handled.
Acute disorders
Signs include: □ vomiting (often unproductive) □ dullness, with lack of appetite and colic □ thirst, but perhaps vomiting water □ vomiting soon after eating.
Chronic disorders
The major sign is intermittent vomiting at variable intervals after eating.
What is the treatment?
If you suspect a stomach disorder, consult your vet as soon as possible. Treatment requires accurate diagnosis; general treatment at home with kaolin preparations will alleviate vomiting prior to your dog seeing the vet.

Gastritis

Simple acute gastritis is a common problem in dogs. It can be thought of as a defence reaction which protects a dog from some of its own baser eating habits. Dogs are attracted to rank-smelling food, bones and poisons. Vomiting this material often avoids serious consequences, but don't bank on this if you see your dog eating something it shouldn't – contact a vet.

The major sign of gastritis is vomiting; if untreated, the dog may suffer from diarrhoea as well. Possible causes include:
● Swallowing poisons (see *First Aid* p.281)
● Ascarid worms (such as roundworm) living in the gut may move up into the stomach. If your dog vomits worms, this means others are present – so give it worming treatment (see p.250).
● Over-eating in puppies may trigger the vomiting reflex.
● Several specific infections cause gastritis, plus enteritis and other symptoms. These include distemper (see p.265), hepatitis (see p.244), parvovirus (see p.247) and leptospirosis (see pp.244 and 259).

Gastric dilation or torsion

In gastric dilation, the stomach becomes inflated with gas. This is a veterinary emergency and may affect any breed. Gastric torsion occurs in deep-chested breeds when the stomach twists, trapping gas inside.

The cause of these problems is uncertain. It is possible that the "wrong" bacteria in the gut cause fermentation and inflation. Some greedy dogs swallow air with their food, and this, coupled with vigorous exercise after feeding, is thought to make stomach torsion more likely. Both these conditions make the stomach taut like a drum. The dog can't settle and is in great pain.

What is the treatment?
Unless treated quickly, the dog may die. The vet can often deflate a stomach dilation by inserting a tube into the dog's stomach, but the vast majority of gastric torsions require emergency surgery.

As a preventative measure, feed deep-chested dogs from a raised bowl and don't exercise them for at least one hour after feeding.

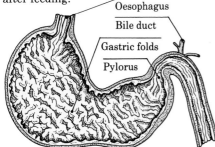

Oesophagus
Bile duct
Gastric folds
Pylorus

Cross-section of the stomach

The oesophagus

The most common oesophageal problems in dogs are associated with malformations of the oesophagus or related structures in the chest.

Vascular ring
Certain congenital disorders of the vessels of the heart can result in a "vascular ring" formed of blood vessels which encloses the oesophagus, preventing the dog from swallowing solids. Most congenital disorders produce the same signs which are:
□ regurgitation soon after eating
□ excessive salivation (drooling) due to failure to swallow □ coughing □ nasal discharge due to food going up the nose.

Obstruction in the oesophagus
A bone can lodge in the chest at the point where the oesophagus passes across the base of the heart or passes from the chest into the abdomen. Foreign bodies lodged at these points may need very delicate surgery to remove them through the chest. Sometimes a vet may be able to remove them with long forceps via incisions in the neck and stomach.

Problems of the pylorus

The pylorus (exit from the stomach) is another site where swallowed objects may stick. In addition, there exists a condition called *pyloric stenosis* where the sphincter, a valve which controls the flow from the stomach, is too powerful and prevents any solids leaving the stomach. This is most often seen in puppies being weaned and given their first solids, although it can also develop as a chronic problem in growing dogs.

The major sign is vomiting of solids; milky foods and fluids normally pass through. The only treatment for these conditions is surgery.

SPECIAL BREED PROBLEMS

Setters and Spaniels – prone to disorders of the pharynx muscles at the entrance to the oesophagus. These may fail to "grab" swallowed food
Scottish and West Highland White Terriers – prone to obstruction of the oesophagus with bones
Boxer – prone to gastric torsion, young dogs are particularly prone to pyloric stenosis
German Shepherd, Irish Setter, Weimaraner – prone to gastric torsion

Disorders of the mouth and teeth

The most common problems occurring inside a dog's mouth are due to new teeth not coming through and the accumulation of tartar. Luckily, dogs aren't especially prone to tooth decay. Affected teeth are usually molars (in old dogs) or ones cracked or damaged due to chewing bones or stones.

Signs of problems include:
☐ temporary teeth not falling out
☐ worn, loose or broken teeth ☐ excess tartar ☐ halitosis (bad breath) ☐ pain on eating ☐ excess salivation ☐ gingivitis.

All these disorders need your vet's attention. Temporary teeth which show no signs of falling out should be removed. Broken or worn teeth can be capped or may need removing. Accumulated tartar should be removed by your vet or it will cause gingivitis (see below.) Loose teeth usually occur through neglect of accumulated tartar, causing gingivitis. If not extracted, they'll cause pain and more gingivitis.

SEE ALSO:

Teeth see *Anatomy* p.23.
The dog's mouth see *Anatomy* p.30.
Teething in puppies see *Puppy-care* pp.136–7.
Dental problems of elderly dogs see *Health Care* p.274.

Canine dentistry
The most common procedures are tooth removal or scaling (tartar removal). Some vets may carry out fillings and cappings, but often, a vet will ask a local dentist to help out.

Gingivitis
Red, inflamed gums usually result from accumulation of tartar causing them to recede and allowing bacteria to invade. In some cases, temporary teeth not falling out when they should cause the permanent teeth to be damaged.

Malar abscess
The signs of this problem are seen on the face. An abscess on the roots of the carnassial tooth causes pain and swelling in front of and below the eye. Consult a vet without delay. Treatment usually involves removal of the tooth and antibiotics to treat the swelling.

Swelling on the tongue
If the salivary ducts beneath the tongue become blocked, a large, fluid swelling appears under one side of the tongue. This is a *ranula* (Latin meaning "frog-belly") and should be drained by the vet. The cause of the blockage should also be removed – it may be a *calculus* (stone) or even a grass seed. Consult a vet as soon as convenient.

PREVENTING TOOTH DECAY

The soft foods we feed our dogs tend to encourage tartar on the teeth, since there is less need for the chewing that helps to remove tartar as it forms. However, rawhide chews, large bones, hard biscuits or suitable toys (see p.148) are all safe items you can give your dog to chew.

Humans rely on cleaning their teeth to prevent decay. If you begin early, you can accustom your dog to having its teeth cleaned, too. Use a new toothbrush (keep this solely for your dog), and brush the teeth exactly as you would your own. Don't use toothpaste – dogs hate the taste. It is easiest to place small dogs on a table. Ask someone to hold the dog's head; you may need to use a muzzle (see p.279). If tartar has already built up, have it removed by the vet.

Disorders of the liver and spleen

The dog's liver has several roles, the most important being ridding the body of poisonous substances. In doing this it often becomes damaged by these substances. The *spleen* is close to the stomach and its main function is storage and re-cycling of red blood cells.

The general term for liver disease is "hepatitis". This can be acute (sudden and serious) or chronic (long-term and milder). Various diseases can affect the dog's liver including the major infectious diseases *leptospirosis* and *canine viral hepatitis* (see p.244). Problems in other parts of the body may also affect the liver – tumours in other areas of the abdomen, heart disease (see p.262) and hormonal problems.

The signs of liver disease are often vague and variable. This is partly due to the liver's capacity and its ability to repair itself; chronic (long-term) liver disease is often accompanied by repair. More than 80 percent of the liver needs to be destroyed before it fails completely.

SEE ALSO:
Liver see *Anatomy* p.31.

Acute liver disease
The signs of this may vary greatly; it may be the culmination of a period of chronic disease. Possible signs include: □ abdominal pain, making the dog dull □ lack of appetite □ vomiting □ high temperature (almost always) □ jaundice (yellowness in gums and whites of eyes) □ haemorrhages in the gums □ pale faeces and dark urine.
What is the treatment?
If your dog shows a combination of these symptoms, don't delay – consult a vet immediately, even at night. The chances of recovery from acute liver disease are poor and delay reduces them still further. For diagnosis, the vet will need to take blood samples and possibly X-rays.

Treatment involves:
● Antibiotics to kill any bacterial infections
● Steroids to build up tissues
● Vitamins
● Intravenous fluids
● Strict dietary control.

Chronic liver disease
This is hard to define and diagnose. It may be the long-term sequel to attacks of acute liver disease, and can affect the brain. Possible signs include: □ weight loss, with or without a poor appetite □ bouts of dullness □ vomiting □ diarrhoea □ increased thirst □ dropsy (swelling of the belly) □ pale faeces □ apparent stupidity □ fits □ pressing the head on the wall or floor.
What is the treatment?
The long-term outlook is very poor; follow your vet's advice. Treatment is aimed at making the dog's life more comfortable. Its diet must be strictly controlled – if its brain isn't affected the dog should have high carbohydrate and low fat levels, combined with good-quality, highly digestible protein like eggs, cheese and meat. But if the brain *is* affected, a low-protein diet is called for. The dog needs steroids, possibly cortisone and vitamin supplements – B complex and Vitamin K.

Spleen tumour
Although tumours of the spleen are quite common, many are benign and cause no problems. If tumours spontaneously haemorrhage into the abdomen, filling it with blood, the dog may die within half an hour from an internal haemorrhage. But minor bleeding may cause nothing more than slight weakness.

The signs of spleen tumours are: □ abdominal swelling □ sudden weakness □ pale gums. Fortunately, if detected early enough, the spleen can be removed, other organs taking over its duties, and the dog can live a normal life.

Infectious canine hepatitis

Also known as Rubarth's disease, this highly contagious disease is caused by a virus. The main sufferers are young dogs, under one year of age. For this reason all young puppies should be vaccinated at around eight to ten weeks (see p.137). The incubation period for the disease is five to seven days.

What are the signs?

Initially, signs are vague. Dogs with only mild cases may simply go off their food and show a raised temperature for a few days. More severe cases become very dull, refuse to eat and are thirsty, but occasionally, a dog will die without warning. Common signs are: ☐ vomiting, with blood seen in the vomit in the later stages ☐ diarrhoea, which may also contain blood ☐ abdominal pain and restlessness ☐ excitability ☐ lack of coordination of the hind legs ☐ convulsions ☐ jaundice (occasionally) ☐ pale gums, with minute haemorrhages.

Other associated problems include kidney damage (this is the last part of the body to become clear of the virus). Recovered dogs shed live virus in their urine for months after infection, which makes them a serious risk to unvaccinated dogs. About 20 percent of dogs show some degree of "blue eye" (see p.256) after infection.

What is the treatment?

Veterinary treatment is essential – your vet may use steroids, antibiotics, transfusions, fluid therapy and kaolin-type preparations.

PREVENTING INFECTIOUS CANINE HEPATITIS

The only way of preventing infectious canine hepatitis is by vaccination. Once a dog has the disease, treatment is limited to relieving symptoms as they occur.

Two types of vaccine are available, living and dead. Live vaccines use a strain of the virus which has been modified so that it doesn't cause disease, and gives lifelong immunity.

However, dead vaccines are more commonly used because they don't produce the undesirable side-effects of some live vaccines (possible kidney damage and "blue eye" reactions).

Leptospirosis

Leptospira icterohaemorrhagiae is one of the two types of leptospirosis in dogs. The bacterium attacks the liver and is also the cause of Weil's disease in man (although dogs aren't thought to be a serious cause of infection). The second form affects the kidney (see p.259). Both are spread through infected urine and the incubation period is about one week. All puppies should be vaccinated.

The acute liver damage is often followed by death which can be rapid or take several days. Signs are: ☐ sudden dullness ☐ high temperature ☐ vomiting with thirst ☐ bloody diarrhoea ☐ jaundice (yellowness in gums and whites of eyes) ☐ small haemorrhages on the gums.

What is the treatment?

Consult a vet immediately. The bacteria do respond to antibiotics, so if treatment is prompt, there's a chance of recovery. Possible additional treatments include:

● Fluid therapy
● Drugs to stop vomiting
● Intestinal sedatives
● Blood transfusions

Observe normal hygiene precautions and wear rubber gloves when handling an affected dog.

SPECIAL BREED PROBLEMS

German Shepherd – prone to spleen tumour
Irish Setter – prone to hepatitis

Disorders of the pancreas

The pancreas performs two vital functions. It produces insulin which helps the body obtain energy from glucose. This is known as an *endocrine* process. The pancreas also produces digestive enzymes – an *exocrine* process. Both functions can be affected by disease. The most well-known exocrine disorder is E.P.I. and the most well-known endocrine disorder is diabetes.

Exocrine pancreatic insufficiency

Also known as E.P.I., this disorder means that the pancreas isn't fully formed. The exocrine section may be reduced or missing. This is usually a congenital problem, and may not become evident until later in a dog's life.

Dogs with this disorder can't digest food properly. They may try to eat their own faeces (because these still smell of food). Signs include: ☐ failure to put on weight ☐ bulky faeces (due to undigested food retaining water) ☐ pallor (due to undigested fat) ☐ dry, scurfy coat due to lack of oil.

What is the treatment?
Veterinary help is needed for a positive diagnosis by checking the enzyme levels in fresh faeces. Treatment requires permanent regular provision of enzymes (mainly trypsin) in tablet or powder form. (Unfortunately these are expensive in the long-term, and many dogs end up being euthanazed.) Special highly digestible oil supplements may be used; these include coconut and safflower oils (see p.168). In addition, vitamin supplements are required.

Diabetes mellitus

The more common of the two types of diabetes is *diabetes mellitus*. More common in bitches, this is caused by the pancreas not producing enough insulin.

Insulin acts on the cells of the body to help them take glucose out of the blood for energy. The different organs in the body of a diabetic dog find it hard to get enough glucose unless levels in the blood are very high. When this happens (particularly after meals), the glucose "spills over" through the kidney filtration system, drawing water with it. Signs include: ☐ heavy thirst ☐ hunger ☐ tiredness ☐ weight loss.

What is the treatment?
All suspect cases should be taken to the vet for blood and urine tests. In mild cases, treatment may be possible by control of the diet alone, reducing levels of carbohydrate and fat. High fibre is important in a diabetic diet to help the dog absorb glucose more evenly. Oral drugs can stimulate production of insulin by the pancreas.

However, most diabetic dogs need regular insulin injections, given at home. There are several different types and dose regimes. Your vet will choose the most appropriate for your dog. You'll be shown how to give the injections and how to use the special kits for monitoring glucose in urine. It is important to stick to the prescribed routine.

Hypoglycaemic coma
Your dog will remain stable under given circumstances but if a feed is missed, the injected insulin has no glucose to "work on" and could cause a hypoglycaemic (low-glucose) coma with collapse and convulsions (see *First Aid* p.280). Too much exercise or activity could produce the same result. Keep honey or glucose syrup to give orally for emergencies. If diabetes remains untreated, highly toxic chemicals called ketones may accumulate in the blood, with possibly fatal results.

SPECIAL BREED PROBLEMS

German Shepherd – prone to exocrine pancreatic insufficiency
Dachshund, King Charles Spaniel, poodles, Scottish Terrier – prone to diabetes

Disorders of the lower digestive tract

The lower section of the dog's digestive tract encompasses the gut (small and large intestines), duodenum, rectum and anus. The main signs of problems and diseases are: □ vomiting □ diarrhoea □ straining. Some dogs have problems establishing the correct bacteria in their gut. This is sometimes due to being prescribed antibiotics but may also occur for no apparent reason. Worms in the small intestine (see p.250) can also cause problems, including fits.

> **SEE ALSO:**
> **The digestive system** see *Anatomy* pp.30–1.
> **Disorders of the upper digestive tract** see *Health Care* pp.240–1.

Acute small-intestine problems
The two acute (sudden, serious) problems which occur most commonly in the small intestine are a lodged foreign body and a condition called intussusception. Both are serious emergencies, needing urgent surgery. If they occur, don't delay – consult a vet immediately.
Foreign body in small intestine
If a foreign body passes through the stomach (perhaps after sitting there for weeks causing a chronic gastritis (see p.240) and occasional vomiting) it may fail to pass through the narrow small intestine where it sticks tight. Signs include: □ acute vomiting □ dullness □ colic □ apparent constipation.
Intussusception
This condition can cause the same symptoms in young dogs as a foreign body. The small intestine turns in on itself and the peristalsis (see p.31) that moves food along drags a section of intestine inside the next section, producing a blockage. The trapped section of bowel often loses its blood supply and dies; it must be surgically corrected urgently.

Chronic small-intestine problems
Some of the chronic (long-term) disorders which fall into this category are difficult to diagnose and treat. Sometimes a partial obstruction may be caused by a swallowed piece of string or cloth. If these lodge, they can cause telescoping of sections of the bowel and ulceration, even peritonitis.
Signs include: □ occasional vomiting and/or diarrhoea □ persistent diarrhoea □ weight loss and variable appetite □ poor coat condition □ bouts of colic. Any condition causing blockage of the intestine requires surgical treatment.

Large-intestine problems
The large intestine (colon) is affected by similar diseases to those which attack the small intestine – tumours, leukaemia, foreign bodies, parasites, and inflammation of uncertain causes. The signs are: □ straining □ production of frequent small amounts of diarrhoea, often containing mucus and/or blood.
One group of large-intestine problems involves the build-up of food in the gut. This may be simple dietary constipation (see p.248) or may be associated with pain from one of the nearby organs, making defecation painful – anal sac problems (see p.248), prostatic disease (see p.261), fracture of the pelvis (see p.267) or arthritis (see p.266).
Occasionally the colon becomes weak and "balloons", encouraging accumulation of faeces. This condition is called "megacolon". It may be congenital, due to chronic colitis, or linked with the development of a perineal hernia, a section of the colon stretching the muscle in the pelvis and eventually producing a swelling on either or both sides of the anus.
What is the treatment?
Treatment of some of the non-specific colitis cases is often long-term and involves drugs. Specific treatment is also needed for infections.

VOMITING AND DIARRHOEA

Most causes of vomiting are linked with gastritis and most of diarrhoea with enteritis. If untreated, either is likely to lead to the other. If your dog is obviously ill or has a temperature more than 1°C above normal (38.5°C), consult a vet as soon as convenient.

Treatment for vomiting

In the absence of more serious signs (see p.229), starve the dog for 24 hours (puppies for 12 hours). Water should be continually available, but only in small amounts – 50–100 ml for small dogs, 200 ml for large dogs. If your dog drinks the whole ration, give the same amount in 30 minutes time, not immediately.

Provided the vomiting stops, give a small meal of light, easily digested food, such as scrambled egg. If the vomiting was frequent initially, it can help to mix a little brandy into this first meal – one teaspoon for a large dog, less for smaller breeds. If this is accepted with no further vomiting, give chicken, lean meat or white fish. Cook it and feed it moistened, mixed with boiled rice (see *Home cooking, meaty diet* p.169). Feed three small meals a day rather than one large one. The next day, introduce more normal food if all is well, but keep amounts small. It is best to take a day or two to get fully back to normal in terms of quantity. You should only feed about two-thirds of the normal amount for the first four days.

Treatment for diarrhoea

Follow the same routine as for vomiting, but omit the scrambled egg, going straight to small meals of chicken, white fish or lean meat as above. Keep the dog on this diet until the diarrhoea improves, then re-introduce the normal diet. If the diarrhoea recurs, start again, introducing one normal diet ingredient at a time (to see if any of them is causing the problem).

Giving drugs

Your vet won't prescribe antibiotics for simple cases of gastroenteritis. Aluminium hydroxide suspensions are good gastric sedatives for vomiting dogs – one teaspoon three times a day for small dogs, one dessertspoon four times a day for large ones. Kaolin and morphine or kaopectate can also be given to dogs suffering from vomiting or diarrhoea (doses as for aluminium hydroxide). Keep one of these handy.

Parvovirus

A relatively new disease, parvovirus has been prevalent only since 1978 when it swept simultaneously across Britain, North America and Australia. This major viral disease of dogs is similar to panleukopaenia in cats.

What are the signs?
In most cases, the major signs are: □ a severe enteritis with haemorrhagic diarrhoea □ acute vomiting, even of fluids □ severe depression □ high temperature. Unless treated promptly, the disease can be fatal. In the initial outbreak, death was common despite treatment and there is still a possibility that an affected dog may succumb.

What is the treatment?
Protection hinges on vaccination. This should be given to all puppies (see p.136) and should be followed up with routine annual boosters.

Treatment is symptomatic. This disease is often acute and dramatic therapy may be needed – fluid given via drips and blood transfusions plus antibiotic cover to avoid secondary infection. Contact your vet immediately you suspect it.

Constipation

One of the most common problems in elderly dogs and those that eat bones is constipation. If you notice it early, before your dog becomes dull and ill and loses its appetite through toxicity, constipation can often be treated at home. The early signs are: ☐ straining ☐ very hard faeces ☐ tail raised for defecation ☐ anus bulging. If your dog is completely unable to pass faeces, contact your vet.

What is the treatment?

If your dog *is* passing faeces, but with difficulty, help it by giving liquid paraffin (one tablespoon twice daily for a 10–15 kg dog, increasing up to two tablespoons twice daily for a dog 30 kg or more). This should lubricate the bowel and soften any blockage. If it doesn't sort out the problem within two days, or if your dog becomes ill, contact the vet.

If the problem recurs, contact the vet. Your dog may have a problem such as a rectal tumour or an enlarged prostate. Elderly dogs that are prone to constipation can be eased by giving bran in the diet – two teaspoons daily for 10–15 kg dogs, increasing to a handful for dogs of 30 kg and over.

RECTAL PROLAPSE

This is a veterinary emergency and occasionally occurs after very severe, untreated diarrhoea or with constipation or rectal tumours. The rectum pops out like an inside-out sleeve and you'll see a lump ranging from the size of a cherry to a bright red sausage hanging out of the dog's rectum. If you notice this, contact the vet immediately. Treatment involves pushing the rectum back through the central hole. If it is a small prolapse you may be able to treat it yourself before getting to the vet but if you can't see the central hole, don't waste time looking. Delay could result in major surgery to remove a section of the rectum.

Action

1 Get the dog to the surgery immediately.

2 Meanwhile, keep the lump moist with cotton wool soaked in warm water.

3 If it is a small prolapse you may be able to treat it yourself before getting to the vet (see above).

EMPTYING THE ANAL SACS

Occasionally, a dog's anal ducts become blocked and the anal sacs need emptying. They may be swollen and painful. You might notice your dog licking the area repeatedly or "scooting" along the ground. Always have the sacs emptied by a vet the first time. If you'd like to try doing it yourself the next time it happens, ask the vet to show you exactly how.

The anal sacs are positioned at 4 o'clock and 8 o'clock either side of the anus, with their ducts leading to the anal rim. The aim is to get your fingers partially behind them and squeeze out the contents. In some dogs, this is difficult or impossible without hurting them. Take these dogs to the vet who may perform the task "internally".

The most acceptable method for dog owners is the external method.

You'll need a helper to restrain the dog. Take the precaution of tying its nose, too (see p.279).

Hold a pad of cotton wool across the palm of one hand and raise the dog's tail with the other. Apply the pad to the rear of the dog. With the middle finger and thumb either side of the anus, squeeze inwards (towards the anus) and outwards so that the contents of the glands are forced out.

Nutritional disorders

Feeding your dog correctly is one of the most crucial aspects of keeping it healthy. Several important diseases are probably due in part to improper nutrition, including hip dysplasia (see p.267). The wrong diet may result in:
● Underfeeding, resulting in lack of energy, loss of weight and starvation.
● Overfeeding, resulting in excess energy, weight gain, and obesity.
● Deficiency diseases, caused by a lack of specific components in the diet.
● Toxicity, caused by an excess of a particular ingredient, such as a vitamin or a mineral.

> **SEE ALSO:**
> **Dietary needs** see *Feeding* pp.162–3.
> **Nutritional requirements** see *Feeding* p.164.
> **Bone growth** see *Anatomy* p.19.

Nutritional bone diseases
Rickets is caused by a deficiency of Vitamin D. The dog can't use calcium properly and its bones become weak and bend, whilst the joints enlarge. It is seen in dogs that grow rapidly, but receive no supplementation in their diet.
Osteoporosis is caused by a diet low in calcium or high in phosphorus (such as an all-meat diet). The bones appear normal but are weak and break easily.

The calcium/phosphorus ratio is very important in any dog's diet (see p.163). *Hypertrophic osteodystrophy* (bone scurvy) is a strange disease, seen particularly in giant breeds. Bone scurvy causes pain and swelling around the growth plates of long bones. It is thought this may be caused by lack of Vitamin C, due to rapid growth and over-supplementation with Vitamin D.

A proper diet should prevent these diseases occurring, but seek veterinary advice if you suspect any of the conditions in your dog. Veterinary treatment may involve giving vitamins intravenously and special diets.

Obesity
The normal distribution of fat on a dog's body includes a thin layer under the skin, other layers between the muscles of the abdominal wall, and some deposits in the abdomen. Except in fit, smooth-coated breeds you probably won't notice the ribs but they should be felt easily; a fat layer of more than 5 mm over the ribs suggests the start of obesity.

Be aware of obesity in your dog and try to avoid it. Surplus weight
● Can cause osteoarthritis (see p.266)
● Makes veterinary examination difficult
● Adds risks for anaesthetics and surgery.

The breeds most at risk from obesity seem to be: Cocker Spaniels, Labradors, terriers, collies, poodles and dachshunds.

TREATING OBESITY

The only way to treat an overweight dog is to give it less to eat. Increasing exercise levels helps but isn't the complete answer. A home-cooked reducing diet is outlined in the *Feeding* chapter (see p.169). In addition, follow these principles:
● No biscuit
● No fats
● Use an all-meat canned food instead of a complete canned diet
● Use bran as a filler
● Include cooked vegetables as fillers
● Try a complete canned "obesity diet" (available from your vet on prescription)
● Give dieting dogs a course of a proprietary multivitamin preparation.

Parasites

Canine parasites fall into two groups: ectoparasites (those which live on the outside of the dog) such as ringworm, lice, fleas and ticks, and endoparasites (those which live inside the dog) including roundworms, hookworms, whipworms and tapeworms.

Most ectoparasites can be treated with suitable insecticidal sprays and creams. Good grooming and a clean environment will also protect your dog from fleas. Wash its bedding regularly.

SEE ALSO:

Worming of puppies see *Puppy-care* p.136.
Heartworm see *Health Care* p.263.

Worming

Regular worming is essential to protect your dog against internal parasites. This involves giving it preparations in liquid or tablet form – a variety is available and your vet will advise you. Adult dogs should be wormed at least once a year – every six months if in close contact with children. Dogs showing any signs of infection should be wormed immediately and all breeding bitches should be wormed prior to mating (see p.190).

Routine yearly treatment for tapeworms is also worthwhile; signs of worm segments in the faeces at any time is cause for immediate treatment.

Ringworm

Uncommon in dogs, ringworm is an infectious fungus which grows on the skin and within the coat. Signs are: ☐ weak, broken hairs ☐ irritated, scaly, inflamed skin.
What is the treatment?
It is important to seek veterinary advice as this parasite can infect humans. Treatment can take the form of special iodine shampoos, clipping the affected area, creams, and a drug given by mouth.

Lice

There are two types of louse – biting lice which chew on skin flakes, and sucking lice which cause more irritation because they penetrate the skin to feed on tissue fluids. (Neither will spread to cats or people.) Lice are grey, about 2 mm long and lay small eggs (nits) which stick to the dog's hairs.

Give repeat treatments of insecticide sprays or baths (at least three at five to seven day intervals) to kill the adults and any hatching larvae.

Fleas

Dog fleas are different to those which infest humans and cats. Fleas can act as intermediate hosts for other dog parasites, but the major problem they cause is skin irritation. When a flea bites, it injects saliva to stop the blood clotting whilst it sucks it up. The saliva contains chemicals which often cause an allergic reaction in the dog. The signs are: ☐ bites looking like small red pimples ☐ black, gritty material in the coat. In some hypersensitive dogs, flea saliva triggers off large areas of inflammation on the animal's back.
What is the treatment?
Spring-clean the house and treat the dog's favourite places with a suitable insecticidal spray. Flea tablets or collars are a good extra precaution, alternatively spray badly affected animals frequently with insecticide throughout the summer months (the flea season).

Ticks

The common tick seen on dogs is the sheep tick. This has a large abdomen that stretches as it fills with blood. It hangs on to the dog's hair and sticks its mouth parts through the skin to suck blood. Ticks are usually found on the underside of the dog, under the forelegs and on the head.
What is the treatment?
Try to remove every tick when you see it.

It is important to extract the head, otherwise an abscess may form. If the head is left in, warm compresses help draw out the infection, combined with antibacterial washes and creams.

Removing a tick

There are various ways of removing ticks, none of them completely foolproof. A good method is to get the tick's head to relax or die by dabbing it with alcohol (such as gin or methylated spirits). Wait a couple of minutes, then use fine-pointed tweezers to extract the tick. Grasp it near (*not* on) the mouth parts. A sharp jerk usually dislodges the tick.

Alternatively, flea sprays can be used locally on ticks. The tick will then die and can be removed the following day. Regular use of a flea spray in tick areas often keeps them away.

Roundworms

Several of these parasites affect dogs but the most important ones belong to the *Ascarid* family. *Toxocara canis* and *Toxascaris leonina* both live in the small intestine. Other roundworms infest the large intestine, blood vessels and respiratory tract.

Ascarids feed on digesting food in the dog's gut, and are particularly harmful to puppies. They penetrate a puppy's gut wall and pass via the blood to the liver and then the lungs. From there they crawl up the trachea to be coughed up and swallowed, again ending up in the gut. Infected puppies may develop:
☐ hepatitis ☐ pneumonia ☐ fits
☐ obstruction in the gut.

As the puppy gets older most of the worms travel to the muscles, where they form cysts. These lie dormant until the puppy (if it is a bitch) becomes pregnant when they migrate to the embryo puppies' lungs. Thus, virtually every puppy is born with roundworm, and must be wormed frequently (see p.136).

How roundworms affect humans

These worms can infect humans, and in a very low number of cases, cause disease. Very rarely, they become encysted in a child's eye, when the eye may have to be removed. Good hygiene and common sense concerning children and puppies should control the problem.

Hookworms and whipworms

Both hookworms and larger whipworms are blood suckers. Both types are visible to the naked eye. These worms can cause anaemia (see p.263), diarrhoea or poor condition.

Tapeworms

The most common dog tapeworm is *Dipylidium caninum*. It is transmitted by fleas in which its larvae develop. Segments of *Dipylidium* are like wriggling rice grains. They tickle the anus and may make the dog "scoot" (drag its rear end) along the floor.

What is the treatment?

Modern tapeworm treatments eliminate all types and your vet will advise on frequency of use. If you see any worm segments in your dog's faeces, treat it as soon as possible. Spray the dog and the house for fleas.

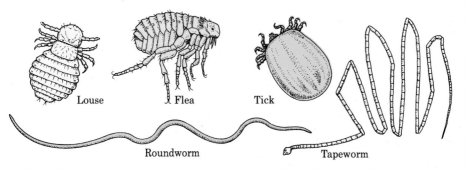

Louse   Flea   Tick

Roundworm   Tapeworm

Ear disorders

It is important to watch your dog for signs of ear disease. Your vigilance can help prevent the spread of infection to the middle and inner ears, and you should know how to examine the ears and how to apply any medicaments. Periodical ear cleaning should be undertaken with care. The proper method of doing this is described on p.254.

SEE ALSO:

Structure of the ear see *Anatomy* p.26.

Examining the ears
Carry out a routine examination of your dog's ears every month – more frequently if it has had any recent ear problems. Establishing this routine makes treatment much easier for you, the dog and the vet.
1 Place the dog on a table (if it is small enough); leave larger dogs on the floor. Restrain the dog (see p.270).
2 Lift the ear flap and look down the canal (a torch may help). Inside the ear canal, you should see a clean surface, similar to the skin on the hairless part of the dog's belly. A little wax is no problem

DISCHARGE FROM THE EAR

A discharge indicates an infection of the outer ear (*otitis externa*).

Things to look for
● Gritty, black material
● Runny, smelly black discharge
● Thick yellow/green discharge
● Pain
● Ear-flap swelling
● Apparent deafness

Possible causes
Depending on the discharge, the cause could be mites (gritty discharge), yeasts (runny, black discharge) or bacterial infections (thick, yellow discharge).

Treatment
These conditions should be examined and treated

by the vet with appropriate medication. Mites: antiparasitic preparation. Yeasts: preparation containing antifungal drugs. Bacterial infections: antibiotics.

Urgency
+++ Don't delay – consult a vet immediately.

SWOLLEN EAR FLAP

A swelling on the inside of the ear flap (small or covering the whole surface) is likely to be an *aural haematoma* (a blood blister formed due to haemorrhage inside the ear flap), often caused by vigorous head shaking.

Things to look for
● Dog shaking its head

● Repeated pawing at the ear
● Tilting the head
● One ear flap at a different angle
● Soft, fluid swellings on inside of ear flap

Possible
● Blow to the ear
● Ear infection causing head shaking
● Fighting

Treatment
Clean the ear (see p.254) and if there's a delay in seeing the vet, bind it to the head with a clean bandage. Surgery is needed to reduce scarring and prevent a "cauliflower ear".

Urgency
++ Consult a vet as soon as convenient.

and should be left alone, but if wax or a hair plug is blocking the ear, it needs plucking and/or cleaning.
3 Smell the ear. A healthy ear has a warm, waxy smell. An unpleasant or strong odour suggests an infection requiring veterinary advice.
4 Reward the dog by making a fuss of it.

Common ear problems
Watch for problems if you own a dog with long ear flaps (such as a Basset) or one with heavy hair growth on large flaps (like a Cocker Spaniel). These flaps reduce ventilation, leading to overheating and excess wax which goes "off" and becomes infected.

Some breeds, such as poodles, have narrow ear canals and are prone to accumulation of wax. Even breeds with wide ear canals and not too much hair in the ears may suffer occasionally from excess wax.

All dogs have hair in their ears which can cause overheating and infection by forming a plug which blocks the ear canal. Remove this by plucking it out with your fingers. Most of the live hair will remain, but dead hair should come out. The ear canal should be clear down the centre as far as you can see. If the opening is still obstructed, you should trim hair away carefully with round-ended scissors.

PAINFUL EARS
There are a variety of causes of painful ears.

Things to look for
- Purulent discharge
- Black waxy material
- Excess hair
- Swelling on ear flap
- Tilting or shaking the head
- Pawing at the ears
- Head painful to touch

Possible causes
- Ear infection
- Excess wax or hair
- Foreign body
- Aural haematoma (see below left)

Treatment
For treatment of discharge, see left.
Accumulated wax and hair should be removed (see *Cleaning the ears*, p.254). Dab calamine lotion on any red areas to soothe pain but don't pour it down the ear.

If the ear looks clean but the dog is in sudden distress, this suggests a foreign body which should be removed by your vet. Don't introduce anything into the ear, even oil.

Urgency
✚✚✚ If there is any inflammation or discharge, don't delay – consult a vet immediately.

POOR HEARING
Deafness is uncommon in dogs but infections may temporarily impair hearing.

Things to look for
- Lack of response to calls for food, walks
- Pain, scratching, head tilt
- Discharge

Possible causes
- Chronic disease blocking outer ear
- Blockage of the ear canal by wax
- Inner-ear infection
- Congenital disorder
- Genetic cause – the same genes which produce albinos can cause deafness

Treatment
Remove any wax or hair blocking the ear canal and have any infections which are present treated by the vet.

Urgency
✚✚ If you suspect infection, consult a vet as soon as convenient.

CLEANING THE EARS

First check the ears for hair plugs. If necessary, pluck out any dead hair with your fingers. Then remove excess wax with an oily cleanser – warm cod-liver oil, liquid paraffin or a special ear cleaner. Don't use powders – they can make matters worse.

Ear cleaning must not be too vigorous or frequent. The ear produces wax partly in response to irritation; too much cleaning causes just that.

Warning When cleaning your dog's ears, never poke the tip of a cotton bud out of sight. You'll do no harm if you keep it in view. Use your fingers as a stop and hold it like a pencil, just above the "bulb".

1 Introduce the oil well down the ear canal using a dropper, then massage around the base of the ear flap to spread it. Look to see if any oil or wax has come to the surface.

2 If it has, remove it with cotton buds or cotton wool. If you see no blood and the dog isn't in distress, continue cleaning until no more wax comes up.

APPLYING EAR MEDICINES

Don't use powders unless given them by the vet – since they can cake. Thick ointments "gum up" the ear, reducing ventilation and obscuring visible signs. Use proprietary drops, cod-liver oil, medicinal liquid paraffin or prescribed medicines.

1 Hold the ear flap to steady the head. Introduce the dropper or tube nozzle carefully into the ear. Squeeze in the prescribed dose.

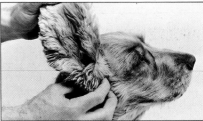

2 Allow the medicine to run down the inside of the ear, then massage the ear canal from the outside to distribute it.

Eye disorders

It is very important to notice any problems in dogs' eyes early. Seek veterinary advice immediately for all eye disorders. Irrigating the eye (see p.257) may relieve discomfort until your dog can see the vet.

Congenital canine eye defects are unfortunately common. They can be extremely painful and you should never breed from dogs with such disorders.

SEE ALSO:

Eye structure see *Anatomy* p.24.
Problems of inbreeding see *Dog Breeds* pp.47–8.
Bandaging the eye see *First Aid* p.283.
Foreign body in eye see *First Aid* p.281.

DISCHARGE FROM THE EYE

The veterinary term for discharge from the eyes is *epiphora*. It is the most common sign of eye disease.

A clear discharge suggests a problem relating to drainage of tears. It can also be caused by irritation and inflammations like conjunctivitis. If the discharge becomes cloudy or *purulent* (thick and discoloured), the eye is probably infected.

Things to look for
● Clear or purulent discharge
● Swelling
● Pain

Possible causes
● Blocked tear ducts
● Conjunctivitis (see p.256)
● Glaucoma (see p.256)
● General infections such as distemper (see p.265)

Treatment
Don't allow hair round the eye to become matted or the discharge to accumulate – a sure way to cause infection.

Until you take the dog to the vet's, bathe the area round the eyes using lint gauze soaked in warm water or a proprietary eye wash.

In the case of blocked tear ducts, the vet will need to flush these out under anaesthetic or enlarge the openings. For treatment of conjunctivitis and glaucoma see p.256.

Urgency
✚✚ If the discharge is clear, consult a vet as soon as convenient.
✚✚✚ If the discharge is purulent or the dog is in pain, don't delay – consult a vet immediately.

SWOLLEN EYE

Swelling in the tissues behind the eye can push the eye forward. The eyeball itself can also swell and be forced out of its socket.

Things to look for
● Protruding eyeball (compare it with the other)
● Glazed stare
● Dilated pupil (due to nerve damage)
● Lids unable to close

Possible causes
● Blow to the head
● Bleeding after a road accident
● Infection behind the eye
● Tumour
● Glaucoma (see p.256)

Urgency
✚✚✚ Any delay could cost the dog its eye – consult a vet immediately.

Blindness

A dog's excellent hearing combined with its memory of the floor-plan of your house may make blindness difficult to spot. A blind dog will manage very well if you are patient and understanding. It can go for walks as usual, but will probably stay close to you. Help by speaking to the dog frequently and not moving furniture around more than necessary. If you have to leave the dog alone in the house, the sound of a radio reduces its degree of isolation.

Third eyelid problems

In some breeds, such as the St Bernard and the Bloodhound, it is normal for the third eyelid to show, but in most dogs there's probably some problem if it suddenly becomes visible or protrudes.

Possible causes include: ☐ painful eye condition ☐ weight loss ☐ scrolled cartilage (a congenital deformity) ☐ prolapsed *nictitans gland* (most common in breeds with loose lower lids).

The signs of third eyelid problems include: ☐ a whitish membrane, usually with a black edge, protruding from the inner corner of the eye ☐ reddish, pea-shaped lump in inner corner of eye ☐ foreign body behind third eyelid ☐ painful eye ☐ red eye.

If your dog develops these signs, don't delay – contact a vet immediately. In the meantime, irrigate the eye to keep it moist (see p.257).

Congenital eyelid and eyelash problems

The most common deformities of the eyelids are *entropion* and *ectropion*, both of which require surgical correction.

In entropion, the eyelid turns inwards, causing the lashes to dig into the surface of the eye. In ectropion the eyelid turns outwards. This causes tears to pool in the pouch formed by the lid, so that the cornea dries out.

A dog's eyelashes may grow in the wrong direction so that they rub on the eyes, causing pain and redness. This is called *trichiasis*. *Distichiasis* is a similar problem where extra hairs on the lid margin rub on the eye. If left untreated they may cause serious damage, even blindness. Fortunately the hairs can be removed by surgery or electrolysis.

Conjunctivitis

This is a painful condition in which the conjunctiva becomes inflamed. The cause may be an infection, a scratch, a congenital disorder, a tumour on the lid, or an irritant such as dust or smoke. Signs include: ☐ tears ☐ screwing up the eye ☐ redness.

If the cornea becomes inflamed (*keratitis*) it begins to look cloudy or even powder blue and completely opaque. This condition is seen in hepatitis (see p.244) and is called "blue eye". The white of the eye may then become severely congested. Finally, chronic inflammation can lead to a film of black pigment spreading across the eye.

If the cause of inflammation is treated in time, the condition can be halted or slowed. The black film can also sometimes be removed by delicate surgery.

Cataracts

These are opaque areas in the lens which can diminish a dog's vision. Some are hereditary whilst others may be caused by a dog's mother being ill or poorly fed during pregnancy. Many dogs develop cataracts in old age, but it isn't always necessary to treat them.

Glaucoma

This is a disorder involving the drainage system of the inside of the eye. It may be caused by: ☐ haemorrhage ☐ inflammation in the anterior chamber ☐ congenital defect. Fluids are continually produced within the eye to nourish it. If their drainage outlets become blocked, the fluids build up, making the globe stretch painfully. The eye becomes severely inflamed and pain makes the dog shed continual tears.

Other signs include: ☐ swelling ☐ pain ☐ sensitivity to light.

If your dog develops these signs, contact a vet immediately. Treatment is surgical or involves special drugs to reduce fluid production, dilate the pupil and improve internal drainage.

Disorders of the retina

The light-sensitive retina can be affected by disease. The most serious involve abnormalities in the retinal structure.

Progressive retinal atrophy (P.R.A.)

In this disease the blood supply to sections of the retina gradually "withers away" and the light-sensitive cells die. The main sign is deteriorating vision. This disorder has two forms – central and generalized – which both lead to impairment of the vision. Central P.R.A. may not cause total blindness but generalized P.R.A. often does. Affected dogs may also have cataracts.

Collie eye anomaly (C.E.A.)

This strange congenital disorder affects collies and Shetland Sheepdogs. It can lead to retinal haemorrhage or detached retina, both of which can cause blindness. Some level of C.E.A. is present in a worryingly large percentage of collies. Fortunately only about five percent of affected dogs go blind and then often only in one eye. The only solution is long-term screening of puppies for future breeding selection.

SPECIAL BREED PROBLEMS

Terriers – prone to luxation (dislocated lens)
German Shepherd – prone to conjunctivitis, scrolled cartilage, cataracts
St Bernard – prone to prolapsed nictitans, scrolled cartilage
Bloodhound, Boxer, Bulldog, Basset – prone to prolapsed nictitans
Collies – prone to Collie eye anomaly, central P.R.A.
Shetland Sheepdog – prone to Collie eye anomaly, central P.R.A.
Golden Retriever, Labrador – prone to central P.R.A., cataracts
Cairn Terrier, Cocker Spaniel, Dachshunds, Poodles, Irish Setter – prone to generalized P.R.A.
Afghan Hound, Boston Terrier, Poodles, Staffordshire Bull Terrier – prone to cataracts

IRRIGATING THE EYE

Use an eye wash, cold weak tea or a boracic acid solution (one teaspoon per cup of warm water).
Warning Don't use cotton wool which may leave numerous tiny fibres in the eye.

1 Hold the eye open with your finger and thumb. Soak a pad of lint in the wash; squeeze over the eye.

2 Lubricate the eye with a drop of cod-liver oil or medicinal liquid paraffin using an eye dropper.

Urinary disorders

The part of the dog's urinary system most commonly affected by disease is the kidney. Kidney disease (known as *nephritis*) is a major cause of death in dogs, so consult the vet immediately you suspect it. Although the signs of individual diseases vary, general signs include: □ abdominal pain □ blood in urine □ swollen abdomen. Often, however, a problem is only noticed when renal (kidney) failure develops, which may be acute (sudden and serious), or chronic (long-term).

Acute kidney failure

Signs are: □ dullness □ vomiting □ lack of appetite □ bad breath □ abdominal pain □ not passing urine. Possible causes are:
- Poisoning (see p.281)
- Acute infections such as leptospirosis (see p.259)
- Secondary to an infection such as pyometra (see p.261)
- Obstruction
- Paralysis of bladder
- Long-term chronic kidney problem.

What is the treatment?
Consult the vet immediately. He or she will use a blood test to assess the severity of the problem. Your dog may need antibiotics, fluid treatment, dialysis, vitamins or anti-emetics.

Chronic kidney failure

Signs vary and may include: □ excessive thirst □ passing a lot of urine □ mouth ulcers □ anaemia (see p.263) □ weight loss and muscle wasting □ bad breath. Possible causes are:
- Minor problems with several factors leading to acute failure
- Tumours (cancer)
- Congenital kidney disorder.

What is the treatment?
Consult your vet who will be able to give your dog steroids and fluid treatment and provide advice on home care. Put the dog on a low-protein diet (see *Special diets*, below) and give it plenty to drink.

To avoid kidney disease, try to ensure no chronic illnesses are allowed to go untreated and that your dog is vaccinated regularly against leptospirosis.

SPECIAL DIETS FOR DOGS WITH KIDNEY DISEASE

Many vets advise low protein diets for dogs with nephritis, to "reduce the strain on the kidneys". In fact, this is often in direct opposition to the needs of the body, which is crying out for good-quality protein. Unfortunately a damaged kidney leaks protein, and if this isn't supplied in the diet, the dog uses its own muscles as a source. Hence the wasting of dogs with chronic nephritis.

Begin restricting dietary protein only on the advice of your vet who can judge the severity of the disease through blood tests. In early cases the slightly reduced-protein "geriatric diet" (see p.169) is generally the most suitable. For dogs that leak vast amounts of protein and develop dropsy (swollen abdomen) and swollen legs a high protein, salt-free diet is needed, along with prescribed diuretics

from your vet.

Increase the rice content of the basic home-cooked diet (p.169) to $\frac{5}{6}$ teacupful and reduce the meat content to $\frac{1}{6}$ teacupful (about 40 g). To make the diet more tasty, add two teaspoons of chicken or turkey fat. Protein levels can be further reduced on your vet's advice by using one egg instead of each $\frac{1}{6}$ teacupful of meat. Eggs provide protein and are very digestible.

Diet supplements
To maintain a low level of phosphorus, substitute calcium carbonate for the bonemeal in the diet supplement. A little salt added to the food helps maintain thirst and kidney flow and compensates for sodium lost via the kidneys.

Other parts of the urinary system
Problems may occur in the lower urinary tract, particularly affecting the bladder and urethra.
Stones in ureter and bladder
Sometimes salts present in the urine crystalize out and form *calculi* or "stones". These rub on the lining of the bladder and cause irritation (*cystitis*, see below). Signs are: □ straining □ passing urine frequently □ blood in the urine.
What is the treatment?
These disorders need surgical treatment. Once your vet has confirmed that stones are present, they can be surgically removed.
Stones in urethra
In dogs rather than bitches the stones can become lodged in the urethra which carries the urine out of the body through the penis. This is painful. Signs are: □ straining □ vomiting □ lack of appetite.
   Urgent veterinary treatment (usually surgery) is needed to remove the obstruction, otherwise back pressure may rupture the bladder or damage the kidney. At this point the pain may disappear but a build-up of toxins will kill the dog unless he is treated promptly.
Cystitis
Infections in the bladder can also cause cystitis, more commonly in bitches. Chronic cystitis can result in stone formation requiring surgery (see stones, above). In mild cases your vet will often prescribe a urinary acidifier such as Vitamin C or chlorethamine, to make the urine less alkaline and less suitable for bacteria to live in. Signs include:
□ blood in urine □ frequent urination

□ licking the penis or vulva.

Leptospirosis
One of the two forms of this bacterial disease, *Leptospira canicola*, attacks the dog's kidney. Like the liver-disease form (see p.244), the organism is spread through infected urine.
What are the signs?
Mild cases may simply be "off colour" for a couple of days. Serious cases may be very dull and vomit as they become uraemic (urea accumulates in the blood due to kidney malfunction). Uraemic dogs often develop mouth ulcers and have bad breath. Later, abdominal colic sets in. Recovery from infection leaves scarring in the kidney and contributes to chronic kidney failure.
What is the treatment?
Have your dog vaccinated regularly. However, if you suspect it in your dog, don't delay – contact a vet immediately. He or she can give antibiotics to combat the bacteria, plus drugs to stop vomiting. Drips, dialysis and transfusions may also be needed, depending on severity.

Urinary incontinence
It is easy to distinguish an incontinent dog which leaks urine in the house from one which is scent-marking (see p.215) or one which simply isn't house-trained. Many incontinent dogs leak urine whilst asleep, leaving a wet patch when they get up. There are several possible causes of incontinence:
● Ectopic ureters – a congenital condition. Puppies may be born with their ureters emptying directly into the urethra and out, rather than into the bladder (see p.29). This can be corrected surgically.
● Urination during an epileptic fit (see p.280)
● Cystitis (see above)
● Prostate disease (see p.260)
● Old age (see p.274).

Reproductive disorders

Some problems affecting the dog's reproductive system, although annoying for breeders, aren't serious. However, there are other conditions which can be life-threatening emergencies.

SEE ALSO:
Anatomy of the reproductive system see *Breeding* p.188.
Bitch's reproductive cycle see *Breeding* p.189.
Mating see *Breeding* p.191.
Eclampsia see *Breeding* p.197.

Fertility and libido problems

Problems relating to fertility or libido can be complex. Apart from making sure your dog is otherwise in good health and within the normal weight range for its size and breed, there's little you can do.

Disorders of the male tract

Several problems can occur in the male dog's system. In general, consult the vet if you notice signs including: ☐ heavy discharge from the penis ☐ bleeding ☐ pain.

Inflammation of the sheath
Young dogs often suffer a mild inflammation on the inside of the sheath. The sign of this is a pale, greenish discharge. If mild, simply bathe off the discharge whenever you notice it.

If the discharge becomes excessive, consult your vet. The problem is caused by an infection at the root of the penis and treatment involves antibiotics given by mouth and antibiotic dressings.

Bleeding penis
Apart from accidental injury, possible causes of this are:
● Bitching injury – dog forced to dismount during mating
● Acute cystitis (see p.259)
● Prostate leaking blood under influence of female hormones (see p.261).

Don't delay – take the dog to the vet immediately. If the problem is a bitching injury, he may have a V-shaped split and need an anaesthetic and some stitches. You can help in the meantime by applying a cold compress to the sheath. Use a towel or a large wad of cotton wool soaked in cold water or wrapped round some ice cubes. Press this tightly onto the sheath, wrap a bath towel round the dog and tie it firmly.

Paraphimosis
The swollen penis may be trapped by the sheath opening and unable to return to its normal size – a tourniquet effect. If the penis doesn't regain its usual size within 15 minutes, try the cold compress technique described above. If there's no response after a further 15 minutes, seek urgent veterinary advice. Surgery may be required to enlarge the opening of the sheath.

Cryptorchidism
Dogs that haven't been castrated but have only one or no testes present in the scrotum are known as "*cryptorchids*" (see p.188). You can't be certain that a dog has a retained testis until about ten months of age. If, after this time a testis has not descended, the vet will remove it surgically; retained testes are prone to cancer. Never use a cryptorchid dog for breeding.

Tumour in the testicles
These tumours may produce female hormones, resulting in odd effects in the male dog – symmetrical hair loss and occasionally, breast development and a pendulous sheath. Consult a vet as soon as convenient – testicle tumours should be surgically removed when spotted.

Prostate disease
The prostate gland is most prone to disease in old dogs. Tumours may develop, or more commonly, the gland becomes enlarged. This internal problem only manifests itself when the dog has problems passing faeces – pain due to the condition leads to constipation.

Any dog with problems or pain on

passing faeces (see *Constipation* p.248) or blood in the urine should be taken to a vet immediately.

An enlarged prostate can be treated with female hormones (even tumours may partially respond to these). To make life easier for the dog, ensure there is always plenty of roughage in its diet.

Disorders of the female tract

A bitch's reproductive system is prone to various ills, many linked to the fluctuations in hormone levels and changes that occur in the womb with each heat.

Signs that something is wrong include: □ abnormal coloured discharges □ excessive thirst □ persistent bleeding or swelling □ nursing behaviour □ production of milk six to seven weeks after a heat.

Pyometra

This means "pus in the womb". Infection usually occurs six to eight weeks after a heat. The bitch may be off-colour and develop: □ excessive thirst □ sometimes an abnormal discharge, yellow, greenish, or reddish and thick □ dullness □ vomiting.

Suspicion of this condition, caused by a combination of these signs, should be reported immediately to your vet. Life-saving surgery is needed to remove the ovaries and womb (ovaro-hysterectomy). Failure to do this will result in death. In some cases, drugs may settle the problem so that the hysterectomy can be carried out when the bitch is over the worst, but it must still be done, otherwise pyometra will recur at the next heat.

Ovarian cyst

The sign of this problem is persistent bleeding from the vulva (a thin, light red discharge) after a heat. If this happens, consult the vet who may administer hormones to burst the cyst or may, with a really problematic case, suggest a hysterectomy.

False pregnancy (pseudopregnancy)

The more common form of false pregnancy begins up to eight or nine weeks after a heat, and may last quite a few weeks. Signs include: □ increased appetite □ odd behaviour – nursing toys and slippers □ hiding away with imaginary puppies □ straining □ breast enlargement □ sluggishness □ displays of affection □ abdominal swelling □ lactation.

Consult the vet – you'll need to decide on a course of action together. False pregnancies can recur after each heat and are thought to occur more commonly in bitches which ultimately develop pyometra. There are various ways of solving the problem. These include drugs which prevent the normal reproductive cycles or surgical spaying (see p.189).

Breast tumour

An unspayed bitch may show cyclical changes in the breasts which can lead to tumours.

If you notice any lumps or swellings in your bitch's breasts, consult the vet with a view to having them removed. Not all breast tumours are malignant but you should check the breasts routinely by feeling them at least every couple of months, particularly following a heat. Benign lumps are often clearer in outline than malignancies, but ask your vet to check any swellings.

Metritis

This is a womb infection which may occur within a couple of weeks of whelping. Signs include: □ purulent, yellow/green discharge □ dullness □ lack of appetite □ vomiting. Treatment involves prompt veterinary prescription of antibiotics or spaying (see *Breeding* p.189).

SPECIAL BREED PROBLEMS

Boxer, Chihuahua – prone to cryptorchidism
Chow Chow – prone to inertia during whelping and difficulty in mating
Bulldog, Pug (and other flat-nosed breeds), – prone to difficulty in whelping

Heart, blood and circulation disorders

Many heart diseases in dogs are caused by congenital deformities. There is a variety of anatomical malformations of varying severity which may involve holes in the heart, transposed blood vessels or connections between vessels.

The general signs of heart disease are:
□ tiredness □ poor ability to exercise □ coughing after a period of lying down (a "cardiac cough") □ "blueness" of the gums □ fainting.

> **SEE ALSO:**
> **Position and function of the heart** see *Anatomy* p.28.
> **Taking a dog's pulse** see *Health Care* p.230.

Patent ductus

A congenital condition may occur where a foetal blood vessel which should be sealed, remains open. This vessel then acts as a shunt between the two sides of the circulatory system (which should not normally be connected). Similar congenital deformities of the vessels around the heart may form a ring which traps the oesophagus, preventing the passage of solids and causing vomiting (see *Vascular rings* p.241). Surgical correction of this type of deformity is often successful.

Heart "murmur"

Inside the heart, between the *atria* and the *ventricles* (see diagram, right) are valves which prevent blood flowing back into the atria when the ventricles contract to pump blood out. Sometimes, due to congenital deformities or age changes in the valves, they may not close efficiently, allowing some leakage back into the atria under pressure. The sound that this blood makes as it squirts back into the atria can be heard through a stethoscope and is therefore called a "murmur".

Murmur on left side of heart
Small breeds in particular seem susceptible to this problem as they get older. A weakness in the *mitral valve* on the left side of the heart causes a rise in pressure in the blood returning from the lungs, forcing small amounts of fluid out into the lung. This hinders the exchange of oxygen for carbon dioxide. Signs are □ reduced exercise ability □ "cardiac cough" (especially when the dog wakes after resting) due to fluid accumulated in the lungs.

Murmur on right side of heart
Similar problems occur when the murmur is due to a failure of the *tricuspid valve* on the right side of the heart. In this case, the fluid collects in the abdomen, producing dropsy (swollen abdomen) and an enlarged liver and spleen. The signs are the same as for a left-side murmur, but with swelling of the abdomen.

What is the treatment for heart conditions?
There are no suitable home remedies for heart conditions in dogs, but it is sensible to watch for and avoid obesity (see p.249), which places undue strain on the heart.

If you're worried about your dog's exercise tolerance, or you suspect a cardiac cough, seek veterinary help. Your vet can control these symptoms with drugs and early treatment reduces the chance of complications.

Sophisticated techniques are available for treatment of heart conditions. Your vet may initially examine your dog with a stethoscope, but may well carry out an E.C.G. examination to detect abnormal rhythms in the heart. These are treated with drugs used for the same conditions in humans. Surgery may be a possibility for some of the less complex congenital abnormalities, especially vascular rings (see p.241) and patent ductus (see left).

New heart valves, as used in humans, aren't fitted to dogs. Treatment is by medical methods, primarily with drugs called "diuretics". By making the dog pass more urine, these move fluid along as it accumulates. Drugs may also be used to strengthen the dog's heartbeat.

Heartworms

Dogs' may be infested by internal parasites called "heartworms" which live in blood vessels. *Angiostrongylus*, the U.K. heartworm, is transmitted via slugs eaten by the dog. Its larvae leave blood vessels in the lung, are coughed up and passed in the faeces.

Dirofilaria, the U.S.A. heartworm, is transmitted by mosquitos and fleas. It is common in some parts of the U.S.A., and lives in the pulmonary artery and the right ventricle.

What is the treatment?
Ridding the dog's body of heartworms is fairly difficult due to the danger of dead adult worms in the blood system causing a thrombosis. Treatment must be carried out in the vet's surgery, usually after supportive care to get the dog in the best possible health before giving drugs to kill the worms.

Anaemia

A condition due to a reduced number of red blood cells and/or a reduction in the amount of *haemoglobin* (red pigment in the blood which carries oxygen). The three major causes of anaemia are:
1 Destruction of red blood cells by:
□ parasites □ poisons □ bacterial toxins □ immune reactions.
2 Loss of blood as a result of:
□ accidents □ poisoning □ bleeding ulcers □ parasites (such as hookworms or whipworms).
3 Reduced or abnormal production of new red blood cells in the bone marrow, due to: □ tumours □ poisons □ acute infections □ chronic septic conditions (such as pyometra or purulent wounds) □ chronic kidney disease (see p.258) □ mineral deficiencies (iron, copper or cobalt) □ vitamin deficiencies (Vitamins B_6 or B_{12}).

The signs of anaemia include: □ pallor in the mouth and round the eyes (loss of normal pink colour) □ gradual weakness □ inability to exercise □ rapid breathing □ being unsettled.

What is the treatment?
If you think your dog is anaemic, consult the vet who will take blood samples to assess the degree, type and cause of the anaemia. Your vet will treat the underlying cause as appropriate and may give your dog anti-anaemic drugs such as iron supplements, vitamins and anabolic steroids. Very severe cases may need a blood transfusion. Once your vet has diagnosed anaemia, you'll be instructed to feed your dog highly nutritious foods, good quality protein, vitamin supplements and liver. Don't overtire your dog during its convalescence.

SPECIAL BREED PROBLEMS

King Charles Spaniel, Pekingese, Poodle – prone to heart murmur
Greyhound – prone to heartworms (due to being kept in kennels in large numbers)

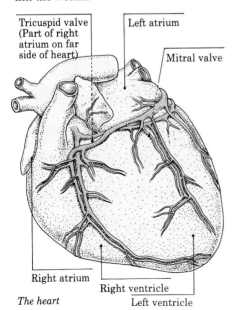

Tricuspid valve (Part of right atrium on far side of heart)

Left atrium

Mitral valve

Right atrium

Right ventricle

Left ventricle

The heart

Neurological disorders

Many problems can afflict the dog's nervous system. The nerves, the brain or the spine may all be affected. Damage to the membranes surrounding the brain and the spinal cord results in *meningitis*; damage to the brain is the problem with *encephalitis*. Both conditions are caused by bacterial infections. Signs of brain damage include: □ fits □ twitching □ tremors □ nystagmus (sideways flicking of the eyes.

> **SEE ALSO:**
>
> **The brain** see *Anatomy* p.23.
> **The spine** see *Anatomy* p.19.
> **Muscle, bone and joint disorders** see *Health Care* pp.266–7.
> **Convulsions** see *First Aid* p. 280.
> **Rabies precautions** see *Housing, Handling and Training* p.152.

Epilepsy

This is quite common, especially in dogs of between one and three years old. It may be caused by:

● Inherited epilepsy
● Previous injury or oxygen starvation to the brain
● Hydrocephalus (see right)
● Distemper (see opposite)
● Tumours.

Some dogs suffer frequent fits, others more occasional ones. There's no set pattern so if two occur close together, it doesn't necessarily mean they're getting worse. However, fits may worsen as a dog gets older, due to the effect of other diseases.

What are the signs?

Strangely enough, fits occur when a dog is relaxed and quiet. They are usually short (about five minutes) and include a period of unconsciousness. For physical signs of a fit, see p.280.

What is the treatment?

For the immediate course of action, see *First Aid* p.280. Long-term treatment means veterinary prescribed anticonvulsants. These may not totally abolish the fits but should reduce their frequency. Dogs having a sequence of continual fits lasting 15–30 minutes should be reported to the vet urgently; intravenous anticonvulsants may be needed.

Hydrocephalus

Literally "water on the brain", this usually occurs through a deformity in the drainage system from the fluid-filled ventricles of the brain. Eventually, the brain tissues are compressed against the skull, and various signs occur which may include: □ fits □ blindness □ incoordination □ dullness.

Successful treatment involves early diagnosis and specialist surgery.

Encephalitis

This means an inflammation of the brain. It may occur due to bacterial infections, viruses like distemper or even old age. Infectious causes are usually very sudden. Bacterial encephalitis often follows ear disease, wounds or skull fractures. Signs include: □ fits □ head pressing □ stiff neck □ pain when touched around the head.

Whatever the reason for its onset, encephalitis needs prompt veterinary treatment since the various causes require different drugs.

Strokes

It isn't certain whether dogs truly suffer strokes like people, but they certainly show similar signs, including: □ sudden collapse □ interference with the function of various parts of the body □ walking in circles □ droopy eyelids □ partial paralysis □ eye flicking.

Consult a vet immediately if your dog shows these signs. Steroids can reduce the symptoms; other drugs can improve the blood flow in the brain. Treatment is often quite successful for a time.

Distemper (hardpad)

This condition occurs most often in young dogs between three and six months old, but can attack at any age.

Infection occurs through inhalation of the virus and is spread around the body by defensive cells trying to capture and kill it. If they fail, the virus attacks the immune and nervous systems and the cells lining the lungs and gut.

What are the signs?

A young, fit dog picking up a very light infection may fight it successfully, showing dullness and a slight temperature. Full-blown cases show a high temperature then a second stage:
☐ dullness ☐ nasal and eye discharge coughing ☐ vomiting ☐ diarrhoea
☐ thickening and cracking of the skin of the nose and pads.

The nervous signs

As the second phase symptoms are improving, about four weeks after initial infection, the nervous system may start to show damage. This can range from slight tremors to full epileptic fits.

What is the treatment?

Antibiotics, cough suppressants and drugs to treat vomiting and diarrhoea are usually required, possibly plus anticonvulsants for dogs with nervous damage.

The real answer to distemper is vaccination (see p.237). Dogs particularly at risk can be given antiserum – very short-term protection which shouldn't be confused with proper vaccination.

Cervical spondylopathy

This disease, whose sufferers are known as "wobblers", tends to affect larger breeds. One (or more) cervical vertebrae are malformed and this, combined with the weight of the dog's head, bruises the spinal cord. Signs include: ☐ trailing the forefeet ☐ scuffing and wearing down nails ☐ wobbling gait ☐ unsteady hindquarters (especially after exercise) ☐ paralysis (partial or total).

What is the treatment?

Take your dog to the vet who will X-ray its neck. Surgical treatment may be possible if the problem is detected early enough. But once paralysis sets in, the future is generally grim.

Slipped disc

More correctly called "disc protrusion", this is a common disorder in short-legged, long-backed breeds. These dogs' discs age more rapidly than in other breeds; the centre of a disc may push through the soft outer layers, damaging nerves in the spinal cord. The signs are:
☐ sudden pain ☐ unwillingness to move
☐ limping ☐ hunched posture
☐ inability to raise the head
☐ paralysis (partial or total).

What is the treatment?

If your dog is in sudden pain accompanied by the other signs, don't delay – consult a vet immediately. Cases showing milder pain or a limp may respond to treatment with drugs, but surgery is indicated for worse cases.

Rabies

This killer viral disease (see also p.152) is transmitted by infected saliva (from an infected dog) being left in a bite wound. Signs include: ☐ inability to swallow
☐ furious running, biting ☐ drowsiness
☐ paralysis. The virus moves back down the nerves to the salivary glands where it multiplies. Affected animals will die; humans in contact with them are in danger and must be vaccinated immediately.

In countries where rabies is present, vaccination will protect your dog. Keep it under constant supervision.

SPECIAL BREED PROBLEMS

Basset –prone to slipped disc, cervical spondylopathy
Chihuahua, King Charles Spaniel, poodles –prone to hydrocephalus
Dachshund, Pekingese, Shih Tzu – prone to slipped disc
Great Dane, Dobermann – prone to cervical spondylopathy

Muscle, bone and joint disorders

Diseases of the muscles, bones or joints are relatively common in dogs – injuries resulting from falls, fights or road accidents being some of the most usual causes. Minor injuries such as sprains may be treatable at home, but if your dog is in pain, contact the vet. Signs are: ☐ limping ☐ pain ☐ swelling.

SEE ALSO:

Muscles and movement see *Anatomy* p.20–1.
Nutritional diseases see *Health Care* p.249.
Skeleton and spine see *Anatomy* pp.18–19.
Splints and bandages see *First Aid* p.283.
Slipped disc, cervical spondylopathy see *Health Care* p.265.

Muscular problems

A muscle disease is called a "myopathy"; inflamed muscle is known as "myositis". There are various causes of myopathy, including bacterial infections. Some are inherited and breed-specific. They have no treatment. Others *do* have specific treatments; consult the vet immediately if you suspect them.

What is the treatment for myopathy?
If you suspect that your dog has mild muscle damage (a slight limp which disappears within 24 hours), try two days' rest. If this relieves it, continue the rest treatment for a while. But if in any doubt, consult the vet.

Eosinophilic myositis
The cause of this disease is unknown. It affects the muscles of the head, causing pain and, later, wasting of the muscles. Signs include: ☐ weakness ☐ stiffness ☐ pain ☐ lop-sided look to the head.
    Eosinophilic myositis needs urgent veterinary help. Your vet can prescribe anti-inflammatory drugs and pain killers.

Joint problems

Arthritis (inflammation of the joints) is fairly common in dogs. The major causes are anatomical abnormalities which may either be hereditary or have nutritional causes (see p.249).

Sprains and osteoarthritis
A sprain is damage to a joint, which may mean torn ligaments or fractured cartilage. This also causes arthritis which, if severe or untreated, can result in osteoarthritis – inflammation of the bone in the joint. Once osteoarthritis sets in, the damage is usually permanent.

LIMPING

The major sign of a limb disorder is a limp. Try to assess the severity of the injury by checking the following:

Things to look for
● Dog carrying its leg clear of the ground or just dabbing it down
● Painful swelling. Both these signs suggest a fairly serious injury

● Dog "favouring" one leg, even if there's no pain or swelling

Possible causes
● Sprain (see above)
● Fracture
● Wound or other injury (see *First Aid* p. 282)

Treatment
However slight the damage, rest your dog until the condition has improved and in most cases, for a week after this. If a few days' rest doesn't cure an apparently minor limp, seek veterinary advice.

Urgency
✚✚ If there's pain or the limp persists, consult the vet as soon as convenient.

What is the treatment?
For first aid, see *Treating a sprain* p.283.
Serious sprains should be rested for
about six weeks, after which you should
slowly re-introduce exercise. You may
find support bandages useful.

Osteoarthritis has no cure so all efforts
should be aimed at alleviating it. Strict
rest is the most important treatment you
can give and veterinary drugs can reduce
the inflammation.

Warning: Pain killers may enable a dog
to use an injured joint which could result
in permanent damage. If your vet
prescribes pain killers, you must also
rest the dog.

Bone diseases
Certain diseases of dog's bones are
congenital, but others are due to some
disruption in the body's provision of
nutrients and oxygen. A fairly common
problem, known as *osteochondritis
dissecans*, is seen especially in large
breeds. Due to inadequate nutrition, an
area of shoulder cartilage dies and falls
into the joint, where it sometimes revives
and grows to form a loose lump called a
"joint mouse". This rubs on the joint,
causing arthritis.

Over-rapid growth is probably involved
in the development of this disease. The
elbow, knee and hock bones can also be
affected. Signs include: □ lameness
□ swelling □ pain □ local heat.

Fortunately, prompt surgery to remove
the joint mouse usually results in almost
complete recovery.

Fractures
A fracture can occur in almost any bone
in the dog's body. Spontaneous fractures
can occur in conditions like *osteoporosis*
where the bones are thin. Signs include:
□ acute lameness □ swelling □ pain
□ local heat.
What is the treatment?
Don't delay – consult a vet immediately
or there may be severe malformation or
failure to heal. (For procedure after an
accident, see *First Aid* p.278.)

Hip dysplasia
This disease is quite common.
Malformation of the hip joint means the
ball and socket connection fits badly.
The head of the femur rubs on the edges
of the joint, causing arthritis.

The problem is most common among
large breeds. There's a strong inherited
component, so many breed societies and
veterinary authorities have set up
certification schemes based on X-rays.
Find out if there's a scheme for your
breed before buying a puppy and ask to
see its parents' certificates (issued at one
year of age).
What is the treatment?
Pain killers may alleviate the problem in
young, growing dogs. Restrict exercise
severely for up to six months, after which
you can gradually build up to a normal
lifestyle. However, more serious cases
will require surgery.

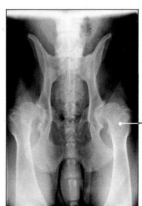

Malformed hip
joint

X-ray showing hip dysplasia

SPECIAL BREED PROBLEMS
German Shepherd – prone to
eosinophilic myositis,
osteochondritis dissecans in elbow,
hip dysplasia
Rottweiler, St. Bernard – prone to
osteochondritis dissecans
Labrador – prone to osteochondritis
dissecans in elbow, hip dysplasia

Skin and coat disorders

Skin diseases in dogs can be complex. A common diagnosis is *eczema* – a general term for inflamed skin – but identifying the actual cause is often difficult or impossible.

The basic sequence of a skin disease is inflammation (dermatitis), causing irritation (itching) which makes the dog scratch with its claws or teeth. This results in loss of hair, more inflammation and more itching – the "itch-scratch-itch cycle". Finally, bacteria invade the broken skin. The most important part of treatment is preventing the dog from scratching; this may call for anti-inflammatory drugs and sedatives.

What are the signs of skin disease?
Major signs of skin disease include:
□ scratching □ hair loss □ reddened skin □ areas wet from licking (often stained brown by saliva in white dogs) □ rashes □ infected spots □ black, gritty material in the coat □ insects in the coat □ mats □ dry coat □ dandruff.

SEE ALSO:

Structure of skin and coat see *Anatomy* p.32.
Parasites see *Health Care* p.250.
Mats and tangles see *Grooming* p.183.
Moulting see *Grooming* p.174.

Mites

Three types of mite can cause problems in dogs:
● Demodex – causes demodectic mange
● Sarcoptes – causes sarcoptic mange
● Otodectes – causes inflammation of the ear

Otodectes is the only type of mite visible to the naked eye and then only rarely; you may see them as tiny white moving dots in the ear.

Demodex
Carried by most dogs, this mite usually causes no trouble, but it may be a nuisance at times of stress and in young animals whose natural defences aren't fully developed. Demodex causes a type of pustular dermatitis in puppies, around the head and shoulders. This often becomes infected – a condition known as "juvenile pyoderma". Signs include:
□ characteristic "mousy" odour □ hair loss □ flaky, oily skin.

What is the treatment?
Unless dogs receive veterinary attention within 24 hours of this developing, very serious scarring can occur. Your vet can prescribe drugs and antibiotics which give effective relief. Special shampoos can control the oiliness of the coat and the characteristic smell.

Sarcoptic mange (Scabies)
More commonly known as "scabies", this problem can affect humans as well as dogs of any age. The sarcoptes burrow through the skin, producing tunnels in which they lay eggs. Although the infection usually dies away in humans, it should still be treated. The sign of this in the dog is an itchy rash of red spots, especially on ears, elbows and hocks. On human skin the "tunnels" can actually be seen.

What is the treatment?
Prompt treatment is important, to avoid human infection and to prevent the dog damaging itself seriously by scratching and biting. The vet will prescribe special chemicals to be applied in insecticidal shampoos every five days for at least four weeks (the eggs take up to three weeks to hatch). The vet may also prescribe drugs to help stop self-mutilation by biting and scratching.

SPECIAL BREED PROBLEMS

Dobermann – prone to demodex and juvenile pyoderma
Dachschund – prone to juvenile pyoderma
Irish Setter – prone to demodex

SCRATCHING

This common sign of skin disease has many possible causes.

Things to look for
- Parasites (fleas, lice and mites, see p.250)
- Bacterial sores – small, infected spots and scaly, red inflamed areas

Possible causes
- Parasite infestation
- Ear disease (see p.252)
- Impacted anal sacs (indicated by dog licking sores at base of tail, see p.248)
- Contact dermatitis (indicated by redness on the belly)

Treatment
Aim to treat the specific cause.
- If indicated, use an antiparasitic bath (if in doubt treat for fleas).
- Wash localized bacterial sores with antibacterial wash.
- Generalized bacterial sores, ear problems or impacted anal sacs need veterinary attention.
- With contact dermatitis, cut off access to likely causes such as nylon carpet, car seat covers, disinfectant on floors. If home treatment fails, consult a vet.

Urgency
++ If the skin is broken and "sticky" or chewed, consult a vet as soon as convenient.

REDDENED SKIN

You may notice this sign before the skin problem becomes fully established.

Possible causes
- Fleas (see p.250)
- Contact dermatitis
- Allergic dermatitis
- Anything causing itching – ringworm, lice or bacterial sores

Treatment
- If the reddened area is very localized, apply calamine lotion.
- If the problem is more generalized, a lanolin baby shampoo will wash out potential irritants and cool the skin. When the dog is dry, apply flea spray. If the problem is still evident after 24 hours, consult the vet.

Urgency
++ Consult a vet as soon as convenient.

HAIR LOSS

There are a variety of factors involved in hair loss in dogs.

Things to look for
- Broken hairs in coat
- Inflamed, red skin
- Bald areas
- Symmetrical hair loss
- Excessive, prolonged moult

Possible causes
- Scratching (indicated by reddening of skin and broken hairs)
- Malfunction in the hair growth cycle (see p.32), indicated by bald areas with no irritation
- Diet

Treatment
To treat scratching, see above. The most common causes of hair loss without irritation are hormonal and need veterinary treatment.
If diet is the problem, multivitamins and extra oil (see p.168) may stop the moult. If there's no response after a few weeks, consult the vet.

Urgency
+ Dietary problems may be treatable at home.
++ Otherwise, consult a vet as soon as convenient.

Veterinary care and nursing

It is a good idea to choose a vet that has been recommended by friends or the breeder of your puppy. Before registering with a vet, find out:
● What are the consulting hours?
● Is there an appointments system or not?
● How early must you phone for a routine appointment?
● Does the practice make house calls?
● What are the arrangements for emergency night calls?
● Are records kept so that your dog's medical history can be sent on to a new vet if you move?

Taking your dog to the surgery
Whenever possible, telephone the surgery to make an appointment if this is the system they use. Withhold food and water from your dog before you visit the vet in case it needs an operation.

Check first to see if the surgery has a separate cat and puppy waiting room. If it has, this is the place for unvaccinated, healthy puppies. Once you have checked in, keep your dog under control on a short lead. Many dogs are tense at the vet's and fights occur easily. Small dogs are often best held on your lap, whilst very sick dogs are often best kept in the car until just before you are called. This avoids exposing other animals to infectious diseases.

The consulting room
Don't let your dog loose as you enter the consulting room; hang on to the lead and keep it under control. Most vets like to let the dog relax first, and will ask you various questions whilst it settles.

Be prepared to tell your vet:
● Your dog's breed, sex and age
● How long you have had the dog
● Its recent history and whether it has recently spent time in kennels
● Whether it has recently encountered any disease
● When it was last vaccinated
● Why you have called and what signs of illness you have observed
● If your dog is eating, drinking and passing urine and faeces normally.

RESTRAINING A DOG

The degree of restraint needed during examination and treatment varies according to the dog and the procedure to be carried out. However, it is usual for the dog to be placed on a table. Hold the dog yourself; it is less likely to cause problems. If you feel it may bite, use a tape muzzle (see *First Aid* p.279).
To restrain a small dog Grasp the scruff tightly including the collar. Don't try to grab the nose – you risk being bitten.
To restrain a medium-sized dog (see right) Tuck the head under your upper arm, place the other arm around the body and grasp one of its forelegs.
To restrain a large dog Place one arm under the neck and fix the head with your other hand by grasping the outer foreleg and leaning your body over its shoulders. Someone else should hold the rear end.

Restraining a medium-sized dog

THE VET'S EXAMINATION

Unless the problem is obviously localized, the vet will examine your dog's whole body, starting at the head and working downwards.

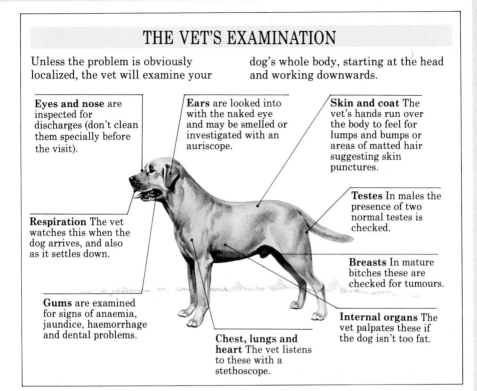

Eyes and nose are inspected for discharges (don't clean them specially before the visit).

Ears are looked into with the naked eye and may be smelled or investigated with an auriscope.

Skin and coat The vet's hands run over the body to feel for lumps and bumps or areas of matted hair suggesting skin punctures.

Testes In males the presence of two normal testes is checked.

Respiration The vet watches this when the dog arrives, and also as it settles down.

Breasts In mature bitches these are checked for tumours.

Gums are examined for signs of anaemia, jaundice, haemorrhage and dental problems.

Internal organs The vet palpates these if the dog isn't too fat.

Chest, lungs and heart The vet listens to these with a stethoscope.

Operations

Procedures do vary from vet to vet, but generally you'll be asked to starve your dog from 6pm the previous evening and give it no fluids after bedtime. On arrival at the surgery, the dog will be admitted by a nurse and you'll be requested to sign a "consent form" permitting the surgery or necessary treatment. The nurse may give your dog a mild pre-operative sedative to minimize the amount of anaesthetic needed.

Most initial anaesthetics are injected. A tube is then inserted into the trachea through which gaseous anaesthetic is passed to keep the dog asleep during the operation. Recovery begins when the gas is turned off and the dog breathes air. This takes about an hour and at this point, the dog is just able to stand. After a minor operation, you'll probably be allowed to collect your pet the same day.

Euthanasia

Unfortunately, your dog may eventually need to be "put to sleep", on the advice of the vet. Your vet can arrange for this to happen at the surgery or in your home; you can ask to be present if you wish. If you have a dog euthanized at home, it is likely the vet will need your help.

The standard method of euthanasia is the injection of a large overdose of an anaesthetic drug. This is usually injected into the foreleg. The brain will often be asleep and the heart stopped before the injection is complete. Euthanasia is peaceful and painless. All the dog feels is a slight prick in its foreleg.

Some owners like to bury their dogs at home, but if this is impractical, all vets have access to cremation services who will individually cremate dogs and return their ashes if you wish.

Home nursing

A sick dog needs gentle care and nursing. Once your vet has diagnosed the illness and prescribed appropriate medication, you'll probably be allowed to take it home where it can convalesce and recover. Your main responsibilities are:
● Providing a warm, hygienic rest area
● Feeding a tempting, nutritious diet
● Giving medicines prescribed by the vet
● Checking dressings or wounds as directed by the vet.

Change your dog's bedding frequently. When the dog needs to go out, just give it enough time to pass urine and faeces before making it come back indoors.

Keeping the dog warm
Make sure your dog is kept warm and out of draughts. Supplement household heating with carefully positioned infra-red or dull-emitting bulbs, placed at least 60 cm away from the dog (test heat with your hand on the dog). Well-wrapped hot-water bottles are useful too (see *Puppy-care* p.130–1).

Feeding a sick dog
Loss of appetite is a common sign of illness in animals. But it is important that your dog eats: it needs nourishment to help it recover.

Sit on the floor beside your dog. Offer it spoonfuls of food or liquid while you talk to it encouragingly. If this fails, spoonfeed as described below.

Nourishing liquid feeds like broth or meat stock help keep up the dog's spirits and maintain its strength. Your vet may instruct you to add glucose or special sachets of power or liquid to the dog's drinking water. Starvation is unlikely but dehydration is a real possibility, particularly in a dog which has had diarrhoea or vomiting. *Make sure your*

SPOONFEEDING A DOG

If the food is pleasant-tasting and your dog placid, you'll probably be able to spoonfeed it on your own. But generally this is a two-person job.
Safety first: After each spoonful, let the dog's mouth open a little to allow it to swallow. Be extra careful with short-nosed breeds like Pugs Pekingese and Bulldogs; these may bite or have trouble breathing; (see *Problems of short-nosed breeds* p.27).

1 The helper kneels by the dog's left side and raises its head by placing his or her right arm round the dog's neck and across the front. With the left hand, the helper should gently hold its nose.

2 The feeder can now spoon food into the right-hand side of the dog's mouth or pour liquids into the "pouch" formed by the side of the lower lip. For more substantial foods, the helper can relax the grip.

dog drinks water. If coaxing fails, give water in a spoon (see below left).

Invalid foods

Unless the vet advises a special diet, feed your dog a variety of tempting, nutritious, tissue-building foods. Choose easily digested foods rich in protein, minerals and vitamins such as:

Liquids

□ glucose (two teaspoons per teacupful of water) □ honey □ beef tea □ calf's foot jelly (warmed) □ proprietary liquid foods.

Solids

□ white fish □ best-quality mince □ cheese □ cooked eggs □ meat- and fish-based baby foods □ mashed potatoes □ cooked rice □ baby cereals.

Giving medicines

Give liquid medicines by spoonfeeding (see below left), but remember few medicines are pleasant-tasting and you may encounter some resistance.

Giving tablets

If your vet prescribes tablets, don't crush them – the centres often taste very bitter. You'll probably need a helper unless the dog is very ill or very placid. As with spoonfeeding, a second person should hold the dog – one arm round the neck to lift its head and one steadying the hindquarters.

The other person should grip the dog's upper jaw firmly with one hand, tucking the skin of the muzzle around and into the mouth with finger and thumb. The other hand containing the tablet is used to push the lower jaw downwards and propel the tablet to the back of the tongue. (If necessary, give it a push with your finger or a blunt instrument.)

If your dog won't swallow tablets given like this, try placing the tablet in the mouth, giving a spoonful of water and closing the mouth to make it swallow. Some dogs will only eat tablets smeared with butter or cheese.

MAKING AN ELIZABETHAN COLLAR

A useful device which you can construct from a plastic bucket – 4.5 litre size for small dogs, 9 litre for larger dogs – this collar prevents a convalescent dog from scratching its head or ears, pawing a head or eye wound, or turning to lick or chew at its hindquarters.

 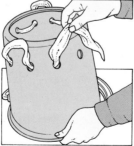 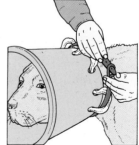

1 With a heated knife, remove the base of the bucket. Make holes round the bottom, 5 cm apart and 5 cm from the edge.

2 Thread a 5 cm bandage through the holes, leaving a loop between each pair, large enough to fit the dog's collar.

3 Insert the collar through the loops. Place the bucket over the dog's head and fasten the collar comfortably.

Care of the elderly dog

The number of years of a dog's life varies considerably between breeds (see *Lifespan* p.123). However, the two chief signs of old age are common to most dogs – greying of hair round the head (especially near the ears and muzzle) and loss of weight.

Elderly dogs lose weight mainly because of a failing liver and kidneys – these problems are accompanied by increased thirst and a good appetite. Once you notice weight loss in your elderly dog, it is worth taking it to the vet for three- to six-monthly checks. Often, a timely course of anabolic steroids will slow down the physical deterioration. Sometimes, these problems are caused by minor attacks of leptospirosis (see pp.244 and 259). If your dog has been vaccinated routinely throughout its life, it may avoid suffering in this way.

Although chronic kidney failure (see p.258) isn't painful, it often culminates in acute kidney failure. If you see any of the signs of acute kidney or liver failure (see pp.258 and 243), consult your vet.

FEEDING TIPS FOR ELDERLY DOGS

A good home-cooked diet for "geriatrics" is given on p.169.
- Make sure you're giving the dog enough food if its appetite is good
- Give easily-digested foods like fish and poultry
- Don't forget the importance of extra vitamins (see p.168)
- Keep drinking water available at all times
- Use bran and/or liquid paraffin to combat constipation
- Add fat (lard, chicken or turkey fat) to the diet to provide extra calories for lean, elderly dogs – one teaspoon for small dogs, four for larger breeds

---

Bowel and bladder problems

Some old dogs become quite constipated – often due to prostate problems (see p.261). Others may lose some degree of control over their bladder; this may be due to cystitis (see p.259). Tumours in the anus may interfere with its function, causing loss of control of the bowel. If any of these problems becomes frequent, consult your vet. They may be painful, or upset a habitually clean dog. There's no need for you to suffer these conditions in silence – all can be treated with some measure of success.

Caring for the teeth

If you're in any doubt about the health of your dog's teeth, mention this to your vet on one of the routine visits. Brushing the teeth and giving material for chewing during a dog's younger years (see p.242) minimizes the build-up of tartar. Elderly dogs may not chew bones any longer, so it is worthwhile brushing the teeth once or twice a week (see p.242). Despite this, tartar is still liable to build up and may need removing under anaesthetic.

Eye and ear problems

Although an old dog's eyesight and hearing often become impaired, its slower lifestyle may compensate for this. Handle your dog gently, taking care not to startle it with sudden loud noises – make sure your dog can see you before you switch on any household appliances such as the vacuum cleaner. Check behind your car before reversing outside your home. For coping with a blind dog, see p.256.

Bone and joint problems

Elderly dogs are often bothered by general stiffness associated with arthritis in some of their joints. This is more of a problem in overweight dogs or large breeds. Ask your vet's advice; he or she may prescribe pain killers which can considerably ease a dog's life.

Keeping your dog healthy

With sensible care, you can considerably reduce the likelihood of your pet succumbing to illness. The principles of owning a healthy dog are:
● Follow the advice on choosing a healthy puppy given in *Choosing a Dog* (see p.127).
● Be aware of any diseases or conditions to which your puppy's breed is prone. Obtain relevant clearance certificates where available and keep a lookout for signs of the problems throughout the dog's life.
● Have your puppy properly vaccinated (see p.136) and keep up to date with annual boosters. For these routine annual visits, prepare a list of any problems or questions you may have for the vet.
● Don't try to boost your dog's growth rate too much through the puppy stage – rapid growth can give rise to muscle and bone problems (see p.162).
● Establish a routine for checking your dog's skin, eyes and ears at grooming sessions. This gives you more chance of spotting any problems early.
● Avoid obesity in your dog (see p.249).
● Keep your dog's bedding and feeding utensils scrupulously clean – hygiene is a crucial factor in good health.
● Keep your dog clean too – check its eyes, ears, nose, mouth, skin, genital and anal areas regularly to ensure they're free of discharges.

Safety precautions

Never let your dog off your property alone. Roaming dogs can be involved in, or even cause, a road accident. Roamers are much more likely to get into fights, upsetting other dog-owners, and may also chase sheep.

Take your dog for walks regularly, even if you have a large garden. A routine walk gives you the opportunity to reinforce basic training lessons (see pp.154–9); always keep your dog under control when it is out with you.

A healthy dog at the prime of life
A fit dog, full of stamina, is the reward of proper feeding, grooming and exercise.

Are you insured?

It is well worth taking out veterinary insurance, particularly for urban dogs whose risk of being involved in fights or road accidents is high. Modern veterinary treatment has paralleled human medical techniques in many of its newer advances, but these can carry high costs. A modest annual premium can ease the burden of unexpected illness and accidents.

ZOONOSES

There are a few canine diseases which also affect humans. These are known as "zoonoses", and the most important are:
● Rabies (see pp.152 and 265)
● Ringworm (see p.250)
● Fleas (see p.250)
● Roundworm (see p.251)
Simple precautions can help avoid all these. Regular worming, use of flea sprays during the summer months and washing your hands after handling a dog with any kind of skin problems, are normal measures to take. If you should ever be bitten by a "suspect" dog in a rabies area, seek medical advice immediately (see p.152).

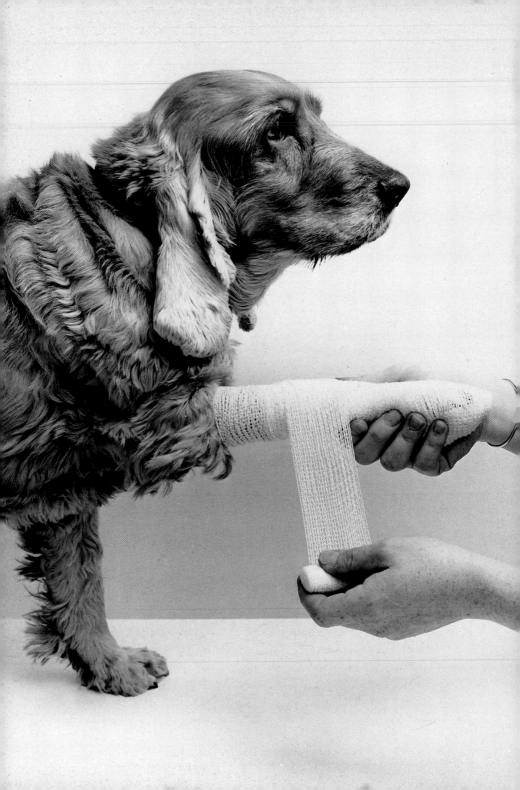

13

FIRST AID

The principles of first aid for dogs are similar to those used for humans. Your own, or any other dog may fall prey to minor accidents that need your attention, and occasionally major ones that need emergency first aid until the dog can be seen by a vet. In the case of a serious accident, try to stay cool and use your common sense to help the animal and calm it down. This chapter covers most of the common problems which may occur; in other circumstances, apply the principles described here until veterinary help is available. Your first aid can save a dog's life, prevent its condition worsening and promote its recovery. Unless you are completely confident that the dog has recovered, take it to the vet as soon as possible. Keep the basic first aid kit in your home and aim to memorize the procedures for dealing with road accidents and giving artificial respiration – you may not have time to consult this book in an emergency.

Accidents and emergencies

One of the most upsetting things that can happen to your dog is a car accident. Dealing with a dog at the site of an accident can be a job for the vet – a dog may need extricating from the underside of a car, or may have become too dangerous (through pain or fear) to be handled by inexperienced people.

In general, though, it is best not to waste time waiting for the vet to arrive. Few vets are equipped with more than a visiting bag out of hours and all specialized equipment is at the surgery. Phone ahead to warn the vet of your arrival and take the dog to the surgery. If the vet is away, he or she can advise the staff what to do in the meantime.

ACCIDENT PROCEDURE
1 Don't panic. Approach the dog cautiously and speak reassuringly (the best person to do this is the owner).
2 Gently restrain the dog with a "lead" made from a belt or piece of rope. Form a noose and drop it over the dog's head.
3 Improvise a muzzle (see opposite).
4 Ensure the dog isn't trapped.
5 Apply necessary first aid. Look for:
● Heartbeat (on left side of chest)
● Breathing movement
● Major haemorrhage
● Gasping
● Pale gums
● Inability to stand
● Obvious fractures
6 Telephone the vet's surgery, stating which of these signs are present.
7 Move the dog carefully (see p.280).

> **SEE ALSO:**
> **Control of bleeding** see *First Aid* p.282.
> **Bandaging** see *First Aid* p.283.
> **Shock** see opposite.

A BASIC FIRST AID KIT

Although many of your own first aid items are suitable for dogs, it is preferable to keep a separate kit.

1 Round-ended scissors 2 Stubby-bulb thermometer (not the family's) 3 Tweezers 4 5 cm and 10 cm bandages 5 5 cm adhesive tape dressing 6 Lint gauze 7 Cotton wool 8 Old socks 9 Plastic bags for keeping foot dressings dry 10 Antiseptic cream 11 Antiseptic wash 12 Cotton buds 13 Kaolin tablets or medicine 14 Calamine lotion 15 Proprietary eye wash 16 Proprietary ear cleaner 17 Medicinal liquid paraffin.

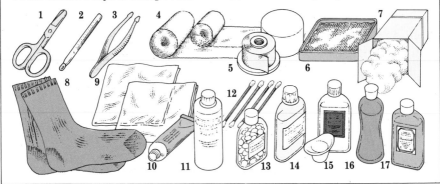

IMPROVISING A MUZZLE

A frightened dog in pain may try to bite, so an improvised muzzle is a sensible precaution. Use a bandage, or a necktie (belts are too stiff).

Watch for the dog going blue or having trouble breathing. If this happens, untie the muzzle, open the mouth and pull the tongue forward. Then keep the muzzle loose and hold the dog's head on your lap.

● **Never** muzzle a dog with chest injuries or one having trouble breathing

● **Never** leave a muzzled dog alone – it may try to remove the muzzle

● **Never** muzzle a short-nosed breed – you may impair its breathing

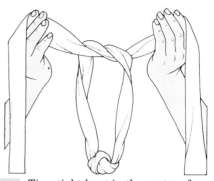

1 Tie a tight knot in the centre of the bandage or tie, so that it "hangs". Make a second, loose knot, about 20 cm above the first.

2 Slip the loop formed between the knots well back over the nose. Pull the second knot tight, so the first catches under the jaw.

3 Bring the two ends down on either side; cross them under the jaw. Take them round and tie at the back in an easily loosened double bow.

SHOCK AND COLLAPSE

If your dog has collapsed, quick action on your part may mean the difference between life and death. For the correct action to take, see p.280. If conscious, it may be suffering from shock. Possible causes of collapse include: □ epileptic fit (see p.264) □ acute infection □ heart disease (see p.262) □ poisoning (see p.281) □ diabetes (see p.245) □ exposure □ heatstroke (see p.281) □ accident injury (see p.278) □ haemorrhage.

DO NOT:

● Give alcoholic stimulants
● Move the dog more than necessary
● Raise the dog's head or prop it up
● Give the dog anything by mouth

SEE ALSO:

Pulse see *Health Care* p.230.
Restraint see *Health Care* p.270.
Convulsions see *First Aid* p.280.

MOVING AN INJURED DOG

Move an injured dog as gently as you can. Transfer the dog to a blanket which can be used as a stretcher. Ideally three people are needed – to support the head, back and pelvis. (If help isn't available, carefully move the dog on to the blanket one section at a time.)

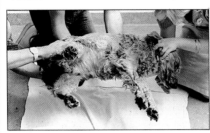

1 If necessary, use a muzzle and lead. Spread the blanket behind the dog and move it gently on to it with the aid of two helpers.

2 Tense the blanket between two people with the third supporting the dog's back and manoeuvre it carefully into the car.

ACTION IN CASE OF COLLAPSE

1 Treat for shock Place the dog in a quiet, warm place and cover it with a blanket. Place a hot (not scalding) water bottle next to it to help minimize shock.
2 Check breathing If it is irregular or non-existent: ☐ loosen the collar ☐ open the mouth ☐ remove any foreign material, saliva, blood or vomit ☐ give artificial respiration (see right).
3 Check the pulse (see p.230). If you can't feel a pulse, try to feel a heartbeat by placing the fingertips on the left-hand side of the lower chest just behind the elbow. If you feel nothing, and the dog is unresponsive, give heart massage by vigorous squeezing of the left-hand side of the chest just behind the elbow – about one squeeze per second. (If the heart stops for more than three or four minutes, there may be irreversible brain damage.) Also give artificial respiration (see right).
4 Treat bleeding Staunch any heavy blood flow (see p.282).
5 Support broken bones (see p.283).
6 Contact the vet Arrange for an immediate veterinary examination.

ARTIFICIAL RESPIRATION

1 Check that the airway is clear, mouth open and clean, tongue forward.
2 Place both hands on the chest, over the rib area and push down firmly but gently to expel air from the lungs. Release the pressure immediately so that the chest expands and draws fresh air in.
3 Repeat at five-second intervals.

CONVULSIONS

The most usual cause is epilepsy (see p.264). This often starts with the dog being generally unsettled, then the fit/convulsions begin. Signs include: ☐ champing and chewing ☐ lips drawn back ☐ foaming at the mouth ☐ collapse and unconsciousness ☐ passing urine and faeces ☐ paddling of the legs.
Action
1 If the dog isn't a known epileptic, telephone the vet immediately.
2 Check that the dog is in a safe place, away from electric cables.
3 Make sure that the dog is comfortable; loosen its collar and cover it with a blanket if necessary. After this, avoid touching it until the fit is over.

4 Keep the room dark and quiet.
5 The fit shouldn't last more than five minutes. Once it is over, wipe the mouth and clean up any urine and faeces.
6 Let the dog have a drink but not much food until it is back to normal. Let it relax in quiet surroundings.
7 Follow the vet's instructions, going to the surgery or waiting for a visit.

DROWNING
Once you have the dog ashore, empty its lungs of water as quickly as possible.
Small dog Pick it up by the back legs and hold it upside down. Swing the dog round very carefully. A helper should then open its mouth and pump its chest.
Larger dog Pick it up behind the ribs, with one arm round the abdomen. Drape the dog over your shoulder while you open its mouth and pump its chest. *Don't* try to swing heavy dogs – you'll dislocate joints and tear ligaments.

HEATSTROKE
If left in an unventilated car in hot weather, a dog may suffer heatstroke. It will be in a variable state of collapse, panting heavily if conscious and frothing round the mouth.
Action
1 Clear froth from the mouth.
2 Douse the whole body with cold water.
3 Rush to the vet's surgery, where treatment will involve more cold water, stimulant drugs and cortisone.

FOREIGN BODY IN THE MOUTH
Restrain the dog (see p.270). If possible, open its mouth as if giving a pill (see p.273), and locate the foreign body. Remove it with your fingers or fine pliers if you can do this safely. If not, try the method described for emptying the lungs of water (see *Drowning*, left). If this fails, don't delay – contact a vet immediately.

FOREIGN BODY IN THE EYE
Stop the dog pawing its eye. If necessary, put a sock padded with cotton wool on each front paw. Restrain the dog (see p.270), and part the eyelids with finger and thumb to inspect the foreign body. If it is penetrating the eye, *don't touch it*, contact the vet immediately.

If the foreign body is sitting on the surface, try to remove it by irrigation (see p.257).

FOREIGN BODY IN THE THROAT
A stick or ball can lodge in a dog's throat or airway. If its larynx is blocked, the dog may have difficulty breathing and may die unless quick action is taken.

Try to remove the obstruction using the same method as for a drowning dog (see left). If this is unsuccessful, the object will have to be removed under anaesthetic by a vet.

POISONS
Fortunately poisoning is fairly rare in dogs, but they're less discriminating than cats and will eat a number of noxious substances. They may also lick off and swallow poisons that have contaminated their coat. Signs include: □ acute vomiting □ collapse □ violent muscular twitching □ fits □ weakness □ bleeding.
Action
1 Prevent further poison being swallowed. Wash off any on the coat.
2 Contact the vet immediately.
3 If you think you know what the dog has swallowed, take some with you to the vet, plus its container.

Don't waste time trying to treat the dog yourself – specific drugs may be needed. Your vet may tell you to make the dog vomit with an emetic. This is only worthwhile if the dog has eaten the poison during the last half hour. Suitable emetics are:
□ washing soda (sodium carbonate) – a pea-sized piece given as a tablet, *not* caustic soda (sodium hydroxide) □ salt in warm water □ mustard in cold water.

Wounds and burns

The most common wounds sustained by dogs are bites from other dogs and cut feet. If you see blood on the coat, first locate the source. If this isn't obvious, feel for matted hair stuck to the skin.
Action
1 If necessary, clip away the hair so that you can see the wound clearly.
2 Control any bleeding (see below).
3 Bandage the wound if possible.
4 Treat for shock. Contact the vet.

TREATING "BURNS"

These are usually caused by spilling hot or caustic liquids on dogs. Other causes include: □ falling into a hot bath □ biting electric cables □ extreme cold.
Action
1 If an offending substance is still on the dog, wash it off with cold water.
2 Apply a greasy ointment such as petroleum jelly.
3 Treat for shock. Contact the vet.

CONTROLLING BLEEDING

To control bleeding, hold a pad over the injury and bind it tightly in place with a bandage. If bleeding continues, apply a pad and bandage to these pressure points:
Forelimb Brachial artery where it crosses the bone above the inner elbow.
Hind limb Femoral artery as it crosses the femur on the upper inner thigh.
Tail Coccygeal artery underneath tail.
Head and neck Push a finger firmly into the groove where the carotid artery meets the shoulder (this can't be done with a pad and bandage).

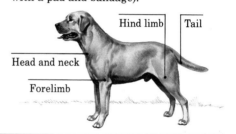

Hind limb   Tail

Head and neck

Forelimb

APPLYING BANDAGES

A bandage can protect an injury and keep it clean until it can be seen by a vet. You'll need an absorbent pad. Use lint, gauze, kitchen towel, even a clean handkerchief, but don't put cotton on a wound – it leaves fibers.

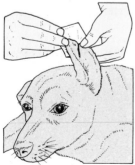

1 Try to close up the wound as much as possible and apply the pad to the site of the wound.

2 Wrap a crepe bandage round it four or five times, using other parts of the dog for anchorage.

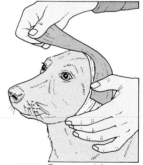

3 Secure with adhesive tape. *Never* use rubber bands – you could cut off the blood suppy.

DRESSING AN EYE WOUND
It is important that the surface of the eye doesn't dry out, so never bind a dry dressing over it. Use an absorbent pad soaked (but not dripping) in warm water. Secure the pad using a crepe bandage wound round the head with turns around the ear to keep it in place.

APPLYING A FOOT DRESSING
1 Insert pieces of cotton between the toes, then swathe the whole foot in cotton. This averts the danger of your stopping the circulation with a tight dressing.
2 Hold the padding in place with a bandage secured with adhesive tape.
3 Cover the dressing with a plastic bag, then a sock. Secure these with more tape above the "wrist."

DRESSING A TORSO WOUND
There are several ways of dealing with injuries to the chest or abdomen.
● A dressing pad can often be secured by bandaging the chest and one front leg.
● If this is tricky, cut a rectangle with "tapes" to tie over the back from a sheet.
● As a stop-gap, a towel or any other suitable piece of cloth can be wrapped round, then the ends twisted together over the back to draw it tight. Hold it in place until you reach the hospital.

TREATING A SPRAIN
Dogs, particularly large ones, are prone to sprains (see p.266). Wrenched and damaged muscle also responds to the same treatment. The most important long-term treatment for severe sprains is weeks or even months of rest.
Action
1 Apply a cold compress immediately – cotton or cloth soaked in chilled water. Change this for a fresh compress every 20 minutes.
2 After a few hours change to a hot compress (soak in water as hot as the back of the hand will bear).
3 Support the limb with a crepe bandage.

APPLYING A SPLINT

Splints can be tricky, but if you suspect a fractured leg, it is well worth applying one if you can. You need a large roll of cotton, battens and a bandage. Try to arrange the limb in its normal extended position, and pad the site with cotton – the more the better.

1 To reduce swelling and assist repair, use the cotton as a bandage, winding it round the leg. Apply a layer twice as thick as the leg, as far up and down it as possible.

2 Once the leg is covered, lay two suitable solid battens on either side of the leg to act as splints and bind them firmly in place with a bandage. Contact a vet.

Index

ACKNOWLEDGEMENTS

Author's Acknowledgements
I would first like to thank my colleague and friend Peter Scott for his tremendous contribution to this book; without him it could not have been written. Also the team at Dorling Kindersley, particularly Caroline Ollard and Derek Coombes for editing and design; their patience, expertise and dedication have been remarkable. Thanks are also due to Miss Horder, Librarian at the Royal College of Veterinary Surgeons – if this lady doesn't know a source of the most arcane information, it doesn't exist!

Dorling Kindersley would like to thank:
Tina Vaughan for design assistance, Linda Gamlin for researching the breeds section, Simon Parsons and Kerry Williamson for checking it, Richard Bird for the index, Bruce Fogle, Jenny Berry, Maxine Clark and Peter Olsen at the Portman Veterinary Clinic, Colin Tennant for training demonstrations and advice, Sue McAllister of the Beaumont Animals' Hospital, Sheila Stevens and Lesley Gilmour-Wood for breeding advice, Animal Fair of Kensington for loan of equipment and Susie McGowan, Mike Snaith and all at MS Filmsetting, Lucio Santoro, Mike Hearn, Chris Cope and Alison Graham.
and also:
Daisy, Tadpole, Gist, Kells puppy, Arklin Kennels puppy, Bicci, Heidi, Guffie and Polly

Picture research
Lesley Davy

Illustrators
Breeds chapter colour illustrations: John Francis of Linden Artists
Other illustrations: Russell Barnett, Kuo Kang Chen, Vana Haggerty, John Woodcock

Photography
Jan Baldwin, Ian O'Leary

Cover
Colour illustrations: John Francis
Line illustration: Kuo Kang Chen
Photography: Ardea/Jean-Paul Ferrero, Sally Anne Thompson/Animal Photography, Ian O'Leary

Typesetting
MS Filmsetting Limited, Frome, Somerset.

Reproduction
Newsele SRL, Milan

Photographic credits
Animal Photography/Sally Anne Thompson: pp.46 (top and bottom), 48, 49, 50, 51, 53, 76, 79, 88, 94, 107, 111, 122, 123, 124, 176(1–5)
Animal Photography/R. Willbie: p.125
Animals Unlimited/Paddy Cutts: pp.14, 90, 148, 198, 202, 204 (top), 205, 206, 207
Ardea: pp.7 (top right), 9 (right), 11 (top right), 219
Ardea/Ian Beames: p.40 (bottom right)
Ardea/J. P. Ferrero: pp.33, 39, 55, 217 (right), 218
Ardea/Clem Haagner: pp.40 (top), 41 (bottom)
Ardea/Peter Steyn: p.40 (centre)
Ardea/Wardene Weisser: p.40 (bottom left)
Beaumont Animals Hospital, Royal Veterinary College: pp.19, 267
Bridgeman Art Gallery (Haworth Gallery, Accrington): p.7 (top left)
British Museum/Michael Holford: pp.34, 38
British Tourist Authority: pp.9 (left), 201, 203 (top)
British Tourist Authority/Barrie Smith: p.204 (bottom)
Bruce Coleman/Mark Boulton: p.203 (bottom)
Mary Evans Picture Library: pp.45, 200
Sonia Halliday Photographs: p.8
Sonia Halliday Photographs/F. Birch: p.11 (left)
Marc Henrie: pp.42, 65, 72, 73, 91, 103, 108, 160, 184
Michael Holford: p.44
The Image Bank/W. Iooss: p.215
The Image Bank/Nicholas Foster: p.216
The Image Bank/Larry Allan: p.217 (left)
Jacana: pp.220, 223
Jacana/J. P. Thomas: pp.210, 225
Frank Lane Picture Agency Ltd/B. Langrish: p.61
Mansell Collection: p.6
Marka, Milan: pp.85, 149
Marka, Milan/Stefano Bisconcini: p.78
NHPA/Lacz Lemoine: pp.77, 120, 275
Panther Photographic International: pp.1, 12 (left), 71, 100
Spectrum: p.7 (bottom)
Spectrum/Anne Cumbers: pp.47, 64, 75, 93, 105, 112, 115, 116, 130, 132, 141, 172, 176 (bottom), 194, 195, 196
Spectrum/Ronald Oulds: p.127
Syndication International: pp.213, 214
Trevor Wood: pp.11 (bottom right), 12 (right), 13, 128
ZEFA: pp.2–3, 41 (top)